5—

310423

MARBORO $1.98
6-23

Elysian Encounter

DIDEROT and GIDE

Elysian Encounter

DIDEROT and GIDE

G. NORMAN LAIDLAW

1963

Syracuse University Press

Copyright © 1963
by Syracuse University Press
Syracuse, New York

ALL RIGHTS RESERVED

Library of Congress
Catalog Card: 63-19193

Composition in Linotype Electra,
with Weiss display.

Designed by Freeman Champney.

Jacket Design by Frank Mahood.

Manufactured in the
United States of America
by the Vail-Ballou Press, Inc.
Binghamton, New York

To Gwen

Acknowledgments

The English translations in this volume appear with the permission of Editions Garnier Frères, Paris: Diderot, *Oeuvres complètes,* ed. J. Assézat et M. Tourneux, 1875–79, 20 volumes; Editions Droz, Geneva: E. Droz, *Le Recueil Trepperel,* 1935 and Diderot, *Le Neveu de Rameau,* ed. J. Fabre, 1950; Librairie Gallimard-Editions de la Nouvelle Revue Française, Paris: Diderot, *Correspondance inédite,* ed. A. Babelon, 1931, 2 volumes and *Lettres à Sophie Volland,* ed. A. Babelon, 1938, 2 volumes, as well as the following works by Gide: *Oeuvres complètes,* ed. L. Martin-Chauffier, 1932–39, 15 volumes; *Journal, Pages de Journal, Journal 1942–49,* 1939, 1946, 1950; *Littérature engagée,* ed. Y. Davet, 1950; *Interviews imaginaires,* 1943; *Ainsi soit-il* ou *Les Jeux sont faits,* 1952.

Grateful acknowledgment is also made to Messrs. Alfred A. Knopf, Inc., New York, for the privilege of quoting directly from their authorized English translations of Gide: *The Journals of André Gide,* trans. Justin O'Brien, 1947–51, 4 volumes; *So Be It* or *The Chips Are Down,* trans. J. O'Brien, 1959; *Imaginary Interviews,* trans. M. Cowley, 1944; *Fruits of the Earth,* trans. D. Bussy, 1949.

The bibliographical notes (pp. 231–244) indicate in detail the sources of shorter quotations.

Contents

Prosaic Prologue

When, in the course of Elysian events, chance brings together the manes of Denis Diderot and the shade of André Gide, the two blithe spirits find much to talk about. Unless their earthly works belie them, they while away many a pleasant eon in conversations as varied in tone as in topic. If these exchanges could be recorded, they would provide a wealth of material for a new series of *Dialogues des morts,* a sequel to Diderot's published *entretiens,* or another volume of Gidean *Interviews imaginaires.* It may be presumed, since these were men of resolute thought and plain speech, that there are some marked divergences of opinion as the discussions range through infinite time and space. But the celestial colloquies undoubtedly bring out, as well as the differences, a surprising tangency of interests and an appreciable agreement in attitudes.

This volume deals with those spiritual encounters in both factual and conjectural terms. It is an examination of intellectual incidence revealed in literary fact rather than a fantasy conjuring up the quintessential Diderot and the ultimate manifestation of Gide.

At first glance, there seems to be minimum reason for picturing Diderot and Gide together. Widely separated in time, they appear to have but slight resemblance in personality or reputation, in literary aims or styles.

"La *combinaison* est analogue ou bizarre," as Diderot once remarked in a study of nature. An adequate interpretation of Diderot's genius, like the definitive edition of his works, has yet to be done. Gide's contribution to modern thought is still a subject of brisk debate and his *Oeuvres complètes* are neither complete nor critically satisfying. With so much to be investigated in each, why a simultaneous study of the two? Why concentrate on rapports rather than lacunae? Is there, in fact, demonstrable incidence or is it merely a question of coincidence?

In spite of an increasing tendency of critics to link their names and to suggest that intellectual bonds exist between Diderot and Gide, none seems to have considered their frequent convergence—in thought or word—as anything more than fortuitous. Browsing through the works of either, the reader is struck by convictions, directions, and turns of phrase usually associated with the other. To the reader blessed with (or plagued by) an associative mind, the discovery invites further search for evidence of an extraordinary relationship between these two unorthodox mentalities.

A rereading of Diderot for Gidean touches and of Gide for echoes of Diderot leads to three results: first, a new appreciation of both writers, thanks to the curious perspective; second, a surprisingly rich accumulation of ideas and comments of the one that are apposite to the other; third, a realization that the standard apparatus and usual terminology of criticism are quite inadequate to the task of defining these *correspondances* of mental disposition, thought process and mode of expression.

Most literary relationships fall into well established

categories. The most frequently reported, perhaps, are those between friends or former friends and those involving international or interlingual ties, complete with contacts in person, letters and books. Other fertile areas are in the realm of influence, such as that of the master on the disciple, the ancestor on the descendant, originator on plagiarist, members of cliques and movements on one another. The Diderot-Gide bonds resist classification. They lie in an intellectual no-man's-land little cultivated to date, that domain of nature where Diderot assumed the existence of "chaînons imperceptibles" (undiscovered links), where the authors' kinship can be inferred from their like responses to similar ideas and problems. This vague harmony of reaction is sometimes described as unconscious affinity. Gide invented two expressions that characterize it more aptly: "influence par ressemblance" (influence through resemblance) and "communion à retardement" (eventual recognition of kinship).

Most methods of exploring such affinities call for an alternating of interest or a bifocal view that is ill suited to our need for a virtually simultaneous concentration on two highly mobile figures. The "double attention" that is essential here has already proved its worth in the theater, where twin spotlights sometimes merge and sometimes separate their beams as they play on equally important characters moving about the stage. In sensationalistic philosophy, Condillac advocated the use of a similar technique to assure maximum understanding of phenomena: "Surveying in this way all our reactions to them, through a series of comparisons and judgments we discover the relationships that exist between them.

The product of these judgments is the idea we formulate of each of them. Attention so directed is like a light reflected by one body and falling on another so that both are more clearly seen."

A modified application of this theory is attempted in the following sections, where a binocular approach is made to Diderot and Gide. It is obviously not our intention to consider *all* our reactions to them; and their divergences of direction will force us, on occasion, to resort to alternation and bifurcation. But we make no apology for this compromise between necessity and the ideal of "double attention"; ours is the practical aim of showing related facets of two multilateral minds. No system, as Diderot pointed out, can lay claim to more than a shred of the robe of Socrates. And every choice, as Gide insisted, entails the rejection of what might have been better.

The seven essays that make up this collection embrace the topics and follow the order that might be expected in the Elysian conversations mentioned earlier. Likenesses of temperament and intellectual disposition are taken as a point of departure. Similarities of approach and of technique, in dealing with questions of major and minor concern, are treated in the second study. After a section on a preoccupation that is sometimes frivolous—the role played by folly in life and in literary exposition—there is a detailed examination of the two writers' presentation of one grimly serious theme, blindness. Problems in personal conduct, individual and social, are surveyed and related. Ideas on death and its consequences are under a separate rubric. An investigation of Gide's admitted acquaintance with Diderot's work follows, with some intimation of the authors' similar places in the history of ideas, the growing recognition by critics of their literary rapports, and an estimate of Gide's debt to the *philosophe.* As an epilogue in lieu of a conclusion (or the "Could be continued . . ." once considered as a possible ending by a Gidean novelist), there is an exemplary dialogue.

Open Minds and Open Questions

The chief sources of light on literary temperament, since Rousseau's *Confessions* and Sainte-Beuve's innovations in critical method, have been autobiography and biography. The personalities of Denis Diderot and André Gide, complex though they are, can be seen to best advantage in their personal accounts of their lives. The daybook of Diderot is his correspondence (particularly his letters to his mistress, Sophie Volland), complemented by an assortment of scenes from his private life appearing overtly in his published works.[1] Gide's is of course his classic *Journal;* it has a variety of supplements, including *Si le grain ne meurt . . .* (*If It Die . . .*), *Et nunc manet in te* (*Madeleine*), and *Jeunesse* (*Youth*), as well as a plethora of confidences to his public, beginning with *Les Cahiers d'André Walter* (*The Notebooks of André Walter*) and ending in *Ainsi soit-il* ou *Les Jeux sont faits* (*So Be It* or *The Chips Are Down*).[2] The facts of Diderot's life, first chronicled by his daughter, Mme de Vandeul, have been elaborated by the scholarly toil of two centuries, notably that of Billy, Venturi, Pommier, Crocker, and Wilson.[3] Of the many critical studies of Gide, those by Fernandez, Pierre-Quint, Archambault, O'Brien, and Brée make most use of the biographical approach.[4]

This rich fund of fact, subjective and objective, should furnish adequate information to those interested in the authors' attitudes. Unfortunately, there is still little unanimity among critics; each has his system, his area of personal preference, his theory to substantiate, all of which are inalienable rights. And for better or worse, the thoughts of Diderot and Gide, expressed with such seeming candor, lend themselves to a generous variety of interpretations. Gide, who claims he writes to be *re*read, is undismayed by the imbroglio: "I do not like explaining my books and I am not upset that people misunderstand them at first; when they are wrongly interpreted, I refrain from protesting. It merely means that much more trouble for my future critics." [5]

The urge of some critics to conclude is matched by the zeal of others to categorize. There is obvious utility in such labels as *philosophe*, encyclopedist, materialist for Diderot, and artist, diarist, *immoraliste* for Gide. But there is something static and restrictive about these convenient terms. Separately or in conjunction, they fail signally to denote several outstanding qualities of dynamic, restive intelligences—qualities patent in Diderot's letters, Gide's *Journal*, and the events of their lives.

The first of these is insatiable curiosity. From it issue most of their other mental attributes, many of their technical procedures, and a large share of their moral attitudes. Their penchant for asking questions, springing from basic desires to preserve open minds and find their own bearings, leads to Diderot's concern with personal and public enlightenment, to Gide's preoccupation with encouraging an unprejudiced outlook in himself and others. When they discover some directions for themselves, they use all their resources to invite, cajole, shock, or prod their readers into doing the same. Their chief instrument, which sometimes resembles a jester's bauble and sometimes a cudgel, is the interrogation mark. In dealing with ethical problems, they have equal disdain for dogmatic premises and absolute solutions.

The two writers have no ready answer to the philosophic question of intelligent conduct in a world that is often unintelligible—the dilemma of all thinking men who reject religious faith as a substitute for understanding. Diderot sees little virtue in established ethics and invents his own ethics of virtue uncodified; to give some semblance of sense to man's revolt against rules of conduct, he suggests the paradoxical behavior of his would-be fatalist Jacques. Gide's anti-ethics of "becoming" and his poised balancing of what he knows he is with what he wants others to believe he is are equally noncommittal. Such attitudes are almost inevitable in men who still value questions even though, like the Gidean Prometheus, they must often say, "My questions go unanswered."

These similar moral positions offer a positive, practical guide to conduct without proposing specious ideals. Most adherents of such codes are philosophers and relativists, in the best sense of those terms. What leads them to value the quest of knowledge above its imagined conquest is a love of wisdom; what makes them more convincing than convinced is their recognition of the relative nature of all interpretations, including their own. Their explorations help them glimpse new worlds to be investigated, added problems, further questions. Each partial discovery is enhanced in value by the promise of what it leaves unknown; a final answer, or what is mistaken for one, is to them an impasse, a mental blind alley that offers two alternatives: to retreat and start again in another direction or to stop abruptly and stagnate. The two are equally repugnant to those who strive to view what is beyond settled frontiers: "Some people head toward an objective. Others simply go straight ahead. As for me, I do not know where I am going; but I am making progress. I am perhaps merely an adventurer. It is only in adventure that people succeed in knowing themselves—in finding themselves." [6] The open minds and open questions of Diderot and Gide support their nomination to this select and inquisitive company, insuring them against cautious traditionalism, involvement in bigoted factions, and election to staid academies. Their works have a scope and diversity that are a measure of their ubiquitous curiosity.

This catholicity of interest suggests to the two like concepts of intelligence and its use. Strenuous thinking is the finest exercise of human faculties; energetic learning —and not the passive storing of facts—is the essence of knowledge. This belief, implicit in Montaigne's remark on the "tête bien faite" (well-trained mind), is at the foundation of Diderot's zeal for enlightenment and of Gide's for self-realization as a personal contribution to progress and artistic achievement. Unrelenting inquiry is the prime function of the mind, which must be kept alert and nurtured unceasingly if man is to improve his lot. Passivity, inertia, and acceptance of dogmatic precepts lead only to mental impotence and the triumph of mediocrity.

Convinced of the efficacy of this attitude in their own

thinking, both writers make it the chief element of their appeal to others. "Jeune homme, prends et lis" ("Take this book, young man, and read it"), says Diderot in a sententious epigraph. Gide gives similar counsel in seemingly opposite terms; in an *envoi,* he tells his imagined protégé that, having read of Gide's discoveries, he must now seek his own truth: "Jette mon livre" ("Throw away this book of mine").[7] Less peremptory, if equally confident, is the Gidean declaration, "I intend to give those who read me strength, joy, courage, defiance, and perspicacity. . . . Develop at one and the same time the critical faculty and energy, those two contraries." [8] The aim, in each case, is to encourage questioning, to issue a challenge to action. Skepticism must be resourceful and dynamic, if it is to be a satisfying way of life. Interrogation must provoke active, unflagging search if the question-mark is to be more than a rhetorical device or a sign of frustrated finality. Man's urge to investigate, not the fear of the Lord, is the beginning of wisdom.

With a persistence that borders on perverse delight, Diderot and Gide pose their embarrassing questions. Gide is unsmiling as he says "Je veux GENER" ("I want to DISTURB people"). His "Tant pis!" ("So much the worse!") is not always casual. And his statement of his religious position in *Numquid et tu? . . .* is a gesture as defiant as throwing down the gauntlet. Diderot's *Est-il bon? Est-il méchant?* is a serious plea for open-minded evaluation based on limited information. His constant intervention in his narratives, to warn the reader to be circumspect, is more than playful teasing. He admits somewhat ruefully that the caution he exercises in his own public avowals is not entirely of his choosing—it is imposed in part by the baleful presence of the censor and uncomfortable memories of his sojourn in Vincennes prison, which cramp his style and limit his frankness to a greater extent than many critics (including Gide) have realized. But they do not stifle his love of challenging questions. Gide is more fortunate. In his day, the outspoken man who asks unconventional questions risks only his reputation.

In spite of their different modes of expression, Gide and Diderot are very much alike in their unawed disrespect—nothing human or divine is untouchable or impertinent to them. Their universal inquisitiveness is urgent, provocative, and frequently defiant. It exasperates the orthodox and conservative as much as it endears the writers to radicals. The irritation is deliberate enough. The identification of their broad intellectual causes with such stultifying doctrines as those of the Marxists and the Communists is an unwarranted, if understandable, *reductio ad absurdum*. Diderot's adoption by the Soviet Russians, despite his friendship with Catherine the Great, is to be attributed to what they call his antihistorical ethics, his internationalist conspectus, and of course his status as a dialectic materialist before Marx and Engels. In the thirties, Gide flouts popular opinion by endorsing communism as a brave new world for the artist. With considerable fanfare, he is invited to visit Russia, which he does in 1936. His Utopia proves to be far from realized—liberty in arts and letters is nonexistent, minds are regimented in every possible respect. Back in France, he writes a disillusioned *Retour de l'URSS* (*Return from the* USSR) and its sequel, *Retouches à mon Retour de l'URSS* (*Afterthoughts on the USSR*), warning his compatriots and others of the peril. The gesture is honest but expensive—his Russian royalties are cut off.[9]

To characterize the Diderot-Gide viewpoint as lack of prejudice is to delimit it unduly. The expression is too negative, although the trait is one both admire. Diderot consorts willingly with the most heterodox thinkers of his day and welcomes the most extravagant ideas. Gide feels that LaBruyère's greatness stems from his having "un esprit non prévenu" (an unprejudiced mind) as had Montaigne and Shakespeare. To speak of tolerance, similarly, is to say too little—the noun is too smug, too flaccid for the attribute. *Disponibilité* (availability), if shorn of some of the ambiguous implications Gide has given it, is perhaps as good a word as any to describe a poised and kinetic disposition of mind, an intelligence that is alert and receptive, critical, and provocative of thought.

The interrogating minds of Diderot and Gide turn frequently to nature and the sciences now called "natural." In an era of lively interest in the phenomena of the universe and in experimental procedures, the *philosophe* associates by choice with professional and amateur scientists. Lectures on chemistry, demonstrations in surgery, studies of anatomy, applications of scientific principles to the arts and trades, even the realms of the monstrous and the occult fascinate Diderot.[10] He wins personal recognition early in his career for his *De l'interprétation de la nature* and later for his *Eléments de physiologie.* In his letter on the blind he suggests a method of reading not unlike the Braille system; in the studies on deaf-mutes, modern techniques of speech therapy and approaches to communications theories are anticipated. As general editor, he supervises the sections on science in the *Encyclopédie,* assuming the personal task of preparing the manual arts and trades division, complete with its highly technical plates. Such incidental works as the *Projet d'un nouvel orgue* and *Principes généraux d'acoustique* are more scientific than musical. When still a schoolboy, Diderot showed his penchant for science by winning distinction in mathematics and physics, fortunately without neglecting his Latin. As a *maître ès arts,* he hoped to continue studies in science and languages, then found himself forced into law for some months. At one stage, he rejected the lancet and scalpel (suggested by his father, who presumably hoped to see his son using the products of the family firm) in favor of the pen. At another, he earned a precarious living as a mathematics tutor and then as a translator of James's *Medicinal Dictionary.* French doctors still pay tribute to Diderot for his long and close association with their profession, stressing his acquaintance with distinguished medical men, his theoretical work in transformism, his part in the controversy between physicians and surgeons, and his public campaign for inoculation. Articles he wrote on hydrotherapy and for the pharmacopoeia are still considered authoritative.[11]

But it is neither for the scope of his interest nor for specific discoveries that Diderot is remembered. He is at his most brilliant in his incursions into theoretical science, particularly in the d'Alembert series; in the *Entretien, Rêve,* and *Suite,* many years before the "inventors," he investigates the principles of transformism, evolution, and teratology.[12] Even his whimsical thoughts often anticipate inventions. After seeing a demonstration of legerdemain, for example, he writes to Sophie, suggesting a device that is not to exist until well after Morse's telegraph—the modern teletype: ". . . some day, communication between one town and another, between one place and another some hundreds of leagues distant. . . . It would simply be a matter of each person having his box; these boxes would be like two small printing presses and everything that was printed on one would immediately be printed on the other. . . ."[13]

Gide's scientific inclinations are less diversified but no less constant. When he reads the proofs of Ramon Fernandez's *André Gide,* he approves especially of the remarks on his urge to be scientific in all matters. Earlier in the *Journal,* he quotes a letter of his mother's concerning her four-year-old son's "mania for standing a long time absolutely still at the foot of a tree, watching snails." Thanks to his herborizing during school vacations, he becomes a surprisingly well informed young botanist. The sight of a row of aristolochia so impresses him, when he is in his twenties, that he mentions them in both his diary and in *Paludes* (*Morasses*), adding symbolic significance to their properties. A half-century later he comments, "I am something of a botanist and look at the plant to find the explanation of the flower." In his early vocabulary, he speaks of choosing some parts of himself for careful development while sacrificing others as "pruning." When he is in his seventies, the metaphor is used of Goethe: "A plant cannot give sap at the same moment to all its buds. This voluntary limitation of his multiple latent faculties remained the secret drama of his life." Likening the failure of his own energy to rise to its erstwhile heights to that of a tree's sap, Gide sees in that failure a first sure indication that he has not long to live.[14]

Apart from botany, Gide's concern with science is largely theoretical. One recurrent preoccupation is the relation of underlying principle to procedure or process. In *Corydon*, for example, the Darwinian protagonist, accused of being a finalist, says, "As a matter of fact, I have always been less concerned with the *why* than with the *how*. But it is sometimes difficult to disentangle the two questions. Nature forms a network that has neither beginning nor end, an unbroken chain of links that you do not know where to grasp." [15] Nearly two decades later, the sentiment is echoed in a *Journal* entry: "Science, to be sure, progresses only by everywhere substituting the *how* for the *why*. But however remote it may be, there is always a point at which the two interrogations meet and fuse." [16] And in one of his last works Gide returns to the theme, now illustrated poetically in the relationship of silkworm to cocoon to moth: "Hence I shall refuse to consider finality in nature. According to the best advice, I shall everywhere substitute, systematically, the *how* for the *why*.—But I am indeed forced . . . to admire the way in which the *how* joins the *why*. . . . Everywhere in nature the solution is inseparable from the problem. Or rather: there is no problem; there are only solutions. Man's mind invents the problem afterward. He sees problems everywhere." [17]

One integral factor of openmindedness is the ability to see several sides of a question at once—the *dédoublement* (dissociation or doubled perspective) that can best be expressed, after multiple interpretation, in paradox, ambiguity, or the open question. Perhaps because of the lack of direction inferred from his bantering remark that "our mind hops and skips, touching everything possible," Diderot is frequently taken to be a jack-of-all-trades, an intellectual dilettante. He accepts the accusation in good part, as though it were a compliment to the flexibility and diversity of his thinking. For he does indeed turn his hand to a strange assortment of chores: writing advertisements for hair tonic, ghost-writing sermons, giving unsolicited political advice to an empress, providing a detailed curriculum for a vast university, contributing to a study in agricultural economics, helping run an international newsletter service, reforming the theater, and grinding out, with minimum aid, a goodly share of the encyclopedia: "The variety of roles I play in this world certainly is strange. Sometimes I cannot help laughing at it. I surely am 'old man Toutatous.' "[18] But his very promiscuity reveals his mental capacity. For it is his restive intelligence that urges him to sample, then to probe not only the several inviting ideas surrounding each question, but also the many implications of each of those ideas.

Not without justification, Gide takes pride in his ubiquity of interests. He too is intrigued by each separate notion, with its rich store of possible meanings and contingent verbal formulations, that contributes to a complex idea. He is fascinated by the curious cohabitation in his mind of the parts of an idea that seem to be in contradiction one with another. As well as the idea divided into its component parts, Gide enjoys the thought with several aspects, each depending on the perspective or perspicacity of the thinker involved. The multiple view of various interpretations of a single idea, fact, or act leads to his predilection for the *en-abyme* (boxes-in-boxes) technique, which he elaborates from the play-within-a-play device and the heraldic system of showing an escutcheon within an escutcheon. This yields the novel within a novel, the diary within a diary, the protagonist created by a protagonist, and the situation repeated in miniature within itself.[19]

If Gide sows his ideas broadcast, it is equally true that he reaps in all directions, which is one of the rewards of *disponibilité*. Among his favorite figures of speech is that of the crossroads, which he uses metaphorically to describe his work and particularly his novel. His mind, he avers, is an open inn at a crossroads, where all thoughts are welcomed as potentially good company, where different opinions can meet in spirited debate. There is a certain exhilaration in the dialogue that ensues when several interpretations contend for acceptance: "Les extrêmes me touchent" ("The extremes meet in me" or "Extremes appeal to me"), he says, giving a personal touch to an old adage. In somewhat different terms: "I always see, almost simultaneously, the two sides of each idea, and the emotion is always polarized in me." And when he talks, twenty-five years later, of systems, including his own: "I let the most antagonistic proposals of my nature gradually come to agreement without violence. Suppressing the dialogue in oneself really amounts to stopping the development of life." [20]

Diderot, too, is given to *polarisation.* Deft paradoxes, antagonistic thoughts, and seemingly irreconcilable viewpoints give special piquancy to his considerations of all matters. And his reactions can contrast simultaneously in mood or level as well as in distance within the same plane: "With my head in the clouds, I notice a straw on the ground." [21]

This aptitude for being at once in two places, at diametrically opposite points on the periphery of an idea, is a source of strength and confidence, rather than a sign of vacillation, to Diderot and Gide. Doubling the advantages of the single point of view, it gives them a conception of truth as an ill-defined median between extremes, a blending in the middle ground of attitudes that can be equally true in that each is only partially valid.

For Gide, the satisfactions this dual vision gives are chiefly intellectual and artistic. "Two really extraordinary faculties of the poet: the permission to yield to things, when he wants, without losing himself; and the capacity of being consciously naïve. These two faculties can moreover be reduced to the single gift of dissociation." [22] Although he does not distinguish it by the same term, Diderot, who says *poète* to mean any creative artist, is well aware of the gift. As a rhetorician, an inveterate debater, and a proponent of chiaroscuro, he puts it to skilled use. His purpose is not only "poetic"; like Bayle and Fontenelle before him, he makes of ambiguity a weapon and a shield in his battle with the censor. This leads Gide, by the way, to chide the *philosophe* for lending such plausible arguments to his adversaries that he seems to weaken his own case. As a critic, Gide has rarely been so obtuse. He fails to recognize that Diderot writing under surveillance is scarcely Diderot at his most expansive, as he can be among his friends at Grandval or at d'Holbach's "synagogue" on the Rue Royale. Plain talk and forthright declaration, admirable as ideals, can invite catastrophe. Prudence dictates that insurgent or heretic ideas be masked; inference, double meaning, and indirection become tactical necessities, however uncomfortable a curb bit they impose.

The inquisitive mind, sensing relationships everywhere, has a natural penchant toward associative thinking. If the inclination to translate ubiquitous interest and multiple vision into action is encouraged and given direction, what could be haphazard woolgathering becomes intellectual exploration. Since Montaigne, adventurers in free thought have been impelled by the urge, which has been called "the simultaneous impulse to range afield and to take one's bearings."

One concomitant of associative thought, for better or worse, is enthusiasm for ideas. Diderot recognizes the trait in himself with the much quoted comment, "Mes pensées, ce sont mes catins" ("My thoughts are my streetwalkers"). His preference, he tells Sophie, is for *idées folles* (extravagant ideas); unusual thoughts appeal to him, banal ones bore him. Meister corroborates these avowals in his portrait: "His ideas overpowered him, they carried him with them, as it were." These observations, taken literally, have perpetuated the legend that Diderot lacked both stability and self-control. It was a legend he helped create during his reported interview with Garat and by his comparison of men from Langres with weathercocks. It must be remembered that he was quite aware of these tendencies and that good-natured exaggeration of his own shortcomings was one of his favorite pastimes as well as a pose for the edification of the public. "A work of art," young Gide notes, "is a matter of exaggeration." Diderot the artist paints himself, sometimes in caricature, in blithe mood. Taken at times for "a bit of an eccentric," he enjoys his role and quips, "Does that do me any harm?"—his version of the Gidean "So much the worse!"

There is the same zest for ideas in Gide, but the pursuit is often limited to ideas that promise personal reward, that can be nurtured and shaped to fruition. The *idée-catin* (wanton thought) appeals to the eighteenth-century man; the man of the twentieth century prefers the *idée-grain* (germinal idea), which must not, on the one hand, be allowed to fall on barren soil nor, on the other, fail to die. In his early days, Gide has for *l'Idée* a respect that approaches idolatry. His provisional literary code begins, "The word must never precede the idea." And he gives long and tender care to each chosen idea, avoiding what he calls "a too hasty manifestation of one's essence." Preoccupations with individual notions, contemporaneous or successsive, have provided biographers with a rich fund of sectional headings: *manifestation, dénuement, renoncement, authenticité* (self-manifestation, impoverishment, renunciation, fidelity to self) become key words along with *le grain.* So do, among others, *acte gratuit, être et paraître, passer outre,* and *devenir* (the unmotivated gesture, being and appearing, going past, and becoming).

To both Diderot and Gide, the greatest virtue of the initial thought is in the aura that surrounds it, in its connotations, implications, elaborations, and overtones.

These associations and extensions of the idea help give new directions to prose, when they are turned to advantage. They are the *sine qua non* of poetry, the source and the substance of imagery. Sustained by strong emotions, perceptive senses, and disciplined expression—all characteristic traits of Diderot and Gide—they blend to yield the stuff of which poems are made. Yet neither author is assured of a place on Helicon by his ventures into verse. As in the Academy, they occupy the supernumerary place of honor—first as "poets" in the eighteenth-century sense of the word, and additionally for their influence on poetry, their "presence" in the poems of others.

Without pretensions to being more than an occasional rhymer—or rhymester—Diderot is a votary and lifelong student of poetry. Horace is his constant companion, Racine is a genius, Shakespeare is "gigantic," Dryden is no stranger to him, and his contemporaries value his astute judgment of their efforts. One of his modern critics, pointing out that Diderot's talents as a poet are far from undeveloped, says ". . . these gifts are there, fully realized and manifested in Saunderson's vision and in the prodigious imagination of the *Rêve*." [23] But it is more for his appreciation of the nature of poetry and the poetic experience that he is remembered. He is, for example, the first to propose the recognition of subtle relationships among the perceptions (*correspondances*) that delight the late nineteenth century. He speaks himself of "sentiments bruns" ("brown" emotions). He is, too, an important forerunner of the Romanticists, the Symbolists, and the Impressionists.[24] In his basic attitudes, he is closer to romanticism than Rousseau, as is being increasingly appreciated: he is truly sensitive to Nature, an advocate of the fullest exercise of the senses, and a lover of his own melancholy, of solitude and of what he calls "the dark zone" (*le sombre*).[25] In his concepts of chiaroscuro and of the vague, complex words beyond comprehension, he anticipates in turn the contrasts of Victor Hugo and the *au-delà* of the Surrealists: "The poet has his chiaroscuro, with its beginnings and its rules deep in his heart." And again: "Ideal painting has in its chiaroscuro something of the realm that lies beyond nature."[26] Since there are for him direct relationships among all the arts, what is said of painting or sculpture is equally true of acting or poetry. Like Verlaine, he is stirred by intermittent sounds, such as those of distant waterfalls, muted drums, and far-off bells, sounds that he transmutes into words with consummate skill. Spitzer sees this as a fundamental feature of Diderot's style: "symbolic rendering of the rhythm of feeling by the rhythm of language . . . an onomatopoeic rendering of feelings which one has been in the habit of dating from Flaubert."[27] Like many poetic souls since Pascal—and the modern "silent" actor—Diderot finds silence laden wth implications, inviting interpretation: "Car le silence même se peint par les sons" ("For silence itself is depicted in sound"), as he comments on young Rameau's pantomime performance. Mornet takes the line as a text for his comment on Diderot the poet: "By a sort of divination, we can already see here . . . the secret relationships that exist for a person of great sensitivity between impressions and feelings that seem to be in the domains of separate senses."[28] Citing Diderot's remark on silence as possibly the most lyric passage of the period, Mornet adds, "It may be said that in eighteenth-century literature there is nothing that heralds more clearly the kind of conception of literature the Symbolists will strive to translate."

Gide the poet deserves fuller treatment than Gide the writer of verse. At his worst, he is no poetaster; in occasional stanzas, he shows adeptness in melding cleverness of idea, and aptness of line. But his contribution to poetry, like Diderot's, lies elsewhere. His exuberant holidays from restraint, his emphasis on intimate experience (carefully recorded), his indulgences of sensitivities and senses and, above all, the richly poetic quality of many of his prose works—all attest to his lyric bent. *Les Nourritures terrestres* (*Fruits of the Earth*) and—to a lesser extent—the later *Nourritures* merit consideration as something more than challenges to sensuousness, much more than stylistic showpieces.[29] In spite of their form, they are not prose works but outpourings of the heart and senses, presented with the conscious art of the poet. According to Diderot's concept, or the Wordsworthian notion of deep feeling "recollected in tranquility," the Gide of the *Nourritures* writes poetically. There is evidence that Gide has not foresworn lyricism nor lost his capacity for the experience of poetry even as he approaches eighty: In his *Feuillets d'automne* (*Autumn Leaves*), he jots down what is, intentionally or not, a prose poem: "Oh, would that my mind could let fall its dead ideas, as the tree does its withered leaves! And without too many regrets, if possible! Those from which the sap has withdrawn. But, good Lord, what beautiful colors!" [30]

Among Gide's tenets is one dear to Diderot—the interrelationship of the arts that confounds the separate senses. It is this concern with synesthesia that leads him to the study of painting, as a sort of structural hygiene, and to an attempt to appreciate Chardin "reverently." The sound of a village piano and the smell of a long-closed house flood his thoughts with suggestions and "harmonies." A stroll through a moonlit garden, through forests, or past lakes, is as poetic an experience for him as those that inspire Rousseau's reveries and Diderot's paeans to nature. Subscribing to the pathetic fallacy in his moments of communion, he sees that the landscape "always assumes desperately the color of my lamentable soul." Recollections of life in North Africa prompt him to say, "I was amazed that nature was so beautiful, and I called everything nature." [31] Visits to the Congo and Chad bring him added delight, sojourns in Normandy, the Midi, and the mountains a quieter but no less real enjoyment of the beauties of the earth. Like Diderot, he finds charm and significance in silence. Pausing on a street in Honfleur, for example, he thinks of Delacroix and muses on the majesty of "the great works of silence." Most of his outpouring of enthusiasm occurs in his youth, from the time of his invention of André Walter through that of his association with Mallarmé and the symbolists to the period of the pleasant strolls with Francis Jammes.[32] Diderot, it will be recalled, philosophizes on nature when young; he responds with increasing lyricism to its pleasures as he ages. He thoroughly enjoys his long walks near Langres and in the countryside near the estates of his wealthy friends d'Holbach, Mme d'Epinay, and Belle. After many years of living by his own choice in Paris, he becomes aware of a distaste for city life and its frenetic activity. Even when he is enjoying a stay in the provinces, however, he has pangs of conscience. He writes to Grimm "That is where I live like a bear in wintertime, sustaining myself by licking my own paw." But he speaks like Rousseau—another "bear," if we believe Mme d'Epinay—in a note to Sophie in praise of the bucolic life: "the dwelling-place of brotherhood . . . our earliest homeland; woods, huts and fields . . . virtually no sign here of those levels of inequality that city people build up in tiers." [33]

When Gide deserts the Symbolist group, he abandons neither the symbol (he invents a multitude of them for his own use) nor poetry in broader terms and other modes. The dadaists, for instance, adopt him as their "uncle"—thanks in part to the spirit of literary libertinism they sense in his writing from *Paludes* to *Les Caves du Vatican* (*The Vatican Swindle*). He virtually discovers Valéry and later encourages him to return to poetry after a long silence; he gives constructive criticism to embryo poets; he rehabilitates reputations of those he considers unjustly forgotten, launches those of unknowns he thinks worthy of recognition. As a writer of prefaces, a literary commentator for a Paris weekly, and an anthologist, he continues his interest until late in life, pausing at one moment (as he works on *Ainsi soit-il*) to wonder whether he is still capable of judging poetry that is truly new.

Gide's own verse is often competent, rich in imagery and rhythmic movement, apt in choice and use of words. His greatest talent, however, is in his faculty for sensing implications and promises of added meaning. There is an invitation to readers to interpret freely and inventively

—calling on poetic as well as witty associations—in his versions of myths, parables, and such quotations as "In the beginning was the Word." As well as objects or instruments of his ironic humor, he makes poetic figures of characters that have become prosaic through long and uncritical acceptance of their legendary postures and gestures. Narcissus, Tityrus, Oedipus, Icarus and Daedalus, Prometheus and Theseus all show the touch of the poet.

The anthology of poetry published in 1949 with Gide as editor was disappointingly conventional and conservative; his *Poétique* had seemed to promise something better when it appeared a year earlier, subtitled "Sur une définition de la poésie." The critical study is an elaboration of Banville's theory of pure lyricism as "that magic that consists of awakening feelings through a combining of sounds . . . that sorcery thanks to which ideas are necessarily communicated to us in a certain way by words that do not however express them." [34] In words reminiscent of Diderot's theorizing on effective presentation ("It is the task of composure to temper the transports of enthusiasm"), Gide insists that "it is a matter of sensations and ideas, but not at all of emotions." [35] After a consideration of the relative merits of Banville's "magic" or "sorcery" and Valéry's ambiguous "charm," Gide discusses, in turn: "incantation" as an element of poetry, sometimes present in prose; his conversations with A. E. Housman on France's great poets, Villon, Baudelaire, and Verlaine; Baudelaire as a contributor to poetic art; Villon "somewhere between the Holy Church and the brothel, with his feet in the mire and his heart in the sky"; the qualities of Victor Hugo's poems. This last section shows that Gide has revised his earlier estimate of Hugo's worth. He quotes himself in the *Interviews imaginaires* as having replied, when asked who he thought was the greatest French poet, "Hugo, hélas!" In the *Poétique*, he makes amends by being more than generous. Despite its brevity and simplicity, the study is a comprehensive expression—almost a manifesto—of Gide's credo.

The reward of the associative spirit in poetry is enriched imagery; the temptation in prose is digression. The author unfettered by rules of thumb (or the traditional rule of three mocked by Gide's Prometheus in his address) is not committed, of course, to strictly logical development of his theme or story. Yet abuse of his right to digress may cost him intelligent readers; however pleasant his peregrinations, the narrator who seems lost himself risks losing much of his public. And a strong sense of discipline is a rare virtue among chain-reaction thinkers. Montaigne and Montesquieu, for example, cause some anguish in those who are fastidious logicians. Stream-of-consciousness writers, pushing associative technique to its extreme point, sometimes contend that their meandering fictions are true representations of thoughts and events in life. The use of logical argument to justify artistic or other disjointedness is also met in Gertrude Stein's resorting to intelligible English to explain how to understand seemingly unintelligible poetry.

Diderot, ever inclined to be lured into interesting byways by an attractive idea, restrains himself when his thoughts are to be formulated and circulated as public information. When the mood is on him, alone or in company, he slackens the rein of discipline and lets his mind canter or gallop. A few of the works that appear during his life show his propensity for choosing detours rather than direct routes. Among them are *Les Bijoux indiscrets* (*The Indiscreet Jewels*), *L'Eloge de Richardson* (*Eulogy of Richardson*), the two major *Lettres* and the *Essai sur . . . Claude et Néron* (*Essay on Claudius and Nero*). But he is at his most relaxed and expansive, hence most digressive, in what is intended for publication only after his death. In the d'Alembert dialogues, continuity of ideas is veiled in seeming incoherence. In *Le Neveu de Rameau* (*Rameau's Nephew*), there is a studied inconsequence that makes an excellent vehicle for presenting young Rameau as a parasitic drifter and unpredictable eccentric. In *Jacques le fataliste* (*James the Fatalist*), ambling and rambling are deliberate devices; digression is the only path that seems open to the characters and their observers, the public. Diderot confesses his errant inclinations to his mistress in one letter: "If I were to try to follow my ideas, a person could have hopped his way around the world on one foot before I finished. The world, incidentally, is about nine thousand leagues around. . . . And may a thousand devils carry off Mariveau [*sic*] and all his insipid imitators like me." He prefers *marivaudage* (bandying of trifles in the style of Marivaux) and its verb, which he coins, to the better known terms used in the *Neveu* to characterize this type of thinking. "I abandon my mind to all its libertine inclinations" has its variants in the correspondence, "for I do meander like Marivaux, a Marivaux who does not know he is one, although I do know I am." And he observes again that "since Crébillon's fairy Taupe, no one has yet been better at the Marivaux approach than I." [36] The self-censure is playful, but it is not altogether groundless. Somewhat more seriously, he attributes his failure to do all the plays he projects to his lack of perseverance and resolution. Without immodesty he could blame his being too busy with necessary chores and with the occasional pursuit of other intriguing thoughts. But the caricature is really part of his public pose—he is far from inconsistent in the expression of his ideas, whatever mental foibles he may have. Few literary men, as a matter of fact, have been more capable of discipline and organization. For physical and intellectual perseverance, his toil on the *Encyclopédie* ranks with the Herculean labors of Walter Scott and of Balzac. His confessions of incoherence and ill-directed effort are no doubt prompted by reflections on what he might have been, had chance and circumstance not made him what he is. At times he is simply teasing or humoring the reader, fabricating a *paraître* (public image) by exaggeration, rather than attempting to portray his *être* (essential personality). In a letter to Catherine of Russia, he gives the lie to his own banter and to those who picture him as spontaneity and instability personified. Discussing the creative process as he knows it from personal experience, he emphasizes the need for skill, toil, and taste. Orderly procedure and cautious pace are necessities. After selecting his topic with care, he mulls over the ideas involved and related—wherever he is, he is "hounded" by his tasks; he documents himself thoroughly, makes various notes, lists (and even numbers) the points he intends to bring out. Next comes a period of corroborative reading and marginal elaboration, followed by reorganization of argument and elimination of weaknesses. The final stage is one of preoccupation with style and effect—as consciously fastidious as Gidean art: "the final polishing-up, the most thorny and difficult of toils . . . especially in a country where a few ill chosen turns of phrase can ruin a very good book." [37]

Gide admits to less struggle between the opposed forces of his associative yet orderly mind. What has been called his classical attitude is his curbing of the inner desire to allow his ideas to wander beyond the point where he can control them. The prospect of expressing his thoughts in print is perhaps the most salutary of influences; on the urge to abandon himself to his thoughts, temptations, and desires, his art often imposes strict discipline. A planned campaign, he discovers, can lead to desirable habits, so he forces himself early in his career to write a small amount each day as a sort of "literary hygiene." Furthermore, if his writing is to be effective, he must manage to control not only his exuberance but also the verbal interpretation of his feelings, schooling himself sternly, ever mindful that one must "never prefer oneself to the chosen end, to the work." He is completely sincere when he notes: "I readily imagine that everyone else works more easily than I." One measure of his skill is the seeming facility of his writing—his artistic anguish, fortunately, is not revealed in a tortured style. But literary conception and gestation are as trying for him as they are for Diderot. He has no peace of mind; he feels his mind "cluttered" with his work; he lives with his undertaking, examines it from many angles for possible shortcomings; he seeks the illusion of "working in the absolute." [38] And only after long incubation, then long cohabitation with its own aspects, echoes, and opposites, the idea reaches the mature stage and, eventually, the public.

This curious aim of simultaneously encouraging thought to grow and expand while constraining its verbal manifestation to ordered form is a major feature of the Diderot-Gide outlook. In Diderot, there is a meeting, almost a conflict, between love of inquiry and wish for intelligibility, essential traits of men dedicated to human enlightenment. Although Gide is prone to indulge his physical desires, he keeps his mind from spending itself in philandering. Intelligibility, from the reader's viewpoint, keeps Gide in check, as it does Diderot—intelligibility closely coupled to artistic effect.

To try to characterize such mentalities would be to attempt to compress quicksilver. Their essence is activity itself, their tendencies are legion, their tenets are relativistic. The products of the two minds are equally difficult to summarize or even to sort into categories. Assézat was not at all satisfied with his six major divisions of Diderot's works (philosophy, *belles lettres*, science, fine arts, *Encyclopédie* articles, letters). Gide was so far from pleased with the headings classifying his works (*récit*, *sotie*, *roman*, etc.) that they were dropped by the publishers. No attempt is made in this volume to discuss all the work or epitomize all the ideas of the two. What is stressed in the following studies is the double vision each has of things and problems. It is an obvious simplification of their multilateral views. An examination of each author's dual considerations of different sides of questions will involve reference to most of the separate works. That is incidental to the main purpose here, which is to show that in emphasizing differences—sometimes by blending, sometimes by balancing opposites—each of these advocates of extremes discovers some techniques, some intellectual bearings, and even some moral orientation.

Extremes and Emphases

An open and venturesome mind yields rich satisfactions: new perceptions, unusual intellectual experiences, discoveries in uncharted territory. At the same time, a "universal" intelligence and an irrepressible spirit impose on an author restrictions that can be frustrating. He may be "requis et délicieusement malmené" ("called upon and delightfully mistreated")—to use Gide's words—by the penchant that possesses him as though it were a devil in his flesh. It is not enough for him to integrate or reconcile the divers ideas in his thoughts; he must transmute them into understandable print. The less orthodox his thinking is, the more arduous the task of presenting it becomes; the greater the intended public, the less the thinker's privilege of explaining at length the complex and subtle ideas he is trying to illustrate.[1]

In diaries and letters, as in simple tales, questions of presentation are not paramount. In those of Diderot and Gide, there are thought-provoking ideas in abundance, sometimes merely mentioned in passing, sometimes promising a future expansion indicated in headings or sketches, outlines and plans. But in works that are to educate or persuade, there is need of skilful argument, spoken or implied, if the public is to be beguiled into scrutinizing the several facets of an issue. Faced with this tactical problem, Diderot and Gide solve it in similar ways. They show contrasted points of view by extensive use of dialogue and they point toward possible lines of thought by emphasis on links that suggest chains and on gestures that may symbolize philosophies. This technique lends itself equally well to the causes of enlightenment and literary art.

During the years of his apprenticeship as a man of letters, Diderot has set patterns to follow. His earliest projects, all translations from English, provide training in skills as well as in patience. Stanyan's *Grecian History,* James's *Medicinal Dictionary,* and Shaftesbury's *Essay on Virtue and Merit* appear in French versions, followed by Diderot's own digest of Shaftesburian ideas in the *Pensées philosophiques* (*Philosophical Thoughts*). These may be mediocre literature, but they reward the young hack with more than his meager pay. First, they acquaint him with the free thinking and outspoken opinion prevalent in England. They allow him to demonstrate the intelligence and capacity for work that commend him for the editorship of the *Encyclopédie.* And, most important among the benefits, they accustom him to the double perspective that is to be the source of his mature technique of exposition. Attempting to understand foreign mentalities, he soon realizes, is an excellent means of improving one's own. A competent Latinist and interpreter of English, he manages to read Italian but shows little interest in learning German or Russian, although he passes through German states and visits Russia in his travels. It must be remembered, however, that French was the language of the northern European court circles of his day. There is slight evidence, by the way, of Diderot's proficiency in speaking any foreign language; his concern is with ideas and their expression in literary form, even in 1749, when reputedly he is annotating Milton to pass the time in Vincennes prison. He recognizes early that translation is far from a menial task, a fact that has been acknowledged by distinguished authors who have attempted it from Dryden to Gide. The point is made in his "Réflexions sur Térence": "There is then but one way to give a faithful rendering of a foreign author in our own language. It is to have one's mind completely imbued with the impressions one has from reading him, to refuse to be satisfied with the translation until it awakens the same impressions in the reader's mind. But is that always possible?" [2] His observations, on the curious interplay of desire for intelligibility on the one hand and frustration by poetic implications on the other, lead to musing on what is essentially untranslatable: harmony, stress, rhythm, pace, imagery, onomatopoeia, and subtle nuance.[3] Gide, who takes up the art relatively late in his career—and without financial motives—also reaps profit from the intellectual exercise of translating English literature into French. To the end of his life, he regrets not having learned to speak English well or German at all, except for a few turns of phrase. In spite of this, his renderings of Shakespeare, Blake, Conrad, Whitman, and Tagore have earned him a respected place among modern translators. The linguistic labor has supplied him, too, not only with extra perspective but with terms (such as "gait" and "serviceability") to which he resorts when French seems inadequate.

In his literary adolescence, although he is a man in his thirties, Diderot experiments in form as well as in topic. He tries allegorical narrative in *La Promenade du sceptique* (*The Skeptic's Walk*), religious disputation in

La Suffisance de la loi naturelle (*The Sufficiency of Natural Law*), amorous fable, oriental style, in *Les Bijoux indiscrets* (*The Indiscreet Jewels*), the licentious tale in *L'Oiseau blanc, conte bleu* (*The White Bird, a Fairy Tale*), and scientific treatises on music (harmonics, a new type of organ, acoustics). There are some distant parallels to these efforts, it may be noted, in Gide's early writing: allegory in *Le Voyage d'Urien* (*Urien's Travels*) and *Paludes* (*Morasses*), skepticism in the *Journal* (see "Religion," 3 June 1893), amorous fable, Gidean style, in *La Tentative amoureuse* (*The Attempt at Love*), and music as a frequent topic in notebooks and diary. It is Diderot's amateur interest in music that cements his friendship with Rousseau, brings the Rameau family to his attention, and later embroils him in the public controversy on the relative merits of Italian and French musicians.

Charged by the powerful Marquis d'Argenson with having written in favor of deism and to the detriment of public morality, Diderot disowns most of his early works as "intempérances d'esprit qui me sont échappées" (inadvertent errors in judgment) or denies his authorship entirely. Although they do contain much literary chaff—Assézat, for example, calls *Les Bijoux* "une incartade de jeunesse" (a youthful indiscretion)—these first efforts at originality contain some grains that will prove productive later, notably the seeds of a libertinism that will grow into full-blown materialism and, especially in the chapter on literature in *Les Bijoux*, the first intimations of mature critical judgment.

Diderot assumes full stature as a literary figure, in full possession of his powers of exposition and dialectic, in the *Lettre sur les aveugles* (*Letter on the Blind*). Three aspects of his approach to problems are here in evidence: an underlining of the relationships among the senses and of the several senses with verbal intelligibility, an emphasis on dialogued presentation, and a stress on the use of twofold interpretation to clarify ideas: "Felicitous turns of phrase are those that are literal for one of the senses, such as touch, and at the same time figurative for another sense, such as sight. They shed a double light for the listener: the true and direct light of the expression and the reflected light of the metaphor." [4] Gide expresses an analogous thought in his *Traité du Narcisse* (*The Treatise of the Narcissus*). Here the poet sees beyond the simple appearance of truth represented to the profane eye by the symbol; he senses the deeper truth of the idea, to which he then gives its proper and inevitable expression, "sa forme véritable enfin, et fatale."

It is Diderot's fondness for spirited discussion that suggests the conversational form he gives most of his writing, beginning with the letter on the blind. The occurrence in titles or subtitles of words such as *dialogue, entretien, paradoxe,* and *réfutation* shows how convinced he is that lively debate can spur intelligent thinking. Even when it is not implicit in the title, contrast is used in most of his work to bring out relative truth. Apart from *Encyclopédie* articles, Diderot uses dialogue as his principal vehicle of presentation in nearly all that he writes after 1748. It serves musical instruction, for example, in the *Leçons de clavecin et principes d'harmonie* (*Lessons for the Harpsichord and Principles of Harmony*), religious argument in the *Lettre sur les aveugles,* moral illustration in the "Apologue du jeune

Mexicain" ("Fable of the Young Mexican") and the *Supplément au Voyage de Bougainville* (*Supplement to Bougainville's Travels*). It is used for character revelation in the *Neveu de Rameau* and for scientific and philosophical exposition in the d'Alembert series. The author admits candidly that dialogue is used with the calculated aim of provoking interest in his topics:

> I have done a Dialogue between d'Alembert and me. In it, we chat quite cheerily and even quite clearly, in spite of the dryness and obscureness of the topic. A second and more extensive Dialogue follows, acting as a clarification of the first, which is called *D'Alembert's Dream.* Those conversing are d'Alembert, who is dreaming, Mlle de Lespinasse, a friend of d'Alembert's, and Dr. Bordeu. If I had wanted to forego riches of content in favor of nobility of tone, my characters would have been Democritus, Hippocrates and Leucippus. But verisimilitude would then have forced me to stay within the narrow confines of ancient philosophy and I should have lost too much by doing that.[5]

The contention that Diderot suggested the attitude of Rousseau's first discourse, made by Marmontel and Grimm and never specifically denied by the *philosophe*, has been refuted many times; but it is still a possibility.[6] Much of Diderot's popularity in social and intellectual circles rested on his witty paradoxes, such as that of the king who went to heaven and the monk who went to hell.[7] The conversations of Father Galiani and "Father" Hoop delighted him as much as his "conversations with his own ideas" (the phrase is Meister's) largely because of their extravagant incongruities and juxtaposition of unlikes. And he proffers ironic solutions to patently insoluble problems, such as the queston of moral conduct in *Jacques le fataliste,* by reconciling incompatibles. Equally paradoxical is his system of adducing testimony that inveigles the observer to accept appearance as truth. The method, illustrated in *Sur l'inconséquence . . .* (*On Inconsistency*) and implicit in several of the problems in ethics (*cas de conscience*) he invents for his friends, is by no means original—it is common to studies in hypocrisy from Molière's *Tartuffe* to Gide's *Faux-Monnayeurs* (*The Counterfeiters*). Diderot refines and exaggerates the approach to such an extent that he sometimes confounds even his admirers by his bland assertions that black is white. Formal philosophers in his times and ours have mistaken the technical—and tactical—device for an ethical position and a moral dilemma.[8] The very existence of the *Encyclopédie* was assured, it should be remembered, by the editor's ability to frame "philosophic" argument in terms astutely borrowed from the enemies of the movement.[9] Anomaly of situation, like verbal paradox, contributes a means of suasion. The chaplain in the *Supplément* shows the absurdity of absolute moral codes, the son in the *Entretien d'un père* (*A Father's Conversation*), the necessity of temporary endorsement of bad laws.

Excelling as he did in dialogue, spectacular effects, and ability to externalize emotions, Diderot should have been a brilliant dramatist. But in spite of his aspirations to fame in the genre and a lasting affection for the theater, his success as a playwright was limited. However, as the author of a comprehensive study of the history, nature, and special functions of the drama and as the theorist of the *drame bourgeois* (middle-class play) he earned a place the plays themselves failed to win for him. For his formulation of the principles of natural delivery, stage grouping and business, and "pictorial" presentation, he is generally considered the founder of modern stage art and technique. A student of what is now called "communications theory," especially of gesture and pantomime, and an ardent admirer of Garrick's genius, he gives particular attention to the process and art of acting itself. His best-known thesis is that convincing performance is the result of shrewd, unemotional calculation and not of "losing oneself" in the role. Expounded in the *Paradoxe sur le comédien* (*Paradox on the Actor*), it is the culmination of painstaking research begun (scientifically and philosophically) in connection with the *Lettre sur les sourds et muets* (*Letter on the Deaf and Dumb*) and elaborated in *De la poésie dramatique* (*On Dramatic Poetry*) and the *Entretiens sur le Fils naturel* (*Conversations on "The Illegitimate Son"*). In his two main plays, *Le Fils naturel* and *Le Père de famille* (*The Father of a Family*), his deftness in dialogue and skill in stagecraft are subordinate to the moral theme. They are overshadowed, too, by the emphasis on the relationship of personal character to status in the home, employment, and society (*conditions*). The visual effects, the positioning and the pictorial groupings on stage (*tableaux*), however, are remarkable innovations. The subtitle of the first—"Les Épreuves de la vertu" ("The Tribulations of Virtue")—and the didactic intention of the second, explained in its dedicatory letter, give some idea of the Richardsonian spirit that pervades the plays. It is that spirit, perhaps, that does most to consign them to the limbo of social-problem dramas, where they will wait a century or more for company from the pens of Augier and Dumas *fils*.

Diderot's conviction that the theater was his true vocation—it was his great regret that the *Encyclopédie* left him so little time for it—comes closer to justification in *Est-il bon? Est-il méchant?* Written nearly a quarter of a century after the others, it has clever dialogue as its prime feature, from the questioning title to the all-inclusive answer in the final scene, where Hardouin-Diderot is judged:

> Is he good? Or is he bad?
> Both in turn.
> Like you and me and everybody else.

Gide's presentation, like Diderot's, is essentially through dialogue. He devotes little space to explanation and description, choosing to stress and illustrate opposed points of view in conversations. The choice of form is most appropriate to expressing his own character, if we believe his statement: "I am a creature of dialogue; everything within me is contention and contradiction." There is constant dialogue of opinion everywhere in his writing, theatrical and other. It is present not only in structure and in verbal argument but in his treatment of plot, theme, and characters. The translator of his journals has pointed out that Gide's life itself is a study in delicate and dynamic equilibrium, with its poise attained through the balancing of the soul and the flesh, life and art, expression and restraint, individual and society, ethics and esthetics, classicism and romanticism, Christianity and religion, God and the devil.[10] The principal irony in most of his tales and plays, as well as in his one novel, lies in the incongruity between intentions and practice, between idealistic hopes and limited attainment. This is as true of dreamy André Walter as of ineffectual Edouard. As the drama of human activity, usually sordid or pathetic, is played by protagonists and their foils, their natures, aims, and intellects are sharply contrasted; and within the sentiments of the characters there is further division and contention. Strong and independent personalities thrive on this infinite variety, while the weak become victims of the others or of their own fears and their need to conform with prevailing mediocrity. Gide does not exempt hmself. A decade before he dies, he regrets the restrictions and fears of censure that sometimes upset the "balancing" of his ideas. He wishes that his thought could still shape itself in dialogue, as it did in his younger days.

Even between his works, Gide strives to maintain a sort of balance: *Paludes,* for example, is to some degree a counterweight as well as an ironic preface to *Les Nourritures terrestres;* the contrast between *L'Immoraliste* and *La Porte étroite* (*Strait Is the Gate*) is deliberate; *Robert,* as the husband explains in his own sanctimonious way, had to be written to correct the prejudiced picture given by Eveline in *L'Ecole des femmes* (*A School for Wives*)—and Geneviève's version is a further corrective to both. In *Les Faux-Monnayeurs,* there is a vast assortment of illustrations (some of them almost clinical studies in moral philosophy) of the unending debate between honesty and hypocrisy—a debate that is sustained not only in verbal dialogue, but in states of mind, in circumstances, and in elaborate patterns of interwoven deceits.

The failure of Gide, not unlike that of Diderot, to win lasting acclaim as a writer of plays stems from his use of what is fundamentally nondramatic material. The contradictions between life and thought are difficult to stage as a serious spectacle and perhaps even more difficult (for anyone less endowed than Molière) as a *comédie de caractère.* Gide's enthusiasm for the theater, his wide acquaintance with that special world, and his perceptive judgment of theatrical talent are as evident in his criticism as they are in his encouragement of such people as Louis Jouvet, Charles Dullin, and Jean-Louis Barrault. With Jacques Copeau, he founded the "Théâtre du Vieux-Colombier," often serving behind the scenes or as a prompter. Like Diderot, he studied the historical development of the theater and was impressed by Shakespearean drama. He stated his own views publicly, notably in his "Evolution du théâtre." [11] He observed techniques of acting with a keen eye, proposed some innovations in stagecraft, and lived to see his dramatization of *Les Caves du Vatican* on the boards of the Salle Richelieu. But his plays, in general, won less public approval than those by relatively unknown literary figures, some of whom he discovered and sponsored.

For Gide, the most significant dialogue is the one he has with his own central ideas. The raw material of his *Interviews imaginaires* and of the many articles once grouped under "critique" and "divers" exemplifies his questioning of his own thoughts and attitudes. Throughout his writing, he uses human illustrations instead of theoretical discussion to present for the reader's consideration his personal problems and those of humanity. This is frequent in the "detached pages" and not unusual elsewhere in the journal. Typical of this open review is the "Dialogue avec le bon Dieu" ("Dialogue with God").[12] Although he offers in it nothing so presumptuous as a "solution," he manages to avoid being completely neutral. Since each man must judge for himself, Gide merely indicates the antipodes of what is an eccentric globe, without specifying the point of balance. It is the privilege (or problem) of the reader to define that point, to establish his own equilibrium between self-realization and self-sacrifice, for example, or logical causation and *inconséquence* (inconsistency), between *être quelconque* (being ordinary) and *être quelqu'un* (being important), or between the predictable and its opposite, the *imprévu.* The same twofold technique presents the struggles that occur in the meetings of opposing forces or issues: the true and the counterfeit; man's salvation by his own effort and the role of Providence; intelligence and faith; sincerity and chicanery.

Dialogue and dialectic provide Diderot and Gide with the foundations and the building materials for their literary structures. What binds the ingredients is a strange compound of consistency and disjointedness they use both in planning and in constructing their works. *Enchaînement* (logical sequence or concatenation) is the watchword of the encyclopedists, as early as the preliminary discourse, which promises to "expose . . . the order and concatenation of human knowledge" to its readers. It is the means and the effect Diderot admires most in the deductions of Hobbes. But any chain can become more interesting as its links become less obvious: "There is nothing incoherent in the mind of a dreaming man or a madman, but it would sometimes be very hard to rediscover the imperceptible links that led to so many disparate ideas. Madness, dreaming, and disjointedness in conversation consist of passing from one thing to another via some common quality."[13] These lines might well serve as an epigraph to a study of Gide's *inconséquences,* if ever it is written as a sequel to his collected *Incidences* (*Angles of Incidence*), *Rencontres* (*Encounters*) and *Préfaces.*

Mention has been made earlier of Diderot's exploration of the scientific chain-of-being theory and of his treatment in the *Rêve de d'Alembert* of material continuity arising from contiguity and movement. In a section entitled "Evolution," Gide shows greater concern with moral and religious evolution than with the physical variety, arguing that it took centuries to form man and much longer to form a Supreme Being. For him, God is the endpoint, and not the beginning, of creation. The same assertion is made in different words in "Dieu fils de l'homme." Diderot, pleased with his discovery of a convenient relationship between succeeding stages of living matter, calls it "an endless concatenation of consequences"—an assertion that has been borne out by modern research. To describe his own danger of getting lost in considerations of his new concept, the *philosophe* uses the labyrinth-and-thread metaphor of which Gide will make repeated use, both in his version of the Theseus legend and as a symbol of the stabilizing influence of Mme Gide.

In his eternal search for relationships, Diderot is as concerned with series of ideas as he is with sequences of physical forms or facts. Struck by the disparities that exist between the logic of nature and the specious presumptions of aprioristic reasoning, he enlists *enchainement* among his forces for philosophic debate on determinism and chance, fatalism and divine guidance, personal freedom and tyrannical authority. As a narrator, he lets seeming incoherence cloak cogent reasoning in the words and acts of young Rameau, in the apparent *non sequiturs* of d'Alembert as he sleeps, in the *Supplément* report on sexual mores on a South Sea Island. He becomes convinced of the existence of a basic unity and consistency of parts within a normal organism and of their lack as the key to monstrosity. Searching for a *système un* (system based on unity), he is more amused than impressed by a thesis that all the arts can be reduced to one, then takes long steps in that direction himself in his art criticism. But his queries, as usual, bring him new questions. Inconsistency and incoherence are often more apparent than real, the vital links are frequently the most difficult to see. What is more, we judge too hastily on the basis of the small fraction of the continuum we can perceive or estimate. There is a surprising coincidence of attitude and form in Gide's meditations on diversity and constancy, and on the inconsistency that veils profound continuity in his *Nouvelles Nourritures*. There is one signal difference; Diderot is talking of the nature of things, Gide of himself.[14]

In the interplay of predestination and chance that is reported in *Jacques le fataliste*, the theme as well as the narrative development accentuates the *décousu*. Disjointedness is used partly to tease the reader, other authors, and the genre, partly to invite divers interpretations, and at times to reproduce with some verisimilitude the multifarious activity and incoherent conversation of daily existence. Jacques calls life "a succession of events" and scoffs at planned routines and belated regrets. Since everything is written in the Great Scroll, which unrolls as the acts take place, he professes a willingness to deal with questions when they present themselves—and not before. This poses some problems for him and his creators. Although Diderot pictures him as "inconsistent, like you and me," he is often shocked by the consistency of Jacques' character—as Gide will be by his Lafcadio when his gesture costs him his freedom of action. Equally disconcerting is the relationship between uncontrollable feelings and the happenings of which they are symbolic presentiments. The upshot for Jacques the would-be fatalist is anything but a resolute fatalism or a reassuring moral code; it is, first, a prudent respect for what may be prescribed on the unseen scroll and, second, an earnest—if unfounded—hope that all will go well, backed by an occasional prayer "on the off chance," as he says. By his sprightly, unpredictable actions and his disconnected arguments, he manages to demonstrate to his master and the reader that calculation as well as chance plays a part in human affairs. The final compromise Jacques makes with probability is analogous to Gide's final truce with motivation. Sheer chance, like perfect gratuitousness, remains ideal only as an abstraction—it is not translatable into action. Rameau's nephew, in like fashion, is characterized by his consistency with himself; even as he illustrates Diderot's contention that "nothing can be more unlike him than he is himself at times," and as he assumes more successive forms than Proteus, he has method in his seeming madness. There is an over-all pattern of relationships among his eccentricities. He plays his role—or his "vile pantomime"—with as much calculation and as deliberate an aim as Jacques. His Parthian shot shows that his engagingly irresponsible stance is as studied a posture as that of the ablest actor, a far cry from complete abandonment to circumstance:

> HE: . . . Good-bye, master philosopher. Isn't it true that I am always the same?
> I: Alas, yes, unfortunately.
> HE: May that misfortune last another forty years. He laughs best who laughs last.[15]

He has a shrewd appreciation of his own times and of how to survive with minimum effort, as well as the will to manage equally well in changing circumstances, present and future. His staid interlocutor cannot help being impressed artistically by his approach to sublime vileness, his quick intelligence, his brilliant interpretive antics, and, most of all, his ability to convert amorality into a rewarding way of life. Far from being a maniac, he has what modern behaviorists would call an integrated and well-adjusted personality. And he has a stature as an amoralist that Gide's Michel fails to attain as an immoral egoist.

In *Le Rêve de d'Alembert,* Dr. Bordeu interprets the sleeping mathematician's mumbled remarks to his supposed mistress, Mlle Lespinasse. What seems incomprehensible to her is brilliantly clear to the doctor, who fills in the transitional thoughts to reveal a comprehensive chain of argument on the life process from its simplest to its most complex forms. When the links are perceived, the soundness of the hidden logic is apparent to the intelligent listener and the implications are sensed even by Mlle Lespinasse.

Gide, too, considers *enchaînement*—as a scientist, an advocate of contingencies, and a narrator. He welcomes it as a dual symbol—of continuity and restriction—that invites as many treatments, extensions, and meanings as the concept of chance itself.

Like some of the characters he depicts, young André Gide believes existence should be planned and that talents must be developed through regular exercise. He sets up programs, agendas, and codes to guide his activities; he admires the directed energies of the dynamic individualist exemplified by Stendhal and formulated by Nietzsche. But when he takes stock of his own resources, he realizes such resolute austerity and purposeful drive are scarcely in keeping with human inclinations in general and his own in particular. It dawns on him that organization carried to excess becomes dull routine. Memoranda and timetables are mocked by events, rational plans are thrust aside by impulsive choices, continuity is broken by unscheduled happenings. With a feeling of deliverance from bondage, he does a series of ironic pictures: a paradise that is boring in its perfection, with a reflection in a river that calls out for its own destruction (*Le Traité du Narcisse*); a planned love affair that proves to be a vain desire (*La Tentative amoureuse*); an organized excursion from organized society to a nonexistent Utopia (*Le Voyage d'Urien*); a social survey of the pointless activity, the mediocrity, the frustration that are the products of a life of *enchaînement* (*Paludes*). In all of these, there are promising glimpses of a positive cure for the negative gloom. Adam, seeking "a little something unexpected," breaks a twig and time is born. Narcissus disturbs his stream with an active movement of the hand. Luc possesses his woman and *inquiétude* supplants chivalry. A melted spot is found in the frozen wastes of perfection. A friend leaves for Biskra on a trip the author has planned for himself, leaving him to search for the *imprévu négatif* in his own sterile life. In germ, the series of preoccupations in the *Nourritures terrestres* is already in these short works—rebellion, adventure, self-indulgence—as the antitheses of renunciation, banal conformity, and acceptance of chains.

After *Les Nourritures* there is a new chain, this time of challenges to continuity as well as convention; following each other closely are illustrations of the *imprévu, disponibilité*, the *acte gratuit*, and the *être d'inconséquence* (person of no consequence). The special role in man's affairs played by the unpredictable is the major concern in *Le Prométhée mal enchaîné* (*Prometheus Ill-Bound*) as it is in *Les Caves du Vatican* (*The Vatican Swindle* or *Lafcadio's Adventures*). The unexpected turn of events contributes, too, to *L'Immoraliste* and *Les Faux-Monnayeurs*; it is present, if incidental, in *Oedipe* (*Oedipus*), *Thésée* (*Theseus*), *Isabelle*, and *La Symphonie pastorale* (*The Pastoral Symphony*). Gide makes even more extensive use, then of his *inconséquence* than Diderot does of his concept of chance. If either author implies a conclusion, it is the relativistic one that few effects can be traced back easily to their causes, but that those causes exist in sequences, however many links seem to be missing from the chain.

In *Le Prométhée mal enchaîné,* Gide proposes a double enigma in the title, suggesting both the inadequacy of his hero's bonds and the incoherence of his own version of the myth. The English translation (*Prometheus Ill-Bound*) seems less felicitous in its ambiguity, since its second meaning might better allude to the printer's binding than the narrator's technique. In any case, Prometheus is only partially freed—his *aigle-conscience* limits his movement until the final scene. The eagle as a living bird is a nuisance; as a symbol of conscience plus consciousness, it is a baleful presence. Zeus, as befits a *miglionnaire,* is unchained—and free to complicate at least two lives through his gratuitous gestures: he gives new personalities to Damocles, the slave of duty, and to Cocles, the opportunist. The reader is to infer, presumably, that Zeus alone is capable of a real *acte gratuit* or a genuine deed of *inconséquence.* Cocles, who is *disponibilité* incarnate, proceeds to fulfill his own possibilities, more helped than hindered by his accidental loss of an eye. Poor Damocles finds his changed status difficult to bear, as he experiences and observes the difference between being *quelqu'un* (a person of consequence) and being *quelconque* (inconsequential). Prometheus himself is a study in seeming incongruities, yet there is logic and progression in his words and conduct: in his address on morals, his discourse on Tityrus and his *chêne* (oak) —or *châine* (chain)—and his disposal of the overzealous eagle. Zeus, however, lacks the human touch—he remains inscrutable, refuses to reveal his motives, and preserves both his prestige and his godly initiative.

Gide pretends, in *Les Caves du Vatican,* to invent an *acte gratuit* that is wholly human, spontaneous, and criminal. When the experiment fails, no one is less surprised than the author. Lafcadio is carefully contrived as a likely candidate for the role of ideal *être d'inconséquence* (an inconsequential character, unhampered by logic), dedicated to *la libre disposition de soi-même* (readiness to take on any project), anxious to *passer outre* (avoid routine ties). But sublimity in inconsistency must involve no plans, no aims, no commitments—Lafcadio is caught in his own trap from the beginning. To be consistent with himself he must be *inconséquent* in all senses of the word and in all his behavior. It is not enough that one act seem unmotivated and unlikely to have significant results: "No doubt this external inconstancy hides a more subtle, inner logic." He suspects he has motives, even as he assures himself he has none. When he pushes Fleurissoire, who is indeed a person of little consequence, from the moving train, he is morally and legally guilty of murder, and he knows the social implications of his supposedly gratuitous crime. The effects on his person, even if he escapes the law, are still more devastating. He is committed by his act to banishment from the ranks of *les subtils* (clever scofflaws); he has forfeited freedom of choice and of conduct and become worse than *les crustacés* (hard-shelled observers of laws), the unthinking marionettes he has long scorned. There is added irony in a discussion Lafcadio has with Julius, who imagines himself to be a *subtil* as he creates a literary character of whom Lafcadio is the physical counterpart.

Caution and consistency in operations, plus inescapable circumstances, are the undoing of Protos, who has a genius for swindles, for covering his tracks, and for disguises. He ends up as a third-rate criminal. In *L'Immoraliste,* Michel, the protagonist, who resolves to be the consummate *immoraliste,* is bound by the chain he forges. He recognizes that his freedom has been paid for in anguish and death by his wife Marceline, even as he justifies his selfishness with "I must prove to myself that I have not gone beyond my rights." Vincent, who sets out in pursuit of pleasure that is "gratuitous, immediate and unmotivated" in *Les Faux-Monnayeurs,* is another victim of misguided belief in *inconséquence.* The *acte gratuit,* then, is beyond the capabilities of humans. At best, it exists only as an ideal concept, with such fictional absolutes as the perfect crime. In the debate with himself on *enchaînement* and *conséquence,* Gide presents the negative side, the case for *inconséquence,* to bedevil those who find consistency, continuity, and causality in everything. He has Édouard paraphrase the idea: "At the present time," he notes in his dairy, "I am very close to seeing in irresolution the secret of not growing old."

In Gidean narrative, there is often a strange complexity achieved through interruptions, interpolations, and digressions. In some respects, this *composition décousue* (technique of disjointedness) is necessary to convey the subtleties of observable *inconséquence.* But with neither Diderot nor Gide does this seemingly casual presentation mean casual literary structure—the form itself is the result of studied care: a telling argument, for example, can be implicit in apparent incoherence; what looks accidental can be prepared for and timed for maximum effect, as it is in the theater; chaotic activity on the surface may hide orderly advancement of a theme. This is particularly true of Gide, who insists on his reader's collaboration. The carefully balanced structure of *Les Faux-Monnayeurs,* Jean Hytier has pointed out, involves three divisions, the first and third of eighteen chapters, the middle of seven. The second, which takes place in Switzerland, is a sort of plateau of conversation; the others, set in Paris, include more direct narration.[16] The neat architecture of the novel may escape the eye of the reader swept along in the maelstrom of events and the complex interweaving of lives that fill the pages. More obvious features are the abrupt halts, tangent developments, multiplication of side-plots, and changes from direct to indirect narrative. Adding to the complication are extracts from diaries and letters, interjected comments by the author among those of the characters, allusions and opinions to be interpreted at various levels. There are challenges to the reader, admissions by the novelist as well as by the story's novelist of the difficulties encountered in the process of creation. Little effort is made to start or finish in the traditional manner or to gather momentum through gradations, much less to indicate continuity by convenient transitions. The chapters seem as autonomous as the several lives that are portrayed; it is as though only accident brings them together. Whether or not the kaleidoscopic amalgam can be considered a novel depends on the reader's definition. Gide was convinced it was, of course, and Hytier's "the novelist's novel" has a nice ambiguity. One of the best characterizations of Gide is that he "may not be a novelist, but he is certainly a born storyteller." And *Les Faux-Monnayeurs* is described with equal aptness as "instead of a novel, the fragments of a novel curiously connected" and "the substance of half a dozen novels." [17]

There is often an artistic *décousu* even in *Journal* entries. Some have incomplete sentences and sketched thoughts, suspension points, and bracketed notes such as "to develop" and "to do." In the *soties* (satirical farces), he puts a premium on sprightly activity, moving from one development to another unexpectedly, from one character to another without warning, at times in and out of the narration himself. In the prose *poésies*, he is equally agile, especially in *Le Traité du Narcisse* and *La Tentative amoureuse*.

Diderot's masterpiece of *non sequitur* narrative is *Jacques le fataliste*, but it is by no means his only exercise in disjointed composition. The private and open letters, the *Pensées philosophiques*, the three d'Alembert studies, the *Neveu de Rameau*, and the *Bijoux indiscrets* all abound in devices later used by Gide. But *Jacques* deserves special consideration, not only for its *décousu* but for its significance in demonstrating what Diderot thinks the novel might be, much as Gide thinks his *Faux-Monnayeurs* epitomizes his theory. Whether or not its primary purpose is to parody the genre, *Jacques* provides a thorough survey, wittily illustrated, of the resources—realized or potential—of narrative fiction. Not the least of these is the good company within the narration itself of author, story, and reader—the first taking advantage of his privileges of intervention and critical comment, the second struggling to get to its point, the third a keen observer and listener, frequently reproached by the narrator for his silent disapproval of either the tale or its presentation. In the manner of the perambulating English narrators, Diderot and his protagonist wander through a maze of incidents and encounters as the history of Jacques's love affair is pieced together and his fatalistic thesis is expounded. Conversation, description, digression, and illustrative anecdote follow one another with little semblance of logic. As attention becomes focused on one development, it is suddenly diverted to something unrelated. The author pauses to discuss situations and his characters' reactions with the reader, sometimes asking his advice on what should follow, more often reminding him that this is a factual account, not to be tampered with by either teller or listener. Long interpolations are frequent—the story of Mme de la Pommeraye is the best known—and there are many short tales and lengthy anecdotes. But in spite of what seems at times like a conspiracy to frustrate both the master and the reading public, Jacques eventually leads his chronicle back to its point of departure, the notorious incident of the injured leg "plagiarized" from *Tristram Shandy*. At the end, Jacques and his interlocutor have traveled far, talked at length, confused their roles, confounded their own philosophies—and solved nothing. Like the characters Gide creates, they find endings and beginnings not far apart. The action moves on at no predictable pace, like life itself; the actors are seen and then move out of sight without climax or dénouement. Caught up in a stream of happenings without perceptible design or control, they go on to new experiences that may well be mere repetitions, on a slightly different scale, of the old. D'Alembert, young Rameau, and the protagonists of the *contes* (philosophic short stories) are seen in episodes, not histories; Jacques and his problem change little in several hundred pages. In similar vein, Gidean characters confirm by their experiences the author's claim that "all things have already been said, but since nobody listens to them, we must always begin again." The writer of *Paludes* (*Morasses*) turns to composing *Polders* (*Dikelands*); the prodigal watches his brother slip away to learn his lesson at first hand; Édouard struggles with a novel that will probably end in "Could be continued . . ."—then turns from young Bernard to admire his younger brother. All are victims of "circular madness," the frenetic rush that leads back to the point of departure. There is a hollow ring, too, in the imagined triumphs of Alissa, Oedipus, and Theseus at the close of their episodic adventures. The first dies, feeling deserted by man and God; the second, blinded by his own hand, leaves Thebes as a nameless traveler, renouncing his possessions, his reputation, and his own personality; and there is a note that is resolute but scarcely joyous in Theseus's remark to Oedipus: "No matter how corrupt you consider man to be, he must play the cards he is dealt."

Dependence on the reader's intelligence, which entails risk as it demonstrates confidence, is a corollary question of presentation on which Diderot and Gide agree. Diderot leaves much to the ingenuity of those who enjoy intellectual effort: "Since it has been my purpose not so much to teach you as to make you use your mind, it does not matter a great deal whether you adopt or reject my ideas, provided you give them your full attention." [18] He introduces *Ceci n'est pas un conte* (*This Is Not a Tale*) to the public with "When a story is told, it is to someone who is listening to it. However little time it takes to tell it, it is unusual if the narrator is not sometimes interrupted by his listener. That is why, in the story you are about to read, I have introduced a character who comes close to playing the role of the reader." Throughout *Jacques le fataliste* he apostrophizes the reader, adding such remarks as, "if you are grateful to me for what I am telling you, be very grateful for what I am not." His parting thrust is "If you are not pleased with what I am disclosing to you about Jacques's love affairs, reader, do better yourself. You have my permission." [19]

Gide stipulates early the relationship he expects between author and reader. *Paludes* has a significant foreword: "Before I explain my book to others, I am waiting for them to explain it to me. Wanting to explain it right away means restricting its sense forthwith. What particularly interests me in it is what I have put there without knowing it, that unconscious share that I should like to call Heaven's contribution. A book is always a matter of collaboration. Let us look everywhere for the revelation of things, but to the public for the revelation of our works." [20] Reminiscing on the composition of *Les Faux-Monnayeurs,* Gide speaks of having no wish to encourage the average, lazy reader. He aims at the "flying fish": "I write only for those who know how to take a hint." He sums up his attitude in the *Journal:* "I took care to indicate only the significant, the decisive, the indispensable; to avoid everything that was 'taken for granted' and where the intelligent reader could fill in for himself (this is what I call the *collaboration of the reader*)." Although he has qualms about his own "excessive continence" and "extreme conciseness," he appreciates La Rochefoucauld: "I like feeling in an author an inner, unexploited wealth which only rises to the surface in the rare writings he gives us." It is a reaffirmation of a position he has held for some time: "All our writers of today (I am speaking of the best) are *precious*. I hope to acquire ever more poverty. (Paradox). In destitution lies salvation." [21]

A final technical device resorted to by both writers—to elicit vivid mental pictures—is gesture. Tactically used, it makes for verbal economy and often illustrates by suggestion what is beyond adequate description. The *geste* that appeals to Diderot and that he tries to capture may be incidental or vital, but it is usually physical, picturesque, and a means of communicating ideas. The Gidean *geste* is one of character, the culminating act that exteriorizes and crystallizes convictions.

Diderot's earliest concern with gestures is scientific and philosophical. Like his associate Condillac, he is impressed by the Lockian theory of sensations and the roles played by the senses. No doubt the two, with their friend Rousseau, have numerous café chats on these popular topics as Condillac works on his *Essai sur l'origine des connaissances humaines* (*Essay on the Origin of Human Understanding*) and the *Traité des sensations* (*Treatise on Sensations*). A few years after the essay, but well before the treatise, Diderot writes his *Lettre sur les sourds et muets.* In it he airs his ideas on the relationships of gesture with thought, theatrical effects, idiom, conversation, mimicry, language in structural form, poetry, and imagery. The dramatic possibilities and artistic technique of pantomime are touched on in *Dorval et moi* (*Dorval and I*), where his *Fils naturel* is considered in detail, and examined more fully in *De la poésie dramatique* (*On Dramatic Poetry*). Diderot contributes to Grimm, for his foreign readers' edification, an article called "Observations sur une brochure intitulée *Garrick* ou *Les Acteurs anglais*" ("Observations on a pamphlet called *Garrick* or *The English Actors*"). His plea for natural acting and expressive, meaningful gesture—already popular practice in England and Italy—leads to the *Paradoxe sur le comédien.* It is in the *Paradoxe* that he enunciates his famous theorem: consummate skill in the interpretation of emotion is possible only for the "cold" actor, who creates (or recreates) the gesture and posture that depict and express that emotion.

In the *Neveu de Rameau,* lively gesture is the key to character as well as a means of showing the communicative power of pantomime. If the extravagant nephew has any legitimate claim to genius, it is in his silent clowning. In virtually everything he writes, Diderot makes telling use of gesture as a revelation of personality and mood. He pictures his own and others' poses, stances, and conscious efforts to elicit desired reactions as *la vie grimacière* (the life we affect), exemplified in his show of attachment to a dressing gown that has seen better days, and again in the mien of a churchgoer who senses she is being watched during a religious service. Unconscious gesture, on the other hand, is equally revealing. It becomes a sort of "second nature" that manifests itself in unguarded moments as *le tic* (quirk).[22] This may be a physical stance, a revealing movement, or the touch of jargon Rameau calls "the professional idiom."

It gives a man the stamp of his trade or indicates his habits and hobby-horses as surely as the distinctive cry identifies the animal.

Gesture often speaks significantly to—and for—Gide. It is his own in "Every time I make a gesture, I calculate: how many times already? I compute: how many times more?" He sees the spirit of Michelangelo fully expressed in the "tense gesture" of his Moses. In the *Journal,* there is a comment reminiscent of Diderot: "In order to express itself the pious feeling invents the gesture, or adopts it, then slips away from under the gesture, and soon the gesture substitutes for it." Of characters in a novel, the "Lui" in the *Interviews imaginaires* says: "What I should like to follow is the effect, on characters chosen at random and quickly abandoned, of a phrase or a gesture." Incidentally, he uses the term "déformation professionnelle" in the *Interviews* and gives several examples of verbal idiosyncrasies in the *Journal.* One of his favorite quirks, the use of a qualifying remark after each phrase, he gets from a tailor's son—it is so good he saves it to use as the basis of a character in a play.[23]

In addition to these mechanical and physical gestures, Gide depicts one that is more complex, an active epitomizing of personality. Its scientific and philosophic aspects are less important to him than its artistic utility. The form is that of the *acte gratuit,* a positive assertion of character, or the *beau geste* of moral affirmation implicit in the blinding of Oedipus. Alike in being dramatic exaggerations, both show the logical expansion of *le geste* from simple gesticulation to something approaching an act of faith. As strong tendencies of the spirit given definition in overt acts, they are counterparts of the climactic deeds of Molière's maniacs.

Diderot and Gide, in brief, are essentially dramatic in their writing. Their staging of the Human Comedy is inspired by the penchant both have for extremes and contrasts. Their presentation involves: twofold perspective and dialogued delivery; themes and characters in which *enchaînement* and *inconséquence* play a large part; disjointed plots; and inconclusive endings. The total effect of the spectacle is heightened by an emphasis on separate gestures, ranging from *un geste* (a casual or incidental gesture), which reveals a simple idea or attitude, to *le geste* (essential gesture), which crystallizes a complex personality.

Fools and Their Play

Since the days of Aristophanes, fools of infinite variety as well as jest have had a prominent place in literature. They range from those born witless to the highly intelligent who encourage madcap activity in word and deed as a temporary relief from the seriousness of life.

At the bottom of the scale are the dolts and louts, the dupes and the *pazzi,* whose wisdom is accidental or whose simplicity confounds the trickster. Next come those whose clever foolishness is calculated to win laughter or reward: the clowns, the jesters, the punchinellos and graciosos. Ranked with or above these are the likable rogues, the Lazarillos and the Scapins, the Frontins, Crispins and Figaros; in the picaresque tradition, they all rely on unscrupulous ruse to promote their masters' and their own causes. Somewhat higher, perhaps, are the serious thinkers who are haunted by guilt as they indulge in unwonted frivolity. The aristocrats are the irrepressible and complex few who are at once the sons of Erasmus and of Panurge. It is with the last group that Diderot and Gide are primarily concerned, although they have a keen interest in the whole hierarchy of fools and shrewd jesters. In spite of their lasting scorn for foolish acts springing from innate or induced stupidity, they confess to a wholesome respect for the tonic value of occasional folly, to an almost diabolical delight in the contributions to human affairs made by intelligent extravagance and momentary madness.

A sense of humor is an indispensable asset of the social commentator who attempts to interpret mankind's foibles with some generosity. It makes for balanced views, allows for comparisons, provides a rich assortment of inferences. It is, incidentally, an antidote to self-esteem and to hasty indictment of others. In its literary expression, humor ranges from gross and boisterous vulgarity to the most subtle of verbal nuance; in its effects, from the guffaw to the almost imperceptible smile. Diderot, living in lusty times and in a highly polished society, enjoyed humor of many types, from the broadest and most physical to the most refined. According to his reports of Rabelaisian banquets and riotous entertainment at Grandval, the d'Holbach country estate, he had a special fondness for jokes and pranks that were rarely subtle. The letters to Sophie were constantly enlivened by his accounts of "foolery of every conceivable sort," "an unparalleled bit of folly," "us vulgar occupants of Grandval," "inhuman outbursts of laughter." An off-color story, or an indecent remark at the dinner table that left him convulsed, was chronicled with similar zest.[1] But he was capable, often in the same letters, of indulging in thoughts and words of such delicate and whimsical implication that their "poetic" humor verges on the precious.

Gide leans toward humor of the quiet, intellectual kind. The incongruous situation and the ludicrous word, the clever rejoinder and the witty ambiguity—even, on occasion, the pun—appeal much more to him than physical horseplay recounted in anecdotes of shocking candor. But he and Diderot meet in their attitudes to *sots* (foolish people), *sottises* (acts of foolishness or stupidity), and the *sotie* (the portrayal of man's follies). They include themselves among the foolish, they recognize the virtue (as well as the perils) of foolishness; and they have a great enthusiasm for the fools' play they witness and help stage.

A volatile temperament and a wide emotional compass make each of them as capable of playing the buffoon as of thinking gravely. Responsive to appeals to the senses, to company, and to environment, they indulge in frivolity as readily as in seriousness, as though to illustrate young Rameau's remark: "There is no great wit without a grain of madness." Among the first of Diderot's characteristics to attract Gide's attention is his *disponibilité*. As evidence of one type of influence, he quotes in an address the *philosophe*'s comment, "When the wind is high, I feel madness in my spirit." Diderot makes no attempt to discourage the legend he creates of his own instability; he seems to take as a compliment Mme d'Holbach's reference to him as "mad or wise." When he finds himself taking life too earnestly, he sees he is a "sot personnage" (silly fellow). When he imposes total abstinence on himself, then goes among heavy drinkers, he considers his conduct unnatural and absurd. There are times, too, when he catches a glimpse of himself becoming presumptuous. Speaking of the human inclination to judge by appearances, he cites the case of an idiot picking up a straw he mistakes for a ray of sunlight, then adds "How many people there are who are just like that madman without suspecting it! Possibly I am myself, at this very moment."[2] All his life he remains "a very estimable fool"—a lesser evil than being what he calls

Falconet, "an extremely vain and very subtle sophist."

On one occasion, as he surveys such past efforts as the *Bijoux indiscrets,* he decides to reform: "I am giving up the bauble and bells forever. And I am returning to Socrates." But the stance is untenable. In the long run, he realizes that he still has his jester's rattle and garb—and that he likes them. From time to time, other attacks of seriousness, ill health, and indigestion lead him to foreswear acts of folly. The resolution soon fades and he continues to take chances, to overindulge his appetites, to make mistakes, and to enjoy being alive. In a salute and valedictory to folly which would have been an excellent epitaph, he writes to his sister: "I advise bad people to feel worried; as for people who are fools in good faith like me, they will be told they have been fools and that will be the end of it." The year is 1778, when both Rousseau and Voltaire die. Diderot lived until 1784.

Terms of foolishness are common in Diderot's allusions to his several amorous adventures. His "sweet madness" for Sophie helps him endure the trying times that follow his foolish passion for Mme de Puisieux, who proves so fickle while he is in Vincennes prison. It is the third of his great loves, Mme de Meaux, whom he asks to refrain—when she sees written on his tombstone "Here lies a wise man"—from revealing his secret by saying, "Here lies a fool."

Gide's personal profession of follies is, from the beginning, less categorical but no less frank, if entries in the *Journal* are taken at face value. He finds his own reactions at a funeral a bit ludicrous, in a scene that seems to anticipate Meursault's first "crime" in Camus's *L'Etranger.* As he draws up his rules for personal deportment, he includes one on straight-faced telling of jokes. He ends a sententious consideration of being and appearing with: "But, after all, what does all this matter!!?" He decides on a kind of "reverse sincerity" as a mode of behavior that will help him to appreciate himself. This endorsement of incongruity, even when it involves him personally, is one key to Gide's disciplined poise.

Sometimes he is troubled by his own lack of sincerity; sometimes he goes to the opposite extreme and accuses himself of pretentious inclinations, which he sees as "the most tiresome, insipid, and almost incomprehensible things in the world when one has got beyond them." A half-century later, he is still concerned: "The number of stupidities that an intelligent person can say in a day is not believable. And I should probably say just as many as others if I were not more often silent." Looking back on youthful excesses he dismissed at the time with "Tant pis!" Gide the septuagenarian muses, "Oh, what a good Mentor I should now be for the man I was in my youth!" There is a vague echo here of Villon's hollow regrets, as well as a reflection of La Rochefoucauld's maxim on the good precepts of those too old to provide bad examples. Diderot has a similar rueful thought: "Ah, we are all very well behaved when we no longer have what is needed to be foolish."

This recognition of their own shortcomings gives Diderot and Gide a generous, indulgent point of view. "Since we are not too sensible ourselves," says the *philosophe*, "let us allow others to be foolish." Gide, after he considers "this contemptible comedy that we all play more or less," concludes, "Hypocrites? . . . Not altogether."

In the maelstrom of Parisian life, Diderot is not inclined to rail against "all the foolishness that is said and done there" lest he be like the fat jostler who complains of the bustle he himself causes in the crowd. Gide is too critical of himself for Olympian scorn—his reaction to the scenes he witnesses is an ironic but understanding smile.

Madcap acts, singly or in series, provide Diderot with much material for a "fool's play." Among his unpredictable and ingenious friends at Grandval are "Father" Hoop, a dour Scot who has studied medicine and done some globe-trotting; Galiani, an Italian cleric with a fund of anecdotes; and the local parish priest, who enters spiritedly into the ribaldries of the group. The fun, games, and practical jokes keep the household in an uproar; some are worthy of Chaucer, Boccaccio, or Rabelais; most have the plausible extravagance and wild activity of a Gidean *sotie*. Diderot's account of one sounds like a publisher's announcement for the *Caves du Vatican*: "The basic material itself is contemptible, but as he treats it, it takes on a great deal of color and sprightliness, becoming an inexhaustible source of good jokes and even, at times, of morals." [3] Mme d'Aine, the mother-in-law (twice in succession) of d'Holbach, is a continual source of diversion to the clan. A delightfully shameless old extrovert, she has a "savage gaiety" that is at its best in rollicking horseplay—astride the surprised priest, screaming for help as she is "attacked" by an unwitting guest, having her seat measured, embarrassing her maid by references to her anatomy, gambling successfully after removing her underclothing for luck. Her distortions of words such as "Socoplie" (*l'Encyclopédie*) and her ludicrous pose as an intellectual rationalist are as much enjoyed as her physical gambols. Among the other guests who like to clown are the Baron himself, "a gay, piquant, indecent satyr," nasty old M. de Bagueville, whose many acts of folly include a dash into a burning house (a gesture Gide's Lafcadio will repeat), and Mme Le-Breton, "a thousand times sillier than she should be at her age." [4]

Diderot rarely uses the term fool in its harshest sense. When he does it is applied to the *crustacés,* whose impenetrable stupidity irks him. His self-righteous brother, for example, and an unwise critic, are indicted for endorsing "sanctified ignorance." Even his daughter is threatened—she hears so much said that is nonsense that Diderot fears he will never succeed in overcoming "this early and harmful incrustation."

Perhaps because the company he keeps is more inclined to intellectual than to muscular exercise, Gide speaks of the attitudes of his acquaintances rather than of their acrobatics. When he writes of oafishness, general or individual, he usually stops short of invective, although he is far from gentle with such critics as Henri Massis: "This fellow gives every impression of being an idiot." He is equally outspoken in dealing with those who distort his words, such as the overzealous proofreader who ruins a good quotation from Diderot by substituting "invents" for "imitates." [5] Personalities, with the exception of his own, interest him less for their separate whims than for the complex imbalance of traits that makes them eccentric individuals. As a result of this, the most striking examples of fools and their play are not in his descriptions of people he knows but in creatures of his own invention, notably the characters in the *soties.*

Part of the fascination of the human scene, for both Diderot and Gide, is the constant interplay of wisdom and folly. "Can a person be wise and foolish at the same time?" Diderot asks Sophie. And why do the stupid seem to succeed and the intelligent fail at times? Leaving the first question rhetorical, he suggests that the answer to the second may lie in the domain of sheer chance. Life is a gamble in which anyone, from cretin to genius, may win; both types sometimes "give up the dice just when their luck is going to change," and it may be assumed that "a lucky fool and an unlucky intelligent man . . . have not yet lived long enough." [6] As though apologizing for his own parade of sagacity, he affirms, "Nothing is commoner than the fool who says something wise." But in this world of fools, it would be overoptimistic to hope for universal intelligence: "Being born in a state of imbecility, in the midst of pain and outcry; being the plaything of ignorance, error, and need; returning step by step to the state of imbecility; from dotage on, living among rogues and quacks." [7] But the mood is transitory. Only at long intervals does Diderot seem to despair of the seed of Adam and Eve, "the two original containers from which have issued so many fools over the years." And even then he has a hypothesis—there may be poor years for crops of men as there are for other crops. In his mellower moments, he is lenient in his dealing with foolishness: "The time when unreason made me furious has gone by. I am getting used to it." Like the Voltairean messenger sent to inspect Persepolis, he reports "What a silly blunder the world is! But oh! my dear, what a lovely blunder! It is one of the innumerable comedies that entertain the Lord." Many months later, he adds a philosophic postscript: "Oh, what a fine comedy this world would be, if we did not have a role in it! If we lived, for example, at some point out in space from which we could observe all the little two-legged aphids people call men!" [8] The kindly impulse prevails, however, over the urge to censure; whenever Diderot surveys his fellow men, his faith in their possibilities is reaffirmed and his own crusading spirit is restored. Here again his sense of proportion saves him from smugness. When he pictures himself as a knight, it is sometimes as an incurably quixotic one: "I still shatter lances championing the human race."

Gide's reaction to folly as a universal phenomenon gets little attention in his diary, where his concentration on sincerity to himself and on literary form precludes the spontaneous evaluations and casual chatter that are characteristic of Diderot's letters. But Gide is by no means unaware of the existence of fools or the high incidence of folly in human affairs. He merely reserves the subject for treatment at length in the genre he invents to accommodate it. It is in his *sotie* that he considers the lighter side of humanity, while presenting some of its grave problems.

Folly is the common denominator of the *récits* and of the *soties*. In the former, it is the subject, which is usually some individual extravagance or self-deception, presented with ironic seriousness of manner and tone. The reverse is true of the *soties*, aptly described by Jean Hytier as "short stories in which good sense wears the guise of folly." In them, partly hidden behind a façade of frenetic nonsense, are some of Gide's keenest observations on his time and on the human race. On them, in all probability, will rest much of his future fame, notwithstanding his aspirations for *Les Faux-Monnayeurs* and the present popularity of the *Journal.*

Whether the *sotie* is taken as a short story, as a genre distinct from the usual ironic tale, or, to use Justin O'Brien's useful term, as a "satirical farce," its chief interest is in its spirit rather than its elusive form. In content and intention, it has more in common with its medieval namesake than with other possible ancestors, such as the philosophic tales of Voltaire and Anatole France. Its critical aim and its mixture of varied ingredients are vaguely reminiscent of Latin satire—and of Diderot's classification under that heading of two of his works. As fanciful on occasion as the *Arabian Nights Tales* and as fantastic at times as *Alice in Wonderland,* it is more than fantasy. And it has little rapport with most twentieth-century examinations of *l'absurde,* in spite of its abundant absurdities. Gide's first allusion to its cryptic nature is in the dedication of *Paludes:* "This satire of what?" He intimates, in the dedication to *Le Prométhée,* that there are many possible interpretations: "May a few rare people like you find some wheat, as you did, among these mad tares." The closest approximation to a helpful definition by Gide himself is in a letter to Jacques Copeau, to whom he dedicates *Les Caves:* "Why do I call this book a *sotie* and the three earlier ones *récits?* To make it clear that they are not, properly speaking, *novels.* Moreover, it does not matter very much to me if people take them to be novels, provided I am not then accused of failing to follow the rules of the 'genre.' *Récits, soties* . . . it seems to me that until now I have written nothing but works that are *ironic* (or critical, if you prefer). This is no doubt the last of them." [9]

There is little resemblance in themes and there is no standard narrative pattern in the three works Gide spoke of as *soties*. Their lengths vary from that of a long tale or a short novelette to that of a novel, but length is one of the few respects in which they correspond to any of the established types of fiction. Gide called *Les Faux-Monnayeurs*, perhaps because it is long and the label is elastic, "my first novel." To some readers it, too, seems a *sotie*, or an expanded *sotie*. *Le Prométhée* and the inner story of *Paludes* are myths, reinterpreted in modern—and very Gidean—style, full of irreverence, anachronism, and play on situation and word.[10] They deal for the most part with the inertia, hypocrisy, and confusion of a present-day world that is ridiculously out of joint. The chaotic nonsequence of events masks carefully plotted development, creating an air of complete fortuitousness that is perhaps their only constant feature. The narrator, too, is as busy as the story, into which he interjects his comments as the spirit moves him. Each of the protagonists has in him an exaggeration of one trait that distorts his nature. The writer in *Paludes* has a vocation; Prometheus has his other self; Lafcadio has a pathological curiosity. But the characters, who think themselves free agents, are controlled both by circumstance and by the author, and they are objects as well as subjects of irony. The wisdom and impudent wit that stamp them are not theirs alone.

As every French schoolboy knows, the *sottie* or *sotie*

is a kind of fool's play that flourished in the comedy of the later Middle Ages. For his own purposes, Gide resuscitates the word and attaches it as a label to his modern tales of apparent fools and seemingly pointless foolishness. Is this device contrived only as a clever anachronism, like the modern background given ancient myth? Or is there a singular appropriateness in the use of the term to describe the manifest madness in our times?

Nothing indicates that Gide had a particular interest in medieval plays of any kind. In all likelihood, he subscribed to the common misconception that the *sotie* was a distinct genre, a brother (or illegitimate child) of farce, vulgar in its language, carelessly improvised, and devoted largely to nose-thumbing at authority, both churchly and civil. Such an impression, however erroneous, lends the word an aura that may have commended it to Gide's use.

The exact nature of the medieval *sotie* becomes generally known only with the appearance in 1935 of the collection known as the *Recueil Trepperel.* By coincidence, that is the year Gide asks his publishers to abandon the system of headings long used for listing his separate works. There is an appreciable irony, if not perversity, in his discarding of the word *sotie* at the very moment that it takes on new aptness. The publication of fourteen previously unprinted *soties* and two known ones corrects the traditional view of what a *sotie* is—and in so doing gives emphasis to the very features Gide stresses in his definition and exemplars of the modern *sotie.* It becomes evident that Gide has a just claim to the throne once held by Gringoire, the most famous *mère-sotte* and director of *sots.* He is a direct heir, though the genealogy is difficult to trace, of much of the best in the early *soties*—as well as of many of their less praiseworthy qualities, real and imagined. In general, for example, he insists on good sense as a basis for dramatized foolishness, as does the motto that frames Jehan Trepperel's trademark: "Everything through reason. Reason in everything. Through everything, reason." The material Gide turns to account, like that of his predecessors in the Middle Ages, is "all humanity, ridiculous and grotesque as it is." His presentation is neither careless nor naive: "The *sottie* can be a dramatic action that is constructed and developed with learned skill. The dialogue is lively and intelligent, the action is brisk, the author uses other means than vulgarity and puns to arouse laughter." [11] With some slight elaboration as to intentions and themes, this definition is as appropriate to Gide's variety of the *sotie* as it is to the older type it describes.

The aim of the medieval play, in addition to entertainment, was social commentary. There were many topics and themes. Slight attention was given to the Church—and even less to politics. Subjects included recent happenings, local and national, changes in laws and regulations, current scandals, and such social evils as drunkenness. Ridiculous figures of all strata were exposed as objects of laughter. By no means all the plays had moralizing aims, but absurdity in its many human manifestations was paraded for public consideration. The number of characters was limited; it ranged from three to eight and was usually about six. The action was brisk and often disconnected. Some *sotties* in fact had next to no story or plot—there was a sort of procession of the performers, enlivened by blows, insults, and asides to the crowds.

Sometimes there were pseudoserious declamations and acrobatic turns. The most popular of the devices involved spoken effects, verbal extravagance, and the jargons of trades and professions. One of the Trepperel *sotties*, for example, provided Rabelais with his character spouting garbled Latin. The general atmosphere of the plays, then, was one of spirited activity, with an abundance of mischievous merrymaking spiced by occasional vulgarity of scene and crudity of language. The real meaning was easily inferred but rarely stated explicitly as a moral. Gide's approach and techniques are similar.

Much of the accepted idea of what *soties* were comes from the fame of Pierre Gringoire's *Prince des sots* (*Prince of Fools*). This is really a three-part play or *jeu*, comprised of a *sottie*, a *farce*, and a *moralité*. Directed against the temporal pretensions of Pope Julius II as an attack sponsored by Louis XII, it is far from being representative of the true *sottie*. In its anti-Roman intention, as in its travesty of the Pope's person, it anticipates the religious *soties* and farces of the late sixteenth century —and the *Caves du Vatican*.[12] But it is quite unlike the *sottie* of pre-Renaissance days.

In the twenty-seven extant plays of the great period (up to 1520), there is little sign of the monstrous irreverence, bordering on sacrilege, that is often attributed to *soties*, both ancient and twentieth-century styles. It is a feature, however, of the merrymaking known as *fêtes joyeuses* in the early Middle Ages. These ancestors of the *sotie* and of modern Fool's Day celebrations were probably related to ancient *saturnalia* and were of two types:

the *fête des fous,* primarily a parody of Church ritual, and the *fête des sots,* which directed most of its ridicule at bourgeois society.[13] A "Fool's Bishop" was elected to lead a riotous parade through the streets, then give a "joyous sermon" from the pulpit. His "congregation" sang lascivious songs to hymnal melodies, used the altar as a buffet for food and drinks, burned shoes as incense. They then enjoyed play with dice, cards, and bowls, danced and banqueted in the nave, and finally staggered cheerily forth to patrol the streets in carts, to a pandemonium of raucous cries and ribald songs. The church was left to be cleansed with mops and prayers before the next service. The imagined supplanting of the true Pope by the freemasons and the libation to which Protos invited Amédée in *Les Caves* reflect this spirit, rather than that of the *sottie.*

The Gidean *sotie,* with so rich an assortment of forebears, is no less an invention of Gide's. If he was influenced, it was in the only sense of the word influence that he accepts—that every artist is indebted to everyone and to no one. Yet there is in his work a compounding of the elements, laudable and other, of the old *sottie* with the mockery of the *fête joyeuse* and the obscenity of low farce. One striking resemblance between the medieval and the modern fool's play is in what an early *Art poétique françois* calls "the irregular variety of incoherent turns of phrase." What Gide adds as his special contribution is a total and artistic atmosphere of incongruity. He accomplishes this dramatically by presenting eccentric characters in disconnected scenes, strange settings, and unpredictable episodes. But the unique savor of the modern *sotie* is in the impression the reader has of Gide's own ironic presence in the midst of the turbulent activity.

Paludes is a study of ludicrous human impotence, of the faceless man of little consequence even in his own unimportant sphere. Among its themes are banality, inertia, and acceptance of the status quo. Matters that are social, spiritual, and moral are passed in absurd review and commented on from the separate points of view of the legendary character in a story, the author of that story, his acquaintances, and the narrator, Gide. Some of the topics are literary pretentiousness, lack of concern for freedom in the individual or the group, insincerity, inability to convert desire for expression and action into results, surrender to circumstances, and escape from responsibility. This bizarre collection of tragic material is presented in tones of mock sympathy, with effects that are both entertaining and revealing. There is ample scope for irony in the successive states of mind: the author's virtuous reaction to his inert protagonist, Tityrus, who will not forsake his *chêne* (oak); his lofty condemnation of Angèle and Hubert for their shallowness; his scorn of his contemporaries for their aimless lives; his justification of his own endeavors; his dismay at the stupidity he sees around him. Typical verbal touches are the smug "It makes no difference to *me*, because I am writing *Paludes*," the definitions and redefinitions of the opus, the punning on *vers* (worms or lines of verse), and Gide's invitations to the reader, in preface and epilogue, such as a blank space to be filled in under "List of most striking expressions in *Paludes*."

Ironic situations are numerous, since the *en-abyme*

technique presents several strata of intelligence, from Gide's down to that of the somnolent shepherd. The most anomalous of positions is that of the young writer, whose failure to recognize his own inadequacies stands in his way when he wants to criticize those of his friends. In his frustration, he resembles Armand in *Les Faux-Monnayeurs,* who thinks of writing a treatise on incompetence but finds himself not quite competent to write it. Other absurdities of his situation are his juggling of his memoranda for the day to match the accomplishments, and his would-be progress from "I am writing *Paludes*" to "I am writing *Polders,*" the beginning and the end of his chronicle. The disparity between projects and results is underlined by the frustrated author's repetitious plea for revolt and for manifestation of talent, when he is capable himself of what is at best only a poor sort of achievement.

The long procession of inconsistencies and incapacities lacks the gaiety and effervescence found in Gide's later *soties.* It is mostly overt criticism of anything and everything, as the dedication implies, with the irony as often snide as amusing. Gide is both puppeteer and commentator, which sometimes keeps him too busy. What wisdom there is in the "play" is to be inferred negatively from the insipid words and pointless acts of the characters and from the questionable support they receive from the narrator. The action, if it can be so called, is slow and relatively easy to follow. It is portrayed in six "days" which correspond somewhat to the *journées* of the mystery plays and the *jornadas* of the old Spanish dramatic poem. Each pictures one of the characters, who are few in number and limited in intelligence. What effects there are spring from dialogue and from absurd situation that is at best mildly dramatic—from the reader's point of vantage, if not from that of the participants. But if the over-all impression is far from sprightly, it is close to the response Gide hoped to elicit from his public as he presented the spectacle of human *sottises* in his first *sotie.*

Le Prométhée mal enchaîné is a boisterous blending of several myths. Loosed from his Caucasian bonds, this "match manufacturer" leaps across the centuries and the map to turn up at a Paris café, where his consciousness-conscience, in the form of an eagle, joins him by crashing through a window. He witnesses and discusses the results of a visit of Zeus, now an Italian tycoon ("banquier-miglionnaire"). Zeus, for no apparent reason, has just dispensed a substantial amount of money and a resounding punch in the face to Damocles and Cocles, chance passersby, who report the incidents to Prometheus and the café waiter. These apparently unmotivated acts, their unexpected results in the lives of the recipients, and the relationships Prometheus has to his chains, his new acquaintances, and his eagle are the preoccupations of the tale. Most important, perhaps, is the gesture of the protagonist in breaking his bonds with the past. He is portrayed as a virtually free man and a reasonably free thinker, whose greatest problem is his *aigle-conscience,* which feeds gluttonously on his liver while Prometheus fails visibly in both health and spirits. Liberation comes eventually when he eats the bird—with no hard feelings, as he points out—saving only a vestigial feather to be kept as a memento and used as a pen. Apart from this final disposition of his baleful companion, Prometheus is involved in an imprisonment and a public address, as well as in the further adventures of his friends: Cocles, supposedly unlucky but always adaptable to circumstances, meets with worldly success and prosperity; Damocles, cursed by his good fortune and his sense of responsibility, comes to an untimely end; the waiter is merely an interested observer of developments, who comments glibly on even the least comprehensible of events.

The action is presented in a dramatic form quite unlike that of *Paludes*. The frame-within-a-frame structure used there (and in the *Cahiers d'André Walter*) will reappear in *Les Caves* and the *Faux-Monnayeurs*, but there is a merciful absence here of scales of values in descending order from protagonist to his protagonist and his protagonist's protagonist. *Le Prométhée* is in three sections of five chapters each, with an extra chapter here and there. The divisions are much closer to being "acts" than those in *Paludes*. The action, too, is much more vivid. Attributes and ideas are translated into visible or palpable effects: the power of Zeus becomes a bank note and a blow. The opportunism of Cocles is evident in his one-eyed prosperity. The wealth and health of Damocles desert him, leaving only worry and death. The blessing and curse of a *conscience* are incarnate for Prometheus in his eagle. Even Gide's bantering justification of the story in the epilogue is in concrete terms. Like Pasiphaë's Minotaur, the product is real and must now be accepted by its parent, even though, in other circumstances, something quite different might have been engendered.

Prometheus, unlike the inept author in *Paludes*, is a clever rascal, notwithstanding his lighthearted manner. His thought-provoking gestures and his ambiguous words are as laden with meaning as those of the court clowns of old. In his early compliance with fate, as in a later decision to shape his own destiny, he is the ensign of intelligent humanity. What he does, silly as it seems, is exemplary; what he says in jest has a broad basis of common sense—of conscience as a light that guides men to their perdition, for example, and of belief in progress and its dangers when it becomes an obsession.[14] For those not too distracted by his display of fireworks or his glow of health, his speeches have a philosophic message—that man's ideal of sacrifice can be more beautiful than rewarding. Much of the story is in dialogue, with personalities aptly revealed through repartee. Zeus shows his temperament as clearly in his comments as he does in his actions. Although he hands out eagles to others, he does not keep one himself. And his gestures do not enslave him: "I launch projects, then I let them go as they will." The pathetic career of Damocles is summed up in his "Once I was nobody, now I am someone." The eagle's change of status is implicit in his early penchant for chatter and his recalcitrant silence when he is given his cue to speak in public.

Disrespect is a keynote of the skillful nonsense in *Le Prométhée*. It is not only lack of respect for Zeus and his company from antiquity, who are warped so deliberately to Gidean form, but for Biblical legend as well—particularly for scriptural imagery and language. The industrialist-financer is, for instance, "the Lord," endowed with initiative, a delight in gambling, and a lack of concern with gain. He is the ultimate in freethinkers. Tityrus, the recumbent Virgilian, has the problem of "planting his seed in fertile ground" and of seeing that his oak "brings forth good fruit in its season," as Prometheus reminds his audience. John the Baptist's words referring to Christ are applied to the eagle battening on the hero's substance; "He must increase, but I must decrease." The bird forces his master to sob repeatedly, "I have asked in vain," uncomfortably reminiscent of the desperate words of Christ forsaken on the cross. Cocles "turns the other cheek" and commercializes his mishap amid references to "thy brother," "my neighbor" and "sustenance," while Damocles ponders the question "What have ye that ye have not received?" He parries with "From whom?" There is a gay insouciance, too, in the funeral oration by Prometheus, whose text is "Let the dead bury their dead."

Indecency is another feature added here to Gide's growing concept of the *sotie*. His indelicate touches are no doubt intended to shock the fastidious. They also serve as trial balloons for later literary ribaldries. One case in point is the nauseating search of Damocles for his bank note. Another is the titillation of the audience by the lewd postcards Prometheus promises to distribute if boredom threatens. These are minor elements in the story, no doubt, by comparison with the monstrous bawdiness of lustier tellers of tales and of contemporary pornographers—Rabelaisian humor is more a foible than a forte of Gide's. The indecencies do, however, enhance the incongruousness of the great anachronism and, in the author's opinion at least, add to the *sotie* atmosphere. In all probability, the scenes are interjected with more whimsical than sinister (or "artistic") intent. If Gide came to regret them for the sake of public relations—as Diderot did his youthful literary indiscretions—it must have been in secret. There is no evidence of such a palinode in his *Journal.* And from *Le Prométhée* on, there are occasional off-color scenes and expressions in most of his works.

Le Prométhée is a *sotie-drame,* emphasizing quick-witted jest and a plainly indicated moral. It veers sharply away from the *sotie-journal* or *sotie-traité* of *Paludes,* with its scorn of "the third person, the one spoken about" and its satire of human *sottises* by a self-appointed judge. The Prometheus story, incidentally, is closer than any other *sotie* to the medieval fool's play in spirit and movement, in spite of its classical reminiscences and its Gidean distortions.

Les Caves du Vatican may be called a *sotie-roman,* or possibly a *sotie-nouvelle.* Amédée's ill-fated crusade to liberate the captive Pope, Lafcadio's ruthless search for proof of his own lack of motive, and the gargantuan swindle launched by Protos are all cleverly woven into an intriguing pattern. The tale is so briskly paced and so full of unexpected turns that it resembles an international spy thriller crossed with a detective novel on Arsène Lupin. Gide's skill as an ironist makes this much more than a well-told story. In narrative form, it is a full-length play of fools, wise and otherwise—and as such, a *sotie* in the full sense of the term. Fanciful exaggeration of the schemers and their dupes, far from making them less credible, lends them an air of plausibility, both in their activities and in their contrasting personalities. This sort of tacit agreement between creator and public is usually met only in the theater and in the fairy tale. Obviously, *Les Caves* has little in common with the latter. The dramatic possibilities of its fantasy were realized by Gide in the theatrical version staged at the Comédie Française, which was enjoying a successful run at the time of his death.

In character depiction, Gide creates something equally new. Lafcadio is probably the least likely of Gidean inventions to be forgotten by readers. He may be a projection of traits perceptible in his author, such as curiosity and experimental individualism (although obviously not in his taste for crime), and he may be an unwholesome example. But he has a personality that is his own, unlike André Walter and even Michel, who move so often in the shadow of their originator. Gide shows a special affection for this bastard son of a Hungarian prostitute and Count Juste-Agénor—or some other "uncle." The charge of moral indecency, frequently brought against Gide, is based no less on his failure to be sufficiently ironic with Lafcadio than on his seeming approval of Ménalque, the libertine who defies public opinion in *Les Nourritures terrestres*. Although Lafcadio's physical ancestry is vague—an advantage of the illegitimate on which Gide often comments—his spiritual genealogy can be traced. If allowance is made for an occasional blank or bar sinister, he is a scion of the dashing and despicable Don Juan, who defies all acceptable standards of society and religion. Julien Sorel is a distant relative—his energies are more shrewdly directed toward gain than satisfaction, and his successive adventures follow an obvious plan. Like the Don Juan of Tirso de Molina and Molière rather than the hero of romanticism, Lafcadio aims at complete self-expression and the ultimate in experience, without concern for decencies or divinities. He is not incapable, however, of an admirable or even heroic action, if the occasion presents itself. This can be seen, for example, in his kissing an old lady and in his rushing into a burning house. He has no desire to be admired or considered virtuous for these gestures, it is worth noting, and physical heroism means little or nothing to him. What makes him a convincing protagonist for a *sotie* is his conviction that he must seek wisdom for himself in a world of fools. " 'Cadio, my boy," he murmurs, "here's the problem: How to tear that fate into bits." The egregious piece of stupidity, the *sottise* that makes him just another *sot* among many, costing him his cherished freedom of action, adds dramatic irony to what might have been a banal case history of a crime without apparent motive, committed by a somewhat juvenile delinquent. Amédée, the misguided victim of scoundrels and circumstances, is pathetic in an unprepossessing way, but none the less an intellectual and a *sot*. "What would have been surprising about it," says the narrator, "if Lafcadio had not taken Fleurissoire seriously!" Julius, too, is a fool. He is of the pompous variety, amply rewarded for his stupid presumption. Protos, finally, is less clever than he imagines. He becomes so entangled in his own net that it will be forever impossible to "operate," to "deal" with the police, or to stay uncommitted—to *passer outre*. Although he is a master of adaptability, disguise, and deception, he loses his touch and his status. In the end, he is a small-time criminal, unable to do more than petty bilking of simpletons—forced to act himself instead of having others act for him, to *agir* rather than *faire agir*.[15]

The verbal devices used in *Les Caves du Vatican* depend to a large extent on ironies of situation. Lafcadio calls himself "an exemplary fellow" as he schemes to confound the "small-timers and nobodies" he sees about him. He tells Julius that the perpetrator of an unmotivated crime (such as the one he himself commits without edifying results) is what people call "a free man." Julius, in his literary speculations on the nature of *inconséquence* and the *acte gratuit,* which he discusses at length with Lafcadio, is a self-constituted authority who is sure he is an expert in such matters. Out of his foolish mouth, too, come words of wisdom that predict the theme of *Les Faux-Monnayeurs:* "We all live counterfeit lives and risk distorting what is best." The unctuous pronouncement is a counterpoise to the motto of the master swindler, Protos-Defouqueblize. "People in civilized society owe it to themselves to lead counterfeit lives."

The indignities to which the Holy See is subjected express the sardonic scorn the author feels. Protos and his elusive gang, the *Mille-Pattes* (Centipedes), use the Vatican to add scope to their scheme. Gide, for whom nothing dogmatic is sacred, implies that the Catholic faith itself is no less a hoax than the unholy plot against which the hapless Amédée takes up arms.

It is in *Les Caves* that the *sotie* reaches its apogee. In spite of the author's assertion that it was to be the last of his "ironic or critical" works, many of its features reappear in *Les Faux-Monnayeurs, Oedipe,* and *Thésée.* Written a generation later, *Thésée* is in many ways representative of the genre. It is a sort of *sotie-mémoire* or *sotie-épître* which lacks much of what distinguished its predecessors: the dramatic liveliness of action, the bold gestures, the incisive ridicule of *sots* and *sottises,* as well as the rollicking ironies of word and situation and the author's stance of impiety and nonconformity. Theseus is no youthful and ebullient prankster, as Prometheus was. Gide himself has outlived the frolicsome mood that pervades even the more serious pages of *Les Caves.* A sober and restrained wit, mellowed by increasing wisdom, marks this whimsical retelling of the Minotaur legend. The narrator is Theseus, whose hope is that it may be brought to the attention of those who can profit by hearing it. His own son, he muses, might have benefited by listening, if fate had not ruled otherwise. The Athenian king, in his exposition of how to succeed in life, has a moral purpose not unlike that of Lord Chesterfield as he wrote to his son, but the exemplary career he envisages is rich in its ironies. Readers who heed warnings against taking the words or viewpoints of a character as those of the artist realize that Theseus is not delivering Gide's personal testament, even—or especially—in his most lofty pronouncements. But there is some reflection in *Thésée* of the author's changing attitude toward human folly. It is considered here as necessary to man's slow progress, rather than a scourge, a mask for wisdom, or a tool to be used by the quick-witted. Through experience, Theseus has learned to esteem personal effort as the way to realization of one's own possibilities. Mistakes and misguided energy are inevitable for the man whose motto is "Achieve your own possibilities. Stay free of commitments to others. Go forward." Each human being must do what he can, with minimum help from others, to justify his existence. His progress may call for challenging God (as it did for Oedipus) or for toiling less spectacularly for the betterment of mankind.

The seriousness of mood in *Thésée* is in marked contrast with the lighthearted atmosphere of earlier studies in folly. Whether the reader should infer a serious moral lesson is another matter. Humanity and the symbolic City of Man take on the proportions of a cult, and Wisdom is enshrined, if all is taken verbatim. Dialogue, the vehicle of wit, is giving way to monologue. The improprieties and the mocking of accepted truths, formerly tossed forth with devilish delight, are now handled with quiet, even delicate, humor. And many readers, who once enjoyed the spirit of *Le Prométhée* and *Les Caves,* are loath to see that Gide has taken his own advice to *passer outre*—he has now "gone beyond" the *sotie.*

There are some minor rapports between the *sotie* and the eighteenth-century *conte philosophique,* but the differences of procedure are considerable. Simple narration, a comprehensive plot (sometimes spasmodic), and a heavily stressed major argument that is intelligible to the average mind are among the main features of the *conte.* Foreign visitors, exotic in garb and reactions, give new perspective on France; Europeans learn of strange lands and planets through reports of real and imaginary travels. The teller of tales takes full advantage of colorful settings and unusual adventures to enliven his story, but he does so without obscuring the main point he is illustrating. Veiled allusion, subtle implication, and delicate irony are much less frequent than open satire of plainly indicated people or institutions, unless fear of the police or the inquisition dictates caution. Until the later years of the century, there is virtually no thrust-and-parry between author and reader or author and characters. Many of the English tales of the period and most of Voltaire's are as straightforward as a simple anecdote, since even the highly intelligent *conteur* wants his ideas and his thesis to reach a large public. His witty subtleties and fine distinctions (*esprit de finesse* and *finesse d'esprit*) are saved for the salon, to impress his intellectual peers in epigram, analogy, or paradox.

Diderot is both part of and aside from the eighteenth-century stream of narrative fiction. He writes some of his stories for immediate publication, others for a select reading public. The former are illustrative tales, not unlike the philosophical short story. Among them are: *Les Bijoux indiscrets,* a framed series of short fictions after the manner of Crébillon *fils; Les Deux Amis de Bourbonne* (*Two Friends from Bourbonne*), written to show that true friendship exists at all levels of human society, especially among the poor and obscure; and *L'Entretien d'un philosophe avec la Maréchale de* * * * (*Conversation of a Philosopher with Maréchale* X), a dialogue on religion and morality which contains the story of a young atheist meeting his Maker. These works have little relationship to the *sotie.* As Diderot points out in *Les Deux Amis,* there are three kinds of tale. All three types aim at entertaining, but they need not all be highly amusing on the one hand nor edifying on the other.

The second general division of Diderot's narrations comprises those not intended for release to the public until after his death. The privileged few making up their immediate audience are members of the *philosophe* group, who read some of them in manuscript, and foreign subscribers to Grimm's literary newsletter, which prints many contributions by Diderot. Apart from these is the vaster public of future generations, for which he claims he writes. And there is one reader who is far from incidental—Sophie Volland, to whom he narrates many a tale he has just invented or heard. The composite of these makes up the audience of the sprightly tales that may be considered his *soties.*

André Billy and Robert Loy, among recent critics, have used the designation *sotie* for *Jacques le fataliste.* The term is apt, to some degree, for such works as the *Rêve de d'Alembert* and the *Neveu de Rameau.* On one or several counts, *Le Supplément au Voyage de Bougainville,* the story of Madame de la Carlière (in *Sur l'inconséquence des jugements publics*) and *La Religieuse* earn places in the genre. All have a serious aim plus humorous presentation; disconnected, spectacular action; earnest argument via witty conversation; flagrant impiety; and unabashed indecency. Even more closely allied to the Gidean *sotie* are the stories intercalated in longer works or in letters: the adventures in ethics of Madame de la Pommeraye, Gousse, Father Hudson, and the protagonist (in *Jacques le fataliste*), and the extended anecdotes of Hoop, Galiani, *et al.*, reported to Sophie from Grandval.

At the time of the composition of *Le Rêve de d'Alembert,* Diderot makes a comment on his work that is an excellent description of the pervading principle and the method of the *sotie:* "It is extremely foolish, yet at the same time deeply philosophical. Wisdom must often be given the appearance of nonsense if it is to get a hearing. I prefer to have people say 'Why, that's not as unreasonable as you might think!' to saying 'Now listen to me, what I am saying is very intelligent.' "[16] In an earlier letter, he speaks in similar words of the *Rêve:* "It's not possible to be more profound and madder." The same thought and verbal pattern appear in his approval of *Tristram Shandy:* "For the last few days I have been completely tied up reading the maddest, most intelligent, sprightliest of all books." And the same work, by the "English Rabelais," which he calls the source of *Jacques le fataliste,* is again triply praised as "this book so mad, so intelligent and so sprightly." [17]

In its shocking interpretation of cloistered life, as that life appeared to Diderot the anti-clerical, *La Religieuse* easily outstrips *Les Caves* for deliberate church-baiting. There is a real similarity, too, in the extravagant hoaxes perpetrated on the innocent Marquis de Croismare and on Fleurissoire, both incidental victims of animosity on the part of the authors toward dogmatic religion. Diderot, Grimm, and friends add zest to their noble acquaintance's quiet life on his country estate by inventing a story of a nun's escape from a convent. The marquis is most interested when he learns that this is the very young lady whose case he has been concerned with since she appealed for dispensation from her vows and lost her plea. He opens his heart and home to her in a series of letters addressed to her supposed place of hiding. The Paris jokesters write in answer until they are obliged (by the impending visit of the marquis) to have her sicken and die. It is not until several years later that they dare confess their deception. During the sustained correspondence, Diderot writes *La Religieuse,* expanding the prank into a lengthy chronicle of the trials and tribulations of the poor religious, and combining the corroborative memoir with an outspoken indictment of monastic life.

In its ingenuity and disrespect for Rome, this scheme outdoes the wildest imaginings of Voltaire, Daudet, or Anatole France. It is not matched in fiction until Protos and his scoundrelly band trump up the story of the Pope's kidnaping by the freemasons, in *Les Caves du Vatican.*

The atmosphere, the verbal pace, and the complication of a *sotie* are all to be found in a detailed description by Diderot of an evening at d'Holbach's estate. The mother of the successive baronesses, Madame d'Aine, plays the *mère-sotte* throughout the conversations, which cover many topics in admirable disorder: Arabs, hegiras, and idolatry; gardens, the feminist movement, and plays; despotism, religions, and philosophy—a strange medley of subjects to begin with. The alphabet follows, then a skinny lover and his shortcomings, then pilgrimages to Mecca, and communion, and some observations on the chambermaid's buttocks, which fascinate the old lady. All this leads, for no apparent reason, to talk on national superstition and the question of enlightenment. Next pass in review the church and the *Encyclopédie;* a local accident; the Koran, the Caliph, tolerance, and monasteries; the separation of Church and State; the local parish priest; the maid's bottom again; sects that are Moslem, Christian, and ancient; philosophy and atheism. Then, in quick succession, a story of three sons, their lives and deaths; God, immortality, and neighbors; Brahmans and divine justice; scientists and philosophies as good missionaries; trouble with the parish priest and lateness of supper. The overwhelming parade of chatter and sense needs only a bit of plotting and the insertion of some physical horse-play—easily transposed from other Grandval reports—to supply material adequate for a full-length *sotie.*

The tale of the *porco sacro* (sacred pig) is equally suitable for at least an episode. It could conceivably be expanded into another *Caves du Vatican.* At a Naples monastery, the sacred pigs are considered untouchable and are publicly supported. One of them is "murdered" by a gang of rogues, who outwit the authorities by disguising the body, saying it is the corpse of a comrade, lighting candles around it, sprinkling holy water, and praying unctuously. There are obvious parallels with devices used in the *Caves*, particularly in the elusive tactics and the sanctimonious conduct of the "Centipedes."

The Roman church and its priests are the butts of many of the salacious stories and extravagant suggestions of the d'Holbach clan: "Father" Hoop tells of a dangerous scheme for uniting Church and State, which could produce little clerics galore; Galiani, known as "that nice priest," has a Boccaccian story of a cardinal's deputy who gets venereal disease; Diderot adds a sketch on an archbishop duping a cardinal by pretending to be a duchess; the Spaniards are quoted as considering the Pope "a little foreign bishop of no authority, influence or consequence." [18]

Although he is far from penitent, Diderot takes some pride in reporting to Sophie that he has just finished an unnamed work (*Le Rêve de d'Alembert*) in which "what will surprise you is that there is not a word in it on religion, nor a single word that is indecent." This is no small accomplishment, since goading the Church has become one of his favorite diversions, both off the record and in print. He has cited, for example, the method used by Venetian priests at carnivals: to attract the crowds from the mountebanks' stalls, they point at the crucifix and cry "Here he is! Here's the real Punchinello, the great Punchinello!" And he claims to prefer the wild exaggerations of Voltaire's fables to "dull and boring harping on Jesus Christ and his apostles." [19] Gaily sacrilegious on all occasions, he applauds Mme d'Houdetot's "Hymn to Breasts" and suggests that the caterpillars eating Sophie's vegetables be "excommunicated." Gide can be equally lacking in respect: Writing *Num quid et tu? . . .* , he finds his own moments of induced religious fervor, once he has recovered from them, nothing but "dishonest play-acting." In his journals, he condemns those who go through the motions of religion without convictions. And he claims, in his exchange of opinions with one distinguished Catholic critic, to have had too long and too close an acquaintance with Christ to try to call him the way people ring one another on the telephone.

Though it has shocked some readers, obscenity is a relatively small factor in Diderot's work, as it is in Gide's. The unsavory scenes, comments, and allusions are part of the total comedy they present, but an incidental part, even by comparison with such spinners of tales as their favorites, Sterne and Dostoevsky.

Nothing divine is sacred, nothing human is taboo to these commentators on fools and folly. The only criteria are the subject's interest and its potentiality for dramatic staging in animated dialogue. Gods and mortals alike are dressed in caps and bells and presented in the *sotie humaine*. Each *sot* has his role, each *sottise* its momentary place in the limelight, whether as an example of man's conduct or a pretext for entertaining argument. Both as occasional fools themselves and as producers of the vast fool's play, Diderot and Gide have a sense of participation and enjoyment denied to Dante in the *Divina Commedia* and even to Balzac in the *Comédie humaine.*

Blindness and Blindfolds

In the serious thought of Diderot and Gide, a major place is given to blindness in its many forms. Treated with an earnestness that approaches morbidity, the theme offers little occasion for frivolity or wit. To both authors, who often clothe seriousness in motley, this problem is no joking matter—it is a tragic physical fact, an object of scientific or psychological study, and a source of limitless philosophical conjecture. It is, esthetically, a useful symbol of the limitation of man's powers and of his inability or unwillingness to welcome truth. In the material world, it represents a process of nature, related to other organic functions and malfunctions; in the spiritual, it can be self-inflicted—if it is dogmatic—or induced, through submissiveness to authority or through faith in something other than human reason.

The literary history of blindness is probably as old as literature. The bodily affliction has always had a mystic aura, suggesting at times the wrath of the gods, at others the gift of "second sight" in lieu of eyes. In primitive tribes and among the civilized peoples of antiquity, symbolic and poetic implications contribute richly to legend and myth. Physicians and philosophers have contended with the problem on the one hand, theologians and artists have dramatized it on the other.

The causes of loss of sight are as varied as the interpretations of the malady and its effects—Oedipus is blinded by his own hand, Saul by the Lord, Milton less sensationally. A paradox that has long been recognized asserts that the physically blind "see" and that others "having eyes, see not." Blindness of mind or spirit is not so dramatic, but it is no less lamentable. Its sources are simple ignorance, lack of opportunity, and unquestioning acceptance of restrictions. The unseeing eyes of its victims are the shuttered windows of the closed mind. Adding modern science and psychological insight to their knowledge of the classics and of the scriptures, Diderot and Gide review both sides of the double paradox. The marked similarity of their attitudes is less surprising than the recurrence of the theme and the significance given the human aspects of the problem.

Eyes played a large part in Diderot's personal history. Those of Madame Dupré de Saint-Maur, mistress of the powerful Marquis d'Argenson, were allowed to observe an important piece of experimental surgery. It was a privilege, as the *philosophe* pointed out, that was denied those with better scientific qualifications. His caustic remarks helped send him to prison. The irresistible glances of other ladies led him into several liaisons. But if Diderot the philanderer was entranced by lovely feminine eyes, Diderot the *philosophe* and amateur scientist was no less captivated by medical aspects of sight. Operations for cataracts and to "restore" vision to those born blind, by such distinguished men as Réaumur and Hilmer, were what doctors call "heroic." The translator of a monumental medical dictionary and editor of a dictionary of arts and sciences could scarcely be expected to pass them by unmoved. The geometry machine invented by Saunderson, the blind mathemathics professor at Cambridge, the pre-Braille alphabet used by Sophie Volland's niece, and the amaurosis reported by Grimm were all material considerations to Diderot, as well as pretexts for philosophic musing.

Diderot's preoccupation with spiritual blindness is patent even earlier than his scientific interest in sightless eyes. He attributes the failure to "see" to the *bandeau* applied by the Church—the blindfold illustrating his deistic argument in *La Promenade du sceptique.* It is implicit, too, in the blind statues seen in Mirzoza's dream (in the *Bijoux indiscrets*), and explicit in a passage he contributed to d'Holbach's *Système de la nature:* "They feel they must be careful to defend their blindfolds. If their eyes so used to darkness are half open for an instant, the light hurts them and they attack furiously the person who is giving them a torch that dazzles them." [1] It is a thesis to which he returns regularly throughout his long anticlerical campaign, part of his war for more light and brighter torches.

Diderot's manifesto as a man of science and an advocate of enlightenment appeared in 1749, with the provocative title of *Lettre sur les aveugles à l'usage de ceux qui voient* (*Letter on the Blind for the Use of Those Who Can See*). It earned him prompt arrest and a stay in Vincennes prison, when an investigation of his writings followed his untoward remark about Madame Dupré de Saint-Maur's eyes. The treatise itself is a daring one. It shows what Assézat later called "inspired insights that prepared the way for the evolution of modern science." D'Argenson was less complimentary at the time. He felt that the author of this *Aveugle clairvoyant* (*Clairvoyant Blind Man*) had "the haughtiness of a fanatic," that the work itself was "an endorsement of deism and a threat to public morality."

The *Lettre* is a twofold elaboration of its title. Real blindness is treated first, more or less factually, in terms that recall the investigations of the senses done by Molyneux, Locke, and Condillac. An exposition of Saunderson's personal philosophy follows—largely invented by Diderot, who blends in his own ideas on such topics as eternity, relativity, ignorance and, finally, the greatness that is possible to a mind unfettered by churchly bonds. In the scientific section at the beginning, Diderot shows that he is an able physiologist and an expert on senses and emotions. He waxes lyrical in his discussion of the compensatory role of other senses when one is lost, and again when he discourses on the interrelationship of the senses and the perceptions.

It is but a short step to more abstract reasoning; opposed though Diderot is in theory to abstractions, they are practical for the blind, who can "geometrize the universe" better than those hindered by eyes. The Sallignac girl, for instance, has no trouble dividing a cube into pyramids in her mind; and able mathematicians find they can solve problems of solid geometry more easily with their eyes shut than open.

Concepts of color and perspective are vague or missing in those who know them only by hearsay, as Gide's Gertrude reveals later. They are apt to seem as strange when put into words as a deaf person's explanation of music he has never heard. Even total confusion is possible, as in the case of a man born deaf and dumb cited in the *Lettre sur les sourds et muets* (*Letter on the Deaf and Dumb*)—when Father Castel's color-harpsichord displayed its ribbons, the *sourd-muet* took the colors to represent letters and their combinations to be words expressing the thoughts of the inventor, whom he imagined to be another deaf-mute.[2] Since the blind resort to transference of perceptions, they substitute for color and distance such palpable impressions as texture, contour, and proximity. They need their souls at their fingertips, according to Diderot, not in their pineal glands (nor in another location he suggests less delicately in an earlier refutation of Cartesian theory).[3] One of the most difficult tasks, when sight is restored, is to divorce touch from visual sensation and to teach the eyes to see, as the tongue is taught to speak.

There is a close relationship between the physical senses and moral sense, among eighteenth-century lovers of logic. Morals and virtues, according to them, derive from organs and sensory feelings. Just as natural law has material foundations, so must any natural ethics or religion that is to be adequate. The prime virtue for the sightless is then honesty; the cardinal sin is theft. Deception is unforgivable, modesty is unnecessary as far as appearances are concerned. Shyness, like conventional behavior in society, is an artificially acquired pose. For a relativist observing the conduct of the blind, it follows that "a person with one more sense than we have would find our ethics less than perfect, to put it mildly." Religion, by the same token, loses much of its appeal if it is stripped of its visual trappings. Its case is sadly weakened when it has to depend on more rational evidence than the testimony of divine presence furnished by the eye. This, at least, is the contention of Diderot, who quotes a statement allegedly made by Saunderson to the imaginary Inchcliff: "What had you and I done to God that one should have that organ and the other be deprived of it?" And on the same note, "If you expect me to believe in God, you must let me touch him." [4] This statement, however apocryphal it may be, has become proverbial among materialists. It both underlines Diderot's skepticism and makes Saunderson the symbol of "those who have been unlucky enough to come upon truth in the dark ages and so imprudent as to reveal it to their blind contemporaries."

The lessons to be learned by questioning intelligent blind people are as rewarding as studies in the restoring of sight and speculation over its results. Oedipus, to Diderot, "probably put out his own eyes so that he might more readily know what makes people see." Among historical figures of unusual perceptiveness in spite of their lack of one sense, Diderot cites Teiresias, who "was well read in the secrets of the gods." His "divine obscurity" is his salient characteristic in Gide's *Oedipe,* it will be remembered, and the source of his disagreement with the king. A related question, that of happiness and its attainment, is also considered here. Restored vision may prove a sore trial to the person who has not known eyesight since birth; darkness is not necessarily a synonym of unhappiness, as Gertrude realizes in the Gidean story. To clinch his argument announced in the title, Diderot warns against taking appearance for reality, pleading with the reader for the openness of eyes and mind advocated by Montaigne's "Que sçay-je?"

The ambiguity of blindness as a term makes its a favorite metaphor of Diderot's, closely related to his figurative use of light. It is applicable at once to keenness and dullness of intellect, to extra senses and lack of sense. Like Voltaire, Diderot finds it an excellent device for philosophic anecdote and illustration. In the epigram "Le Borgne" ("The One-Eyed Man"), the affliction is a physical pretext for revelation of stoic wisdom. The aged protagonist accepts the loss of an eye with "That leaves all the less to do, now one of them is closed." The outlook makes the Diderot character an ancestor of Gide's Cocles, who capitalizes on his seeming loss. He is less closely related to his one-eyed contemporaries in Voltairean *contes*.

There are many allusions to blindness in its various forms in the letters to Sophie Volland. Typical is the case of a woman blinded while protecting her husband from the violence of a mob. Her ungrateful spouse and daughter "make tears flow from those now sightless eyes." At the very time that Diderot is pleading the cause of inoculation with Sophie's mother "chance bestows on her a poor creature blinded by ordinary smallpox, to give support to my request." Grimm's threatened impairment of the optic nerve evokes three sympathetic comments from his friend; then, when the crisis is past, a fourth that is less cruel than it sounds: "I warn you in advance that his cane and dog are ready for him."

Little Mélanie Sallignac, the daughter of Sophie's sister, is discussed at some length in the addition to the letter on the blind, and mentioned on occasion in letters to the family. Other references relate blindness to morals. The Chinese love of common sense and decency is given the stamp of approval, for example, in "They would be quite right if they said they have two eyes, we have one, and the rest of the world is blind." [5] Quite undaunted by his self-contradiction, the *philosophe* presents virtue in the opposite light in the later *Eléments de Physiologie*. A maxim in the "Mélanges" ("Miscellany"), entitled "Aveugles" ("The Blind"), says: "They have imagination; the fact is that vice exists only in the retina." The dictum can be collated with the recurrent quotation from scripture, in *La Symphonie pastorale*, of the pronouncement on newly opened eyes and the perception of sin.

In politics, monarchs are particularly susceptible to ignorance through self-deception: "What monstrous blindness is visited on those unfortunates who open their eyes only to gaze on an idolatrous cult of their own persons!" [6] At the other extreme, the "fanatic disciples of liberty" are indicted for their egalitarian love of lawlessness and reproached for their kind of blindness in "Les Eleuthéromanes" ("The Mad Pursuers of Liberty"). Giving the metaphor even broader application, Diderot quotes Seneca's remark, "All men want to be happy. But all are blind when it comes to examining the question of what makes happiness." [7]

The image of blindness is so constant and so useful in philosophic argument that it is almost a tic. Diderot symbolizes the role of chance by reference to the old blind man of classical fable, standing beside a ditch, winnowing nude children, roses, and snakes. And the *philosophe* makes the figure of speech universal with the plea to blind victims of circumstance to refrain from judging: "Let us pardon Nature. Nature is blind."

The only ray of hope that remains in this benighted world, according to Diderot, is the light of knowledge. Men must remove the blindfolds they have too long endured, put their trust in their common sense, and depend on wholly human faculties. They will then, and only then, be able to interpret a material universe and to cope with its forces. It may take decades, even centuries, for this to come to pass, but the goal makes the struggle worthwhile. The thought is epitomized in one major section of d'Holbach's *Système de la nature,* supposedly contributed by Diderot, which points the way to progress with the apostrophe, "No, mortals blinded by terror! The friend of nature is not your enemy!"

Along with this assortment of attributions of blindness to things factual, scientific, religious, and moral is a repeated use of the Oedipus legend. Saunderson is the most vociferous and sensational of Diderot's blind characters, but the tyrant-philosopher is his most frequently used illustration of blindness and its ambiguities. The awful gesture of the Greek hero is stamped indelibly on Diderot's mind, as it is on Gide's; all else in his dramatic life seems secondary or anticlimactic. It is, however, the pathetic plight of Oedipus, not his hope of serenity, that looms large in Diderot's thoughts when he sees, in an English play (probably Lillo's *Fatal Curiosity*), "a spectacle that is more terrifying than that of blinded Oedipus bending down to grope about for his children." [8] He adds a variation to the theme in a moral message for the sister of his mistress: "Please ask Uranie why she does not put her children's eyes out. Ignorance is the mother of all our errors. Is it good to come to know the truth? Or is it better to wander about in darkness?" [9] The procedure, he suggests in one of his essays in verse, has already been adopted by the Church. If salvation is to be assured to the devout, "What has to be done/ So says the cowled one/ Is to gouge out your eyes."

Unlike Gide, Diderot does not glorify Oedipus at the expense of Teiresias, whom he mentions only as a "blind philosopher" and a seer of unusual insight. The king's ill-starred birth, his successful career following his unknowing patricide, his "complex" that has taken on so perverted a meaning and, finally, his human solution of the Sphinx's riddle evoke little reaction in print from Diderot. The tragic pitting of a noble and innocent man against the conspiring fates provides regal drama to Aeschylus and Sophocles and a pretext for argument to Gide and Cocteau. It intrigues Diderot primarily for its possibilities in pantomime and in striking use of gesture. No doubt Oedipus appeals to him as a victim of infernal machinations—of circumstances, the only "gods"—and as a symbol of free-thinking individual man, but his *condition* hardly commends him to a writer of contemporary bourgeois dramas. Diderot evidently knows the legend well, as a classical scholar and as a theatergoer. The Brumoy version of the Sophoclean play is mentioned in one of his letters; he undoubtedly is acquainted with the versions by Corneille and Voltaire, as well as with the two by Houdard de la Motte and, in all likelihood, those by Seneca and Dryden. Although he feels no urge to do an *Oedipe* himself, it is obvious that the story is not lost on him as a classic example of human enlightenment by spectacular gesture.

In fine, physiological blindness presents the first challenge to Diderot's thought, with the Bible providing the paradox on which he bases his ambivalent speculations. Literary reference, though useful, is but one of the several means he uses to convert the divers connotations of blindness and blindfolds into weapons that support his philosophic contentions.

An interest in blindness does not send Gide to prison. But as an ailment, a theme, and a figure of speech, it is as vital to him as it is to Diderot. His approach, however, is more esthetic than didactic and his emphasis is somewhat more on anomalies than on combating ignorance and dogma. But his intentions are essentially the same. In its variety of implications, the realm of the blind is admirably suited to Gidean treatment. It suggests the opaque, the transparent, and the translucent as much as utter darkness; it applies to unreasoning faith and reasoned understanding; it accentuates such opposites as renunciation and egoism, appearance and reality, hypocrisy and integrity, counterfeit and valid specie. It is as much a meeting place of ideas as Gide's own mind.

As a twentieth-century student of darkness and light, Gide is less impressed by medical research on blindness than by the effects of the affliction and of its cure on personality, on religious attitudes, and on moral points of view. The theme appears, in one form or another, in most of his works. The chief questions at issue are religion and personal ethics; science, sociology, and metaphysics are given less attention. He turns to the Bible and mythology for reinforcement of his argument. His imagination, rather than his observation of clinical cases, furnishes what evidence he needs. When analogy can give a desired effect, it is introduced; where contrast serves better, opposites and polarities meet in dialogue.

One of Gide's best-known tales, *La Symphonie pastorale*, was first called *L'Aveugle* (*The Blind One*) in his journal. An essay in interpreting both real blindness and blindfolds, it is a *récit* rather than a *lettre* on the blind for the use of those who can see. Its intention is clear. In a less broadminded country than France—or in less lethargic times—this seemingly innocent story of Gertrude, a blind waif, the ward of a charitable country preacher, would have been stamped by religious critics as "highly dangerous." The bucolic tragedy of an operation to give sight to the girl veils a study in tragic hypocrisy on the part of the minister, whom Gide presents as indulging in "one form of self-deception."

Like the other *récits*, *La Symphonie* delivers a trivial message with portentous seriousness. Its plot is an excuse for ironic commentary on human stupidity and on refusal to see what is patent. The reader is left to draw inevitable conclusions on the deceit, insincerity, and smugness of lives that seem exemplary. Implicitly, if sometimes by negative illustration, the narratives of Gide appeal for new standards of honesty, a new appreciation of man's capabilities, a casting off of what stultifies and deforms his personality.

The pastor in the *Symphonie* represents intellectual dishonesty in the cloak of religion. He is as sanctimonious and as confident of success as the would-be confessor in the letter on the blind. Gertrude's naively honest reaction to her new-found sight—as she admits her attempted suicide and her love for young Jacques—reflects the author's sentiments on the need for integrity without religiosity. It does so as plainly as Saunderson's pronouncement sums up Diderot's view of "unnatural" religion. There is, at the same time, a certain irony in the reader's reaction if he realizes that the writers' evangelical zeal has carried them, in their contrived indictments, to exaggeration verging on self-satisfaction, as the guardian fails to justify himself and the confessor to have Saunderson recant.

In this story of a Swiss-Protestant family, atmosphere and plausible fiction mingle with digressions and asides: on the medical history and the education of Laura Bridgman, as recorded in her doctor's journal and in *The Cricket and the Hearth,* inspired by her life; on Condillac's animated statue; on the difficulties of reading by the Braille system for those impeded by sight; on Gertrude's concepts of colors, shades, and distance. The last bear striking resemblances to Diderot's observations, based on his study of real cases of blindness from birth.[10] The plot itself is an elaboration of the Biblical paradox on opening of eyes and minds. In the words of St. Paul: "For I was alive without the law once: but when the commandment came, sin revived, and I died." [11]

Only the barest intimation is given of the household drama. Comic relief, too, is rare. Spoken ironies are numerous but restrained. The pastor's wife, for instance, sighs: "What do you expect, dear? It was not willed that I be blind." The minister hoodwinks himself by rationalization, fervent prayer, and continual quotation of the Bible, while contending that "it always strikes me as unseemly to use the authority of the Good Book as a protection for my behavior." He pleads for the girl's soul to be released from her "opaque body" by a ray of light "shed by Thy grace, O Lord." For Gertrude's benefit, he paraphrases the words of Jeremiah: "Those who have eyes are they who know not how to see." He recalls at convenient moments such texts as "If ye were blind, ye should have no sin"; "God is light and in Him there is no darkness"; "I am the light of the world: he that followeth me shall not walk in darkness." [12] The pious verbal background sets off both his self-blinding and the girl's progress toward light. For the two moral problems are studied simultaneously. The guardian's ability to recognize his vicious tendencies shrinks progressively, and the ward's appreciation of the awful truth increases, as she seeks happiness and finds catastrophe. The world has much to offer her as she visualizes it at a concert or to the sound of a brook: "These ineffable harmonies did not paint the world as it was, but as it could have been . . . if it had not been for evil and sin."

As Gertrude acquires knowledge, the Cornelian dream fades. Finding her imaginings suspect, she broaches the question of whether the happiness she owes her protector is based entirely on her ignorance. Then, echoing Oedipus, she concludes, "I do not want that sort of happiness. You must understand that I do not . . . insist on being happy. I prefer knowing the truth." When vision is physically possible, she does know the truth, as Oedipus does when he becomes sightless. But the moment of revelation brings her no peace of mind or certain direction for the future, as it does to him. The world, in spite of its natural beauty, is now unbearably ugly. People have care and anguish graven on their brows. Instead of the happiness and the new life she hopes for, she encounters sordidness and a realization of sin. Only an early death can deliver her, as she follows St. Paul's prescription to the letter.

Of the treasures Gide unearths in his delving into

mythology, none is more satisfying than Oedipus. Among the gods and men resurrected from the days when "a few myths were all that were needed," as his *Traité du Narcisse* puts it, only Theseus approaches the Theban king in frequency of appearance on Gide's pages. The reborn Zeus, Prometheus, Narcissus, Sisyphus, Daedalus, and Icarus have their little scenes in the vast play; Cocles and Damocles wander on stage and off. But Oedipus strides in early and is still a member of the company after half a century. The sympathy is not hard to understand—Gide feels drawn not to the sage, the despot, or the plaything of the gods, but to Oedipus the man, Oedipus the resolute individualist. His role as a self-made orphan and his incestuous love merit only passing comment. What matters in the king's life, for Gide, is the defiant gesture that costs him his sight and gives him his vision.

The Gidean and Sophoclean plays are as far apart in mood as they are in time. The power of the malevolent gods pales in the modern version; their victim's chief struggle is now with himself. A few vestiges of the classical drama remain: some names, the outline of the plot, and the yearning for *sophrosyne*, "a modest measure of prosperity and the right mind, without which true happiness is not to be won." [13] The tale Aeschylus tells is of mortal guilt and divine retribution. Sophocles pictures a worthy man crushed by the divinities as though he were a sinner. *Le Nouvel Oedipe* (*The New Oedipus*), as Gide first intended to call his play, is a paradoxical inquiry into happy ignorance and anguished revelation. In notes written some thirty years before the work appears, Gide reminds himself: "Oedipus deserves a place by himself, in the meditation on the theater: antipodal to Macbeth."

Oedipe is a strange patchwork of the serious and the frivolous, yet it is not a burlesque, a tragicomedy, nor a *drame* in the eighteenth-century sense. Whimsical elements heighten the climax of the blinding and prevent too great an accumulation of tragic doom; the sombre atmosphere Gide creates by emphasizing the king's ignorance and deliverance is pierced here and there, but not dissipated, by flashes of incongruous wit. Several minor issues infiltrate the story, too, but interest is concentrated on the dark major theme—the conflict of human and ecclesiastical powers. The latter-day Oedipus is a versatile fellow who runs his own race and rides several of his creator's hobby-horses at the same time. In a single act, for example, he admits to being "inconsistent, like all impulsive people"; he congratulates himself on his own perspicacity, turning aside criticism of his "savage individuality"; he voices his scorn of those who do not attempt to emancipate themselves. Later developments testify to his ability to "avoid commitment" and to dictate his own terms for considering renunciation and acceptance of his fate, as befits a new and very Gidean Oedipus.

Gide seems to have forgotten his own words of distaste on viewing a new interpretation of what he calls "Sophocles's lady," *Antigone:* "Suffered unbearably from the ultra-modern sauce in which was served up that wonderful play, which remains beautiful more in spite of Cocteau than because of him." The pot seems somewhat harsh with the kettle, when some of the ingredients of Gide's own "sauce" are considered: the Tartuffe-like entrance of Teiresias, speaking unctuously of "a day in His sight"; the equally anachronistic "Something is rotten in the state"; the nasty talk of the incestuously inclined boys; the juvenile restiveness; the parade of indecencies to shock the stodgily conventional reader. Even Cocteau's *Machine infernale* can scarcely surpass this as a masterly distortion of the Oedipus myth, intended to serve personal ends and demonstrate personal technique. For it is only in the final act that *Oedipe* becomes a philosophic consideration of "eyes that see not" and of minds gifted with sight. The spectacular act of *dépassement* (going beyond the expected) is what is significant for Gide, even more than the hero's new understanding of the nature of things and his final attainment of *sophrosyne.*

The confrontation of the king and the priest accentuates the differences in their two types of blindness: that of Oedipus in his contented ignorance is curable, that of the dogmatic Teiresias is not. The ruler progresses from an ignoble darkness to an admirable one; his counselor persists in his blindness by accepting his lot without question. To readers who insist on seeing the work as a treatise on free will and determinism, Gide explains it as "the struggle . . . between individualism and submission to religious authority . . . of individuality against religious ethics . . . the opposition between the perspicacious antimystic and the believer." [14] Oedipus, blinded by his own hand, undertakes an intensive search for spiritual happiness, rejecting the easy kind of salvation preached by Teiresias, who is blind in his faith. In the contest between the man who submits to God and the one who believes only in man, it is his calculated act that wins Oedipus the advantage over the priest.

As well as the major treatments of blindness in *La Symphonie pastorale* and *Oedipe*, there are many *Journal* entries on the topic—some thirty referring to Oedipus alone. It is a preoccupation and a symbol as early as the first notebooks, as late as the preface to Hogg's *Confession of a Justified Sinner*. The allusions have little pattern, but they offer many parallels with Diderot's illustrative references. There are a few medical histories and mentions of cases. More often blindness and its cure are adduced to point up contrasts—between the neglect and implementing of intelligence, between ecclesiastical controls and personal convictions, between human stagnation and advancement.

Traveling in Brittany, Gide's semifictional André is impressed, in his youthful and guileless way, by the waters that have been blessed by a local saint: "Blind people came, and the opaque leucoma fell from their dampened eyes." After the poet loses his Emmanuèle, he asks divine guidance: "What is needed is a faith that is humble, credulous and completely simple. After all, is it really sure that it leads to blindness? Is it really true that people must go blind to see Thee, and that, on the other hand, those who sought carefuly would not look, Oh God, upon Thee?" [15]

Blindness to the obvious, trusting in appearances, taking things naively at face value, all are ridiculed in the *soties*. The author of *Paludes* comments on Angèle's illusion of happiness: "If blindness is combined with mediocrity, it is still sadder." He returns to this theme of his story to summarize it in an axiom: "Being blind to believe oneself happy." In *Le Prométhée,* the match manufacturer brings light to men as well as fire—and Cocles "sees" the road to success only after his partial blinding. *Les Caves* is as much a tale of mistaken trust in first impressions as it is of episodic adventure and of the effort to *passer outre.* Its only specific reference to blindness concerns Anthime's experiments with rats: in an ironic preview of the spirit of *Oedipe,* Gide has Anthime enlighten the animals by blinding them. Lafcadio and Protos, dealing with dupes who believe what they see, depend more on their shrewdness of mind than on their eyes to give them insight.

If, as Gide avers, the *récits* are a series of ironic studies, it is equally true that they are all studies in blindness of various types: Michel's, in *L'Immoraliste,* is of the self-imposed kind: Alissa's, in *La Porte étroite,* comes from wearing a voluntary blindfold; the prodigal son returns with broadened vision, while his young brother must still learn to see when he leaves; in *Isabelle,* the whole romantic illusion springs from failure to see simple facts in a reasonable light; the three perspectives on the same events given in turn by Eveline, Robert, and Geneviève (in *L'Ecole des femmes* and *Robert*) are family variations of "blinding by love"—as Robert calls it—or of astigmatism or tubular vision. In *Thésée,* Oedipus adds a memoir to his personal history: "I put out my eyes to punish them for failing to see evidence that was plain enough, as they say, to put my eye out.—Nobody understood the cry I uttered then 'Oh, darkness! My light!'—They took it to be a complaint . . . at that very moment the sky within me was lighting up with stars." [16]

Reading the autobiography of a girl born blind, Gide finds that hypocrisy is not limited to those able to see physically. Her figures and turns of speech are damning evidence against her; she speaks in clichés based on visual sensations she could not possibly have experienced. Presumably, such lack of sincerity is not beyond forgiving in those who stay blind. They have a special privilege, as Gide points out both in *La Symphonie pastorale* and in *Numquid et tu?* . . . ? "If you were blind, you would be without sin. But now you say 'We see.' That is why your sin continues to exist."

Few are immune to blindness or exempt from the charge of it when Gide is in critical mood: Diderot is accused of *aveuglement* in the *Journal;* in the *Interviews imaginaires,* Victor Hugo is criticized in his own words, for "seeing beyond the world that is real." During the Second World War, a contemporary writer fails to appreciate the meaning of the fall of France and Gide remarks: "One thinks with sadness of the satisfaction of Chardonne who is blind to the present." Even Goethe, whose work intrigues Gide, is severely treated: "It is the custom to rhapsodize over his thirst for clarity; everybody admires his last words: 'Mehr Licht'. . . . On the contrary, I should choose to deplore this horror of obscurity, which I hold to be Goethe's most serious weakness and error. It is at the point at which he approaches Voltaire. . . . Why did he fail to overcome his horror of darkness and fail to put more questions to the 'Mouth of Shadow' in an effort to seize upon some of its secrets?" [17] This is the attitude Oedipus expresses in his "Oh, darkness! My light!" and that Diderot encourages in "Poets, be dark!" But even darkness must be intelligently interpreted and blindness used to good effect; in *Littérature et Morale,* Gide speaks in tones that recall those of Diderot preaching "virtuism": "I like blindness to evil to come from being dazzled by good. Otherwise virtue is ignorance—poverty."

In his own way, Gide is a deeply religious man, in spite of his rejection of churchly dogmas and cults. The scriptures intrigue him both in their wisdom and in their imagery. His writings abound in quotations on blindness, light, and darkness. From time to time, he debates with himself the worth of the spiritual vision that is possible for those willing to sacrifice their right to reason. In his moments of elevation, he feels strongly drawn toward a rather special Christianity. But he always finds he has a few reservations and confesses that salvation through surrender is beyond him: "The difficulty comes from this, that Christianity (Christian orthodoxy) is exclusive and that belief in *its* truth excludes belief in any other truth. It does not absorb; it repulses." [18] If he is to lose himself, he would prefer—like the men of the Age of Reason—that it be without benefit of blindfolds. Religious light may suffice to guide Claudel and other trusting Christians out of the labyrinth, but Gide feels reassured only if he has a firm grip on the strong thread provided by his own reasoning. This, by the way, is the lesson Diderot sees in the Theseus legend—only experience and knowledge of nature can supply the thread and defeat the Minotaur.[19] To Gide, as to Diderot, religion's influence on conduct is more likely to be harmful than helpful. "God is virtue"—the words are Gide's, not Diderot's—sums up his religious outlook when he is in his late seventies. For him, blind faith in the Christian

God is no less a superstition than the African belief in the efficacy of masks. In religion as in art, he prefers that nothing be taken for granted. He knows what he calls the "palace of faith" too well to care to venture into it: "One has to check too many things in the cloakroom. I am willing to give up my purse, but not my reason—my reason for existing. One enters there with eyes closed; with eyes blinded." [20]

Theseus is speaking for himself and not for Gide in his valedictory address to the city he has built. In at least one respect, however, he and Gide are agreed. He has a proper respect for the gods as well as for bulls, but little inclination to follow the example set by Oedipus or the urging of Teiresias: "To see God, one must cease seeing the world." He is quite content, he replies, to stay a "child of this earth." [21] Gide echoes the sentiment in his reply to a suggestion that he join the church:

> He.—Then what is keeping you from doing it?
> I.—It is that gesture of blind belief the Church insists on: faith.

And the argument is repeated, both in substance and in form, later in "Dieu, fils de l'homme": "In order to *believe*, you must put out your eyes. You must cease looking, if you are to see the object of belief." [22]

Gide admits, then, of only two sources of spiritual light that do not call for a *bandeau* or a more permanent *aveuglement:* the Bible and man's effort to humanize God. The first has beams of wisdom, often clouded by ambiguities but still perceptible to the keen searcher, "Reason itself brings me to the Gospel, as love does. Why then deny reason?" The scripture "needs no commentary," he says in *Numquid et tu?* . . . , and "every human effort to throw light upon it only dims it." To help answer the question of how to assure God's coming closer to humanity, Gide has a modest proposal—he suggests, first of all, ridding humanity of the inhuman God of harsh judgment and dark threats of damnation. The God who turns a deaf ear to subservient pleas is to be supplanted by Christ the Man, who understands men and whose life is full of voluntary sacrifice, of promised joy and forgiveness, and of exemplary light. In "Dieu, fils de l'homme," there is a reaffirmation of the credo expressed in his foreword to *Numquid et tu?* . . . : "I have not been converted. I am neither a Protestant nor a Catholic; I am simply a Christian." He is a Christian, that is to say, by special definition and according to his own lights. Gide's is a personal faith that has self-expression as its basis, enjoyment of an immediate and material eternity as its reward, and reasoned self-discipline as its cross.

Blindness is as prevalent in administration and in politics as it is in matters social, moral, and religious. Writing of current affairs, Gide uses many turns of phrase that relate to sight or the lack of it—some of them so common that their metaphorical sense is scarcely noticed. The inhuman failure of the African exploitation companies to see the plight of the natives, for example, is equaled by the disregard of the legislators when Gide campaigns for reform of the laws. Courts and their procedures place the blindfold on the figure of justice. The adherents of political parties—particularly fascists and communists—are deluded by their limited vision. Those who could not sense the nation's unpreparedness for World War I must surely have been blind. Those who advocate a back-to-the-land movement to save France in 1940 are frightening in their *aveuglement.*

Blindness, then, is a universal affliction to both Diderot and Gide. Its tragic results are alleviated but slightly by the increased perception that it sometimes brings, or by the enthusiasm possible for those who negate the existence of reality—an attitude Gide illustrates by citing the case of the nightingale, which supposedly sings better when blinded. The paradoxes inherent in blindness and the contrasts of its extensions provide an admirable symbol—at times an unconscious figure of speech—for use by observers and commentators on the problems of mankind. Its converse and cure, enlightenment, is the goal of *philosophe* and modern humanist alike.

Dilemmas and Directions

The moral dilemmas of Diderot and Gide complicate their lives, permeate their works, and direct a large part of their thinking. Diderot's philosophical quandary is that of all who deny the existence of divine providence and reject systems, while still feeling a need for some sense of direction in their behavior. Gide sums up his problem succinctly: "I am torn by a conflict between the rules of morality and the rules of sincerity." Their ethics must be appreciated, in each case, in the light of a long life and a voluminous literary output; too much stress on any incident or pronouncement, as Gide has frequently pointed out, distorts the total impression.[1]

In the quest of principles to guide their own and humanity's conduct, both authors break with family traditions of piety and conventionality. They find established codes and patterns inadequate to their own needs and strike out in new directions without fixed goals—directions that can be revised and corrected as circumstances change. For their orientation, they rely on man's capacity for progressive improvement through the use of intelligence, and for discovery of successive (but always provisional) objectives. Each admits without regret—as Gide remarks in a study of literature and morals—that "in the world of morals, there is never an absolute victory." The ethical manifesto of either could have come from the pen of the other: "Laws and rules of conduct are for the state of childhood; education is an emancipation. The wise man lives without a rule of conduct, according to his wisdom. We must try to reach a higher immorality." The words were actually Gide's, confided to his *Journal* when he was in his early twenties. The sentiments are those Diderot expressed tô his somewhat scandalized father during a visit to his home in Langres.

The indignant outcry such attitudes have evoked from conservative critics is understandable. Provoked is perhaps a better word, since the authors are deliberate in their public admission that they are "immoral" by moral conviction. Each professes to seeking for himself—and in so doing implies that others should seek—a higher morality than accepted systems of ethics, religious or lay, offer a thinking man.

A confusion of terms adds to the imbroglio. Both writers can be described (with varying degrees of aptness) as moral men and moralists, as *moralistes* and *immoralistes*, as *moraliseurs*. They are moral men legally because they can distinguish between right and wrong in simple matters and moral men ethically since they prefer virtue to vice. Because they sometimes pass judgment, in spite of firm resolutions, on human conduct—and particularly since they encourage others to good behavior—they are moralists. When their insistence on virtue approaches sermonizing, they become *moraliseurs*. As observers of and commentators on mores, whether or not they evaluate them, both are *moralistes*. The word *immoraliste*, given such popularity by Gide, is still not accepted in correct French usage; it implies one who knows what accepted standards are, but opposes them. The authors, like Gide's Michel, are active rebels. Young

Rameau, on the other hand, is an *amoraliste* (or would be, if the term existed)—his stance is one of unconcern and nonchalance rather than of defiance and revolt.

As an individual and as editor of the *Encyclopédie*, Diderot is subjected to many attacks. Even when the point at issue is fundamentally religious, the charge on which he is arraigned is moral. Supporting deism, in his day, is tantamount to challenging public decency. The Jesuit *Journal de Trévoux*, irked by professional jealousy —its editors are preparing their own dictionary—takes advantage of the public mood. Its accusations are voiced in terms of malevolent influence rather than of plain heresy. Various condemnations and prohibitions of the publishing enterprise are contrived on ethical grounds. Among the pretexts are Diderot's "dangerous" contributions to the sensationalistic ideas of the Sorbonne thesis presented by the abbé de Prades, and his condoning of the behavioristic views expressed by Helvétius in *De l'esprit*. Fréron, Palissot, and other adversaries of the *philosophes* make much capital of their righteous horror at seeing society debauched by immoral enemies of the public weal.

Gide's noxious influence on French morality (especially on the minds of the young) has long been a topic of spirited debate. His rejection of Christianity is less often the given reason for censure than his defense of homosexuality. He responds in various ways to his accusers. For Henri Massis, who pictures him as a sort of antichrist, he has only scorn. Béraud's violent article in the *Nouvelles littéraires* is "very amusing." He is more disposed to discussion with other "right thinking" men, even to the point of commending them for some of their ideas and thanking them for helping reveal what he stands for. One of André Rouveyre's articles, for example, is "extraordinarily perceptive," although Gide finds the argument on his supposed "deleterious effect" unconvincing and factitious. François Porché, the author of *L'Amour qui n'ose pas dire son nom* (*Unnameable Love*), receives a series of letters from Gide thanking him for sympathetic treatment but indicating many errors of judgment—in particular that of failing to recognize that Gide's play *Saül* is more "dangerous" than his *Immoraliste.*

Pointing out courteously to one Father Poucel that it is a serious error to consider any one work representative of an author's total ethics, Gide admits that, from the church's point of view, "It goes without saying that all my recent works are plainly worthy of being condemned and damned." With exasperating patience he reminds the cleric that the *Narcisse, Saül,* and the early *Nourritures* are youthful points of view and that other works similarly show stages and changes of attitude. Then, with increasing asperity of tone: "Obviously, the simplest thing to do is reject everything together, and to let *Corydon*, the *Faux-Monnayeurs* and *Si le grain* . . . drag my complete works down into your hell." [2]

Religion, which Catholic philosophers consider inseparable from ethics, does help Diderot and Gide in their search for their moral bearings. But its role is a negative one. A devout home environment, a sanctimonious brother, an uncle with a canonry he may pass on, a Jesuit education, and two narrow escapes from becoming a cleric himself—all these add up to a conviction in Diderot's mind that the priesthood is not his vocation.

Young Gide grows up in a puritanical atmosphere of prayers, scripture, and strait-laced behavior, personified in his mother and in the worthy family retainer, Anna Shackleton. By the time he is twenty-three, "completely virgin and utterly depraved," he has stored up enough observation of religion to last him the rest of his life. It is not surprising that he explores "the slippery paths of unbelief" and undergoes the "ravages of free-thinking"—to use the words mouthed by his pious character Robert as he laments his late wife's wasted life. Diderot brings dismay to his relatives, who see in him the promise of a distinguished career as a prelate; he confounds them by moving from Christian faith through natural religion to deism, then to atheism.[3] Gide follows a similar path, passing through a period of glorification of nature (which is for him a kind of pantheism) and of hedonism to arrive at the idealized materialism that is his unique brand of Christianity—a cult of deified man as the successor to an anthropomorphic God.[4]

As they rid themselves of their religious bonds, Diderot and Gide feel freer to make their own inquiries into ethics. Disdaining metaphysics and abstractions, each explores physical and physiological principles, Diderot in terms of philosophic sensationalism, Gide with a more personal interest in gratification of the senses.

Sexual conduct is a matter of personal hygiene to Diderot. It is a human question that affects individuals emotionally while assuring animal continuity, but it has no other ethical significance. He is not insensitive to the appeal of the flesh himself—he marries for love and has lengthy liaisons with some of his successive mistresses, but there is no evidence that he is inordinately libidinous.

In his letters to Sophie and other friends, he talks of the sexual act and of amorous adventures with a candor that now seems shocking, but must have seemed less so to eighteenth-century readers. He acknowledges, too, the power of the passions—without either enshrining or deprecating them. It is the function of the intelligence, he believes, to interpret feelings, to thrive on both the sensations and the judgments that follow. He asks only for common sense and balance in the indulgence of passions, with some enthusiasm and occasional folly to enliven the routine of existence. Of man and his urges, he says, "Surrounded by reefs, buffeted by a thousand adverse winds, can he possibly make port? Yes, he can. He has his reason to control his *passions*, light to show him the way, rules to guide him, vigilance to sustain him, effort and prudence within his capabilities." [5] This temperate view, voiced in the *Encyclopédie* article "Passions," seems more characteristic of the solid bourgeois (or the churchman) than of the menace to public morality and would-be Casanova. On the other hand, pronouncements in the *Encyclopédie*, even in signed contributions, do not necessarily express the convictions of the writer. It may be said, however, that Diderot regards sex as a natural phenomenon and an aspect of behavior. It becomes a problem only when it threatens to impair health or when it is given ethical values that are not part of its nature. As is well illustrated in the *Supplément au Voyage de Bougainville*, ethical judgments are illogical and pointless. The subtitle states the theme: "On the Disadvantage of Attaching Moral Ideas to Certain Physical Actions Incompatible Therewith." A similar defense may be alleged against the charge of obscenity that is leveled at Diderot for sections in *Les Bijoux, La Suite de l'entretien,* and *Jacques.*

Sexual inversion and perversion both have a place, though not a major one, in Diderot's work. Gide draws attention to a comment, in a letter to Sophie, on a lustful interest aroused by Diderot's seeing a boy at the baths. Although the *philosophe* uses the first singular pronoun ("Never write 'I' again," Gide reports Oscar Wilde as saying to him) that is slight evidence for presuming that Diderot was a homosexual, or even that he was a potential invert.[6] The incident may well be reported, suitably garnished with an air of authenticity, as one of his vivid "problem cases" in ethics. Another possibility is that he hopes to encourage Sophie to talk of her affection for her sister, which strikes him as unnatural. It would be equally specious to see allusions to sensuality and sexual inversion in Diderot's remarks on youthful masturbation or in such exaggerated comments as "I forgive everything passion leads to. . . . I have always been a defender of strong emotions." Or again, "We must never break away completely from our status as animals."[7] It is plain that the *condition animale* to which he refers is not the homosexual penchant in the animal world on which Gide expounds in his *Journal.* Diderot's one treatment at length of sexual perversion, the frank exposé of convent life in *La Religieuse* (*The Nun*), is far from being an endorsement of the practices he depicts. Even Citizen Naigeon, Diderot's literary executor and a rabid anticlerical, regrets that a good editor did not prune out, before publication of *La Religieuse,* "the depiction that is very faithful, no doubt, but also very disgusting, of the Mother Superior's infamous love affairs." The judgment is at once a tribute to Diderot's skill in description and an admission of Naigeon's critical ineptness. For Diderot writes as an indignant *philosophe*—the case histories of the sadistic Superior and the other Lesbians are introduced as evidence, to prove that the cloistered life is a crime against natural instincts. He resorts to artistic exaggeration to support his plea for a change in public attitude. This technique of shock propaganda will be commonplace in later centuries—Gide will use it in *Corydon* to persuade his readers toward a more radical revision of standards. But in *La Religieuse* sexual adventures and episodes are used merely to illustrate the argument. They are no more the point at issue here than in *Le Supplément,* the tale of Madame de la Carlière, the d'Alembert sequence, or *Jacques le fataliste.*

The story of saccharine Suzanne's misadventures during her unwilling tour of convents resembles the sad sagas of Richardson's heroines and of Marivaux's worthy but insipid Marianne. Diderot outdoes the other novelists, however, in the reactions he elicits from his readers. Others evoke sympathy, ranging from mild dismay to tears of anguish: he provokes virtual empathy, enhanced by moral indignation. He directs attention toward the causes of the naive nun's plight—the depravity of her selfish parents is surpassed only by that of the institutions to which she is confined by a monstrous conspiracy. Manouri the lawyer speaks for human decency as well as for Diderot and his marionette, Suzanne: "Taking the vow of chastity is promising God the constant infraction of His wisest and most important laws; taking the vow of obedience is renouncing the inalienable prerogative of mankind, liberty. If one observes these vows, one is a criminal; if not, one is a perjurer. Cloistered life is for fanatics or hypocrites." [8] The author himself, in the middle of the account of homosexual practices, intervenes as a *raisonneur* to present the sensible point of view: "That is the effect of withdrawal from the world. Man is born to live in society. Separate or isolate him from it and his ideas will become incoherent, his character will be changed, a thousand ridiculous affections will arise in his heart. . . . Put a man in a forest, and he will become wild; in a cloister, where the notion of necessity is combined with that of servitude, it is even worse." [9]

It is the broadly philosophic intention of *La Religieuse* that impresses Grimm, who is more astute than Naigeon: "A work of genius . . . a work of public and general utility, for it was the most cruel satire ever done on the cloister." The praise is not without bias, of course—Grimm was Diderot's closest friend and a fellow-conspirator in the hoax that led to his writing the novel.

Gide's preoccupation with sexual questions, more personal and better publicized than Diderot's, constitutes a large part of his early and lasting moral dilemma. An avowed pederast, he wages an open campaign for the removal of social stigma from "Greek love," while looking with some hauteur at homosexual inversion, effeminacy, and sodomy, and scornfully applying the term "Lesbian" to what he calls "double inversion" among heterosexuals.[10] The problem is discussed in detail in *Corydon*, a series of four Socratic dialogues that serve as his manifesto on sex, in *Si le grain ne meurt . . .* , his memoirs covering the period before his marriage, and in

Ainsi soit-il, his revelations from beyond the grave. The theme is infused into many other works, notably the *Journal*, *Les Nourritures terrestres*, *Saül*, *L'Immoraliste*, and *Les Faux-Monnayeurs*.

As has been said, he convinces himself (if not the public) that *Corydon* is his most important work and that *Saül* deserves much more attention than it has been given. Of *Si le grain ne meurt* . . . , which he intended as an honest chronicle of his youthful experiences, he writes, "Put the case that I am writing it for a penance." The preface to *Corydon* makes his feeling of compulsion clear: "The indignation that *Corydon* will probably arouse will not prevent me from believing that the things I am saying here must be said. Not that I feel that everything people think must be said, and said at any time at all—but this specifically must, and it must be said today!" [11] Some years before, he wrote: "After all, what I say about it here, I thought, does not make it so. It *exists*. I am trying to explain what exists. And since people do not generally want to admit that it *exists*, I am examining, I am trying to examine, the question of whether it is really so deplorable that people should say that it does exist." [12]

The four sections of *Corydon* report conversations between the narrator and a brilliant young doctor whose homosexual proclivities are shocking Paris. The interviewer, surprised to find Corydon masculine in appearance and tastes, lends a willing ear to his long and technical discourses on the importance of homosexuality in literature, the arts, and the sciences. The argument is summarized in Corydon's final words: "From the age of thirteen to twenty-two years, for the Greeks, is the period of loving companionship, of shared exaltation, of the noblest emulation. Only after that, according to their vows, the boy hopes to become a man, that is, thinks of women—that is, thinks of marrying." By the doctor's prescription, Gide became a man at the age of twenty-six, when he married his cousin; he did not, however, forswear homosexuality. This contributed to many years of anguished marriage, later chronicled in *Ainsi soit-il,* until his wife died in 1938, without issue. Gide's one child was a daughter, born in 1923 to him and a literary friend, Madame Van Rysselberghe.

Reconsidering *Corydon* during the forties, Gide still ranks it as his most significant book, "but also the one in which I find the most to be said again. The least successful is the one in which it was most important to succeed. I was no doubt ill-advised to treat such serious questions ironically." He remains faithful to the work to the end, declaring a few years before his death that, if he is elected to the Academy (on his own terms), one of his first acts will be another preface to *Corydon,* his most "serviceable" work—he uses the English word—and the one that is to prove "most helpful to human progress."

Si le grain ne meurt . . . , ripening for years in Gide's mind and manuscript files, appears in print two years after the first limited edition of *Corydon.* To an English friend, he writes, "Why I wrote this book?—Because I felt I *should* write it." He enlarges on this in the vein he uses to guarantee the worth of *Corydon:* "I wrote this book to 'create a precedent,' to offer an example of outspokenness, to enlighten some, reassure others, force opinion to take into account what people are ignorant of, or pretend to be ignorant of, to the great detriment of psychology, morals, art . . . and society." [13] The autobiography bares his intimate history with a candor rare in literature, for better or worse, since Rousseau's *Confessions*. Years earlier, soliloquizing on his aims, Gide wrote, "I do not want to move to pity with this book; I want to *embarrass*." Noting that it was not "some almost unhealthy obsession," he went on: "The difficulty comes rather from the fact that I must artificially revive a problem to which I have found (as far as I am concerned) a practical solution." [14] Although the reference was actually to *Corydon*, the problem was that of *Si le grain . . .* as well. To avoid indirect discourse—and disregarding warnings by both Proust and Wilde—Gide presents his case in the first singular, even considering as an alternative title *Et ego*. Along with other facts, he lists his sexual experiences from his first impulses as a small boy until he is in his mid-twenties. With Rousseau-like aplomb, he reassures the public (and himself) that his is a worthy cause: "I am not writing these Memoirs to defend myself. I am not called on to defend myself, since I am not accused. I am writing them before being accused. I am writing them in order to be accused." Having stressed the sincerity of the undertaking ("the whole object of my story is to be truthful"), he reviews his attachments and experiments in several hundred pages, then reiterates his purpose: "But I am not trying to make my ethics prevail; it is not my apology I am writing, but my story." [15] When his exemplary tale has been told, his scorn of hypocrisy demonstrated, and his "practical solution" discovered, Gide can say, "I foresee a time when *ethical* problems will interest only a few timid souls."

While Diderot and Gide look on sexual behavior as an aspect of human experience that varies from person to person and from place to place, they differ sharply in their opinions of its relative importance in each man's ethics. Diderot usually dismisses it as an incidental factor, Gide feels it is a vital force in determining moral directions. It follows that the remainder of the moral dilemma—in which sex plays a small role, or none—concerns Diderot more and Gide less. But in spite of the disproportion of parts, their total attitudes are similar. They are convinced that the intelligent man must be guided by some basic principles (even though they cannot be formulated) if he is to achieve his own best possibilities and offer guidance to others. Their ethical positions, epitomized in Diderot's "virtuism" and Gide's self-realization, are different only in terminology and in the benefits sought—to oneself and others in the first instance, to oneself as representative of others in the second.

It is sometimes argued that a resolute materialist can have no basis for conduct other than fortuity, since he must by definition reject providence and free will. The devout insist with particular vehemence that materialistic monism and moral responsibility are incompatible, that human faculties alone cannot insure mankind's salvation. Diderot disagrees. Foregoing divine surveillance and the promise of eternity in favor of practicable decency, he puts the pursuit of virtue at the center of his personal morality, suggesting that the performance of unselfish actions to help others is man's best hope in his civilized life. Surpassing at times his faith in reason, this faith in virtue sustains much of his work. It is a prominent feature of his theory of drama, his plays, and his art criticism. It is evident in his letters, his articles, and his advice to rulers, parents, educators, and authors. But it is not a blind and fanatic faith in man's goodness. Diderot's enthusiasm for Richardsonian virtue seconds his philosophic penchant—it does not supplant it. As a sensationalist, he demonstrates his concept of "feeling matter" in *Le Rêve de d'Alembert.* From material to moral sensitivity—that is, from consciousness to conscience—is but a short step for the *philosophe.* It is simply a matter of adding judgment to observation. As a believer in gradual progress through education, he maintains that human conduct is susceptible to modification and improvement, provided that men are proffered attainable goals in lieu of such ideals and abstractions as Paradise. Shunning metaphysical speculations on rewards in the afterlife, he proposes the immediate and perceptible satisfactions of virtue. In so doing, he adopts a moral stance that is humanistic and humane. The position is as far from being static as Gide's cultivation of an energetic individualism in moral affairs, and it is equally dependent on personal effort.

The Diderot-Gide rapport is apparent in one definition found in the eulogy of Richardson: "What is virtue? In every aspect, it is self-sacrifice." Thoughts come to mind of Gide's emphasis on "losing" oneself and renunciation, on preferring others—and artistic tasks—to himself, and on accepting what is beyond control. Diderot asserts that virtue is everything, while life is nothing. He recommends the point of view even to a princess, to whom he dedicates one of his plays: "The habit of virtue is the only one you may acquire without fear for the future." Occasionally, he sounds like Rousseau in full cry: "It is the contemptible conventions that pervert mankind, and not human nature that should be accused. What is there actually that moves us as much as the report of a generous deed? Where is there a miserable fellow who can listen unmoved to the anguished cry of a worthy man?" [16] As for creative works: "Oh, how beneficial it would be for humanity if all the imitative arts agreed on a common goal and competed with the laws some day to make virtue loved and vice hated!" At the sight of an audience's emotional response to a moving tableau, Diderot waxes lyric: "Upon my word, humanity is lovely to see at the theater! Why must people bid one another goodbye so soon! Men are so good and so happy when decency joins them in attitudes, blends them, makes them as one." [17] And he never fails to be impressed by the noble qualities he sees in man at his best: "I have the greatest confidence," he writes to Falconet, "in virtue, talent, and probity, and until now this confidence has never proven unfounded."

When confronted by amorality incarnate in Rameau the younger, Diderot is constrained, as his interlocutor, to praise Theophrastu, La Bruyère, and Molière for teaching people "to know their duties, to love virtue, and to hate vice." The parasite turns aside the lofty sentiment with, "The voice of honor and conscience is very weak when the bowels are crying out." Illustrating the relative nature of moral judgments, he continues: "I'll tell you what you're like, you fellows, you think that the same happiness suits everyone. What a strange fantasy!

– – – You decorate this eccentricity with the name of virtue; you call it philosophy. But do virtue and philosophy suit everyone? He has them who can, and maintains them if he can." [18] While recognizing that there are different tastes in morals as elsewhere, Diderot makes it clear where his own preference lies. In a letter to his mistress, he contrasts a young libertine and himself: "His taste comes down to this: I like vice; and mine to this: I like virtue. That is the way it is with all judgments—they finally are reduced to one of these statements or the other." The M. Hardouin of *Est-il bon? Est-il méchant?* —Who comes closest to being Diderot's Corydon—explains his ambiguous ethics by saying, "I serve the cause of vice, I slander virtue . . . but it is counterfeit virtue."

Gide's extolling of virtue is as constant as Diderot's. It is interrelated with his ideas of renunciation, strength (the Latin "virtus"), and individual achievement. Philoctetes states the author's outlook in the treatise on the three moral codes: "Only step by step can one attain higher virtue." He answers significantly when Ulysses asks, "Have you no admiration for virtue?" by saying, "Yes, for my own." His ethical quest is announced in "Oh, virtue! In your bitter name I seek some slight intoxication." He admits his failure in "Virtue I no longer believe in, Néoptolème." In the section of *Le Prométhée* called "Chronicle of Private Morality," the failure is extended beyond personal conduct. The narrator blandly states, "I shall not speak of public morality, since there is none." Throughout his writing, Gide in turn endorses and regrets this individualistic response to the appeal of human virtue. One "unpublished comment" is typical:

"Considering then . . . that nothing was doing more to make me prideful than my sense of virtue, I became horrified of that very virtue and of everything I could take pride in, of overything that allowed me to say: I am not like you, common man! But I realize that this excessive renunciation, this negation of virtue through love of virtue itself, will seem to be only a despicable piece of sophistry." [19]

In the *Journal,* the word and the image recur so frequently that the reader suffers from a surfeit of virtue, which can be as boring as vice. Fortunately, Gide's sense of balance restrains him from doing a novel on unalloyed virtue or virtue triumphant, eighteenth-century style. During the First World War, however, he does sketch a theme for "the story of him who would deny his virtue." It is to be a story of exaltation, self-sacrifice, disillusionment, and luxurious living; the protagonist is envisioned as "a man, equally capable of passions, even of dissipation, and of virtues." [20] Other applications of the term are to the Germans' practical genius for war, the visionary and unmethodical approach of the French to major problems, plant intelligence ("a school for virtue"), and "virtue . . . become flesh."

Although the names Gide gives it vary widely, the basic idea of virtue haunts him, and the search for an adequate definition in personal terms constitutes much of his moral adventure. The history of his career could be written in his ethical catchwords: *stratégie idéale, choisir, manifester, être pour paraître* (ideal strategy, choosing, manifesting, existing in order to present a desired image). These catchwords alternate with *sincérité, authenticité, fidélité, personnalité.* The *acte gratuit,* for a time, shares attention with *renoncement, dénuement, sacrifice,* and *acceptation.* There is a preoccupation with *progrès, sérénité,* and *humanité.* And everywhere in the kaleidoscope of terms come *nourritures, plaisirs, satisfactions.* The compound of all these is Gide's concept of virtue, which has its fullest meaning for him in his last years. While it cannot be taken as a definitive moral system, it is for him a satisfying and comprehensive "provisional morality," which he accepts and propounds.

Late in life, perturbed by man's continuing need of a code that does not include false premises—such as Providence—he gives his idea of intelligent conduct: "It requires much virtue to achieve that state of total atheism; even more to remain there. The 'believer' will probably see in it nothing but an invitation to license. If this were so, hooray for God! Hooray for the sacred falsehood that would preserve humanity from collapse, from disaster. But cannot man learn to demand of himself, through virtue, what he believes demanded by God?" The attitude and the phraseology might well be those of an eighteenth-century manifesto. It becomes even more obvious in a later paragraph that the enshrinement of virtue is the essential point: "That strange game that we are playing on earth (unintentionally, unconsciously, and often unwillingly) will be won only if the idea of God, on withdrawing, yields to virtue, only if man's virtue, his dignity, supplants God. God has ceased to exist save by virtue of man." [21]

A year after his Nobel Prize is awarded, he reports a discussion of his extreme views with a liberal Catholic, who obligingly suggests that their differences are purely semantic: "What they call God you are free to name Virtue if you wish." Gide finds this too facile a solution. He makes his own proposal: "God is virtue. But what do I mean by that? I should have to define; I cannot do so. I shall manage to do so only subsequently. But I shall already have accomplished much if I remove God from the altar and put man in his place. Provisionally I shall think that virtue is the best the individual can obtain from himself." And if this is not enough to make life tolerable in this "frightful world," he adds, "up and at the demoralizers!" [22]

Vice and virtue have their interest, then, for Diderot and Gide, both in theory and in personal practice. Closely allied to that interest are their notions of social morality. Diderot contends that ethics become significant only in society, since acts not affecting others have nothing but physical meaning. Rameau voices that opinion forcefully: "Moreover, you must remember that where something as variable as morality is concerned, nothing is absolutely, essentially, generally true or false." He elaborates with: "I say vice, because I'm speaking your language; for if we were to have it out, we might find that you call vice what I call virtue, and virtue what I call vice." [23]

The common sense of the sycophant's sally is not lost on his serious interrogator. For it is not the word but the principle of virtue that Diderot endorses; "the word that kills" can emphasize artificial distinctions and create differences where none exists. Lofty nomenclature may veil vapid abstractions, which he calls "words empty of sense," but useful concepts likewise may be hidden by inappropriate labels or by too elaborate definition. Categorical virtue and absolute vice exist only for the metaphysician. In life, virtue and vice interpenetrate each other. The same act, according to circumstances and the attitudes of those who pass judgment, can be one or the other, or both at once.

Personally, and with full awareness of his bias, Diderot persists in looking on virtue as "a mistress to whom one becomes attached as much because of what one does for her as of the appeal she seems to have." For practical purposes and for evaluating the actions of others, he prefers terms less categorical than virtue and vice, good and evil. If the proposition is accepted that man is a product of material forces, it follows that human liberty does not exist, so that, as his frequently quoted letter to Landois puts it, "There is no act deserving of praise or blame; there is neither vice nor virtue, there is nothing to be necessarily rewarded or punished. What then distinguishes men? Beneficence and maleficence.– – – –But even if beneficent or maleficent man is not free, man is nevertheless a modifiable creature." [24] Such distinctions as there are in ethics are completely artificial, however convenient they may seem: "To tell the truth," he confides to Sophie, "I believe Nature is not concerned either with good or with evil; it is wholly taken up with two aims: the preservation of the individual and the propagation of the species." [25]

Gide, reacting in much the same way to ethical distinctions, finds words a poor substitute for deeds. If social progress is to be made, "I consider it awkward, unprofitable, uninstructive to stand (solely) on the plane of *good* and *evil* in order to judge human actions, or, more exactly, in order to appreciate their value. The comfortable and reassuring idea of *the good,* such as the middle classes cherish, invites humanity to stagnation, to sleep." [26] As a positive step, Gide suggests a mode of human behavior that seems a direct borrowing from Diderot's Jacques, who tempers his theoretical fatalism with practical foresight: "The determinism from which it seems clear that our mind, any more than our body, cannot possibly escape is so subtle, corresponds to such diverse, multiple and tenuous causes, that it seems childish to try to number them, and even more to get rid of them. And I admit that man is never free; but the simplest and most honest thing is to act as if he were." [27]

Opinions, institutions, and laws that infringe on human rights are as much concerns of Diderot and Gide as are broader questions of social relationships. The theme of *Sur l'inconséquence* . . . is public opinion, "that ugly beast with a thousand evil heads and the same number of evil tongues." In *La Religieuse,* the cloister is shown as a crime against both society and the individual. *Le Supplément* is a study of the rapports of morals, climate, and customs. The letter to Landois and the *Entretien d'un père avec ses enfants* (*Conversation of a Father with His Children*) give Diderot's theories of crime and punishment, liberty and social responsibility, laws and personal freedom; the *Essai sur les règnes de Claude et de Néron* (*Essay on the Reigns of Claudius and Nero*) is a compendium of ideas on social philosophy and, according to Meister, "one of the best books on ethics extant in our language."

Diderot's father ("a man with excellent judgment, but a pious man") is the soul of bourgeois respectability, yet he discusses his son's unorthodox views without cant:

> —The fact is, father, that strictly speaking there are no laws for the wise man.
> —Lower your voice. . . .
> —Since all of them are liable to exceptions, it's up to him to decide in what cases one should submit to them and when one should disregard them.
> —I shouldn't be too upset if there were one or two citizens like you in a town. But I shouldn't live there if they all thought the same way.[28]

Gide's "intelligent man," who attains "higher immorality" by living "without ethics, according to his own wisdom," is obviously a relative of Diderot's wise young man.

Modification of society's outlook and correction of existing evils are Diderot's aims. He scourges inhuman customs, not individual "sins": "When it comes to accusing gods or men, I prefer accusing gods." To complement this pronouncement on religion, he makes a profession of faith in civilized man that is strikingly similar to assertions by Voltaire: "If today there are more acts of trickery, more falsehoods and more licentiousness than ever, there are also more sincerity, more uprightness, more genuine attachment, more sentiments, more delicacy, more lasting passion than in earlier times." [29] The exculpation is completed in *Sur l'inconséquence:* "And then I have my own ideas, possibly accurate and certainly strange, on certain acts that I consider less as vices of man than as consequences of our absurd laws, which are the sources of social conduct that is as absurd as they are, and of a depravity that I should gladly call unnatural." [30]

Gide's reactions to the spectacle of society are markedly similar to Diderot's. His judgments, too, are given as suspended sentences. If civilization is to be saved, in his opinion, it will not be by the masses but by intelligent individuals: "The question of society? Of course. But the question of ethics comes before it. Man is more interesting than men." Prometheus gives the maxim added meaning with, "I don't like men; I like what devours them." And during the Nazi occupation of France, Gide admits sadly: "The stagnation of the greatest possible number of representatives of a second-rate humanity in a second-rate everyday happiness is not an 'ideal' to which I can lose my heart." [31] But he does believe in the possibility of gradual improvement: "Man's progress is only within himself." Though man moves but slowly toward a better world, Gide's confidence in his resources and his ideas rarely flags: "What I blame Rousseau for is speaking of 'laws of nature' when it is a matter of human affairs. Natural laws cannot be modified; there is nothing that man institutes, there is nothing human, that cannot be modified—beginning (or rather: ending) with man himself." [32] Even in the darkest days following the German invasion, when Gide is tempted to submit to the imposed regime, he still sees one glimmer of hope: "It devolves upon man alone, in the final reckoning, to solve all these problems which he alone has presumably raised." [33]

As a *philosophe* who has been a student-at-law, Diderot points out directions for reform of the administration of justice. Via Doctor Bordeu in *Le Rêve* and in his much-quoted letter to Landois, he advances a theory of remedial and "penitential" punishment that has been implemented in modern penal practice. He concurs with those who feel that the deliberate criminal must be punished to deter him and others from future crimes; at the same time, he insists that all circumstances be considered in determining the seriousness of the offense, urging that the sentence imposed be commensurate with both the crime itself and the possibility of encouraging criminals to lead better lives.

In spite of his disavowals of concern, Gide has a strong sense of responsibility as a citizen. It leads him to accepting the mayoralty of his Norman village—with a bizarre complication that he recalls in *Jeunesse.* On a return visit to La Roque after an absence of fifteen years, he learns the truth of *l'affaire Mulot,* the case of a laborer condemned "unjustly" to prison during his term in office, supposedly for perjury. It transpires that he was actually sentenced for a sexual offense involving a minor, but the constituents had not dared tell their mayor, who was then in his twenties.

Gide's interest in justice continues all his life. He attends the Court of Assizes, scans newspaper reports, and enjoys conversations on legal matters, writing indignantly of inequities he encounters. He speaks out plainly for what he believes is right in the Dreyfus case and other *causes célèbres.* He initiates a campaign against alcoholism (long before the Mendès-France milk crusade) in his village. He senses the dangers of political upheaval in North Africa. And, on his return from the Congo and Chad, he makes a public issue of the need for reform in the administration of colonies.

Giving even greater scope to their moral observations, both authors speculate occasionally on the world's ills and their eventual cures. Each feels inclined, when his spirits droop, to give up the blithe hopes he has for mankind and the quixotic causes man has espoused. As they feel the years encroaching on their energies, they sometimes concede that resignation to the inevitable is the best assurance of equanimity, once "the age of struggling with the angel is over." One says, "Oh, what an unpleasant thing life is!" and the other, "I have had my fill on this earth." But neither can bring himself entirely to abandoning hope. Diderot seems to speak for both when he says, "People must cherish a beautiful trust in the future to be attached to it."

In short, the moral attainments of Diderot and Gide are not in the goals they achieve but in the directions they discover. A complete answer, for either of them, would be as sure a sign of defeat as a last-minute conversion. Realizing that ethics are always relative to circumstances (which are themselves in flux), they look for paths to follow, not for rules, preferring a dynamic attitude to a static position. They are, by definition, "immoral" in their defiance of accepted standards and in their insistence that inherited conventions are inadequate for either present or future use. The only promises of progress they see lie in love of virtue, in refusal to take as answers what are patently unsolved questions. In *L'Humanisme de Diderot*, Jean Thomas has epitomized the ethical dilemma they face, both for themselves and for their fellow men: "We need a law that is universal and yet suited to each of us, founded on both learning and intuition, capable of reconciling the happiness of the individual and the balance of society, of assuring material progress and saving the ideal.[34] It is such a "law" that Diderot and Gide try to sense—and to intimate to their readers—in their moral explorations of sex, virtue, good and evil, society, laws and justice. By routes that are sometimes parallel, sometimes divergent, and sometimes identical, they proceed in similar directions. Discussing together what Gide calls "the stages in a slow advance toward the light," they may well say to each other what Diderot once wrote to a friend: "We are both extremely worthy people; we have the same ethical principles and very different types of behavior. The fact is that principles are a matter of judgment, and behavior is a matter of character." [35]

Mortality and Eternity

Diderot died in 1784, in his seventy-first year, at his fine new apartment on Rue de Richelieu. Death came as a dramatic climax—the family scene was a tableau worthy of a *comédie bourgeoise*—to a busy life, a measure of quiet contentment and an encyclopedic list of physical ailments. The final cause, in the medical sense, was thought to be apoplexy. Recent diagnosis reveals that it was a coronary thrombosis.[1] Tradition has it, on the word of his loving daughter, that his refusal to renounce his atheistic ways was unequivocal and that his last utterance was quotably philosophic. The funeral was lavish. Interment was at the church of Saint-Roch. Survivors included his wife, his daughter, and his son-in-law.

Gide died of pneumonia in 1951. He was in his eighty-second year. Like Diderot, he had enjoyed a relatively peaceful later life and retained full use of his senses to the last, despite recurrent illnesses and disabilities. Like Diderot, too, he died unregenerate and in Paris, at his modest apartment on Rue Vaneau. Like the *philosophe*, finally, he approached and met death in his own dramatic way, leaving a legend of fittingly profound last words. There were no religious services. Burial was at Cuverville. He was survived by his daughter and his son-in-law.

Roger Martin du Gard, one of Gide's closest friends, makes a statement (refuting the rumor that Gide was tempted to recant on his deathbed) that could well have been made by Grimm, with no other change than the substitution of Diderot's name: "Gide died, with his immediate family present, in a state of very confident and very conscious agnosticism. It was not without regret, but certainly without hope or fear. Whether this is deplored or not, it is fitting to recognize what is a *fact* honestly." [2]

The mortal statistics given above fail to convey the vital concerns that preceded the events: advancing age, the proper manner of dying and the nature of what (if anything) comes after the grave. All of these recur in the thought, conversation and writing of both authors, especially in their later years. Their ideas and comments range from whimsical to morbid, but their reactions are essentially similar, both in general and in detail.

Diderot paraphrases Montaigne in observing that a commendable apprenticeship for death is to be found in philosophy, "habitual and deep meditation, that carries us away from all that surrounds us and overwhelms us." To him, the aging process, like everything else in the material universe, is subject to the laws of nature, which are immutable, inexorable, and philosophically acceptable. Death itself is a necessary part of the "general chain" in which the individual's existence is but a link. In physiological terms, there is a continuity of living matter that is dependent on (and often unaware of) the disappearance of the single organism. The normal, the adaptable, and the modifiable entities are allowed to carry out their little lives, while the sports and the patently unfit are eliminated ruthlessly. Diderot surmises that even if he is an "hors d'oeuvre" himself, not monstrous enough to suffer early extermination, he will eventually be swept away by what he calls the "universal torrent." Meanwhile, there is much to be done. And if any man does what good and learns what truth he can, if he encourages thinking, promotes virtue and justice, and if he is fortunate enough to enjoy some earthly pleasures, he earns the right to "scorn life." The moment, the place, and the circumstances of his death, since they cannot be foretold, can be matters of complete indifference to the *homme de bien*, the upright man.

Although Gide does not pretend to be a formal philosopher—Diderot once called philosophy "momentary old age"—he is increasingly fond of philosophizing as he grows older. His cosmology is egocentric. The material universe in flux, the relentless continuity of nature, the relationships of infinite time and space to man's existence are significant to him, first in terms of how they affect him, and second in their rapports with mankind. An eclectic approach to many systems (conformity, hedonism, naturalism, agnosticism, even communism), yields an unformulated complex of attitudes that is peculiarly Gidean. The agglomerate contains too much subjectivity—the lyricism Gide calls poetry—to be simply monistic or materialistic and too little profound concern for society to be broadly humanistic. The chain of being, for example, impresses him less in its infinite extensions from the past into the future than in its perceptible links and their possible reshaping. Agreeing with Diderot that man is indeed a modifiable organism, he contends that the supposedly fixed laws and inevitable processes of nature can themselves be modified, accelerated, or redirected by human means. Using the analogy of the plant, carefully pruned to assure its most effective production of flower, fruit, or seed, he proposes "cultivation" of man's potentialities—notably those of the creative artist. In his "ideal strategy" and numerous memoranda under the rubric "Morals," he emphasizes the stripping away of all that hinders maximum growth of what is most promising, then the nurturing and fertilizing of what can yield unique significance and beauty. The forces of nature, unfortunately, seem to conspire with those of conventional society to prevent such individual achievement, even when it would be to the benefit of humanity. But the man of courage, talent, and conviction can be "authentic," true to what he has chosen as his own best. By leaving as little as possible to chance and to the influence of others, he can "make a rent in that fate," as Lafcadio says, and shape his life and works to manifest what he is, or what he wants to be thought to be, when his career ends: "A man's life is his image. At the hour of death we shall be reflected in the past, and, leaning over the mirror of our acts, our souls will recognize *what we are.*" [3] The self-portrait, then, must be scrupulously honest as well as striking. What is difficult is conceiving clearly and early what picture we hope to paint; what is frightening is that each moment, word, and movement adds an indelible stroke to the canvas. Gide decides to portray himself through the use of what he calls "reverse sincerity": "All our life is spent in sketching an ineradicable portrait of ourselves. The terrible thing is that we don't know this. . . . We recount our lives and lie to ourselves, but our life will not lie; it will recount our soul, which will stand before God in its usual posture." Even death itself, as Mauriac points out nearly sixty years after this declaration, is not a matter of nature taking its course. For Gide, whom he calls an "old Ariel," it is "an episode, and not the least successful of episodes (as though he had arranged it himself) in that fate that was not submitted to but conducted and orchestrated—and with what mastery!" [4]

The *sophrosyne* that was the supreme attainment of Greek philosophers comes to Diderot and Gide almost uninvited; the equanimity and serenity that mark their last decades of life seem anticlimactic after their frenetic and contentious careers. They have the time, the means, and the wit to relax and to take stock of their experiences and their prospects.

Diderot's espousal of unorthodox causes and his enthusiastic commitment to experimental ventures give way gradually to a mellow outlook characterized by indulgence and expansiveness. He has several bouts with failing health, often the aftermath of gluttonous banqueting; there are occasional outbursts of impatience or exasperation; now and then he has moments of depression, when he questions the value of his long struggle against almost insurmountable odds. He uses the myth of Sisyphus—as Camus will later—to symbolize man's effort. More frequently, his metaphors are in the parlance of gambling. Life itself is a gaming-table, for example: "We insist on staying at that table like unlucky gamblers who are ruining themselves as they go on saying 'By Jove, luck simply *has* to change.'" [5] An inveterate gamester himself (he once outlined a French adaptation of Moore's *The Gamester*), he refuses to accept Pascal's wager but takes many others: "I'll not know until the end whether I have won or lost in this vast gambling den where I shall have spent some sixty years with the cup in my hand, *shaking the dice*." [6] At times, he verges on morbidity as he reviews the pointlessness of human existence: "Life lasts so short a time," he writes to Sophie, "our real needs are so limited, and when we go away, it matters so little whether we have been someone or nobody." But he hastens to assure his mistress that such sombre sentiments are prompted less by conviction than by indigestion.

The sprightly touch or the wry turn of phrase usually saves Diderot when he threatens to become pompous. He looks on the flight of time and on man's mortal estate as cosmic jokes, which he appreciates even though he is himself an incidental butt. When he speaks of life as a farce, it is with a cheerful sense of his own incongruous part in it. Like Gide, he gives considerable attention to the image he wants to present to his contemporaries and to posterity. He is, too, equally adept at posing. His "releases" for the edification of his public are as carefully contrived as Gide's for effect. But he does not do an "authentic" self-portrait. He presents instead a series of self-caricatures. Among the whimsical sketches of "the true Diderot" are the man who has done nothing worthwhile, although he is well on in his forties—the way he sees himself when he writes of Richardson's death—and the man who has tried everything. He sees himself as the undistinguished *père Toutatous*, as faceless in the crowd as Cocles is before his blinding. He asks Sophie, "Can a person be wise and foolish at the same instant?" He is sure that he is, and incurably so, even as he writes penitently, "Be reassured, dear, the days of that sort of foolishness are past for me."

In a maxim reminiscent of La Rochefoucauld, Diderot remarks that men are wise once they no longer have the energy to be foolish. A belated infatuation confirms his opinion that he is not yet a "sage," although he is sometimes mistaken for one; experience proves only that he is "a dull oaf, just like anyone else." His discovery of his own mediocrity and ineptitude is a repeated phenomenon. He reduces his status as a patriarch to an incident in which he portrays himself running into a door. To his granddaughter's comment that he is *always* bumping his nose, he adds his own: that he seems to have done little but "nose-bumping" all his life. When Grimm observes that his friend was made for another world than ours, Diderot confesses, "Before long, I shall have been a stranger in this one for fifty years, living an imitative life that is not my own, endlessly adopting for myself the behavior of others, like a dog that learns to walk on its hind paws." [7] After a failure to keep a social promise, he calls himself a "bear," then adds, as if to burlesque Rousseau's unhappy existence, "An anchorite does not live as retired a life as I do." The simile appears again in his depiction of the excessively calm and meditative sojourn he has on a country estate: "That is where I live, like a hibernating bear, on my own substance, licking my paw."

One of his late contributions to the gallery of pastiches is of Diderot the emotional man: "I suspect that my sensibility has increased. Everything moves me, everything affects me. I am becoming the worst old crybaby you ever saw." In still another guise, he is as lyrical (and perhaps as sincere) as Rousseau in his advocacy of a return to nature, "the domicile of brotherhood": "As soon as we return to our earliest home—woods, cottages and fields—we immediately take on its ways of life. There are no longer virtually any of those types of inequality that place citydwellers one above another." [8]

Probably the best-known of all his sketches are those of himself as a Langres weathervane, spun about by the many winds, and of the man of affluence and connoisseur of the arts, lolling in his lavish new quarters, grateful to his imperial benefactress, but musing wistfully over memories brought back by his worn and ink-stained dressing gown. The artfully contrived "revelation" in the "Regrets sur ma vieille robe de chambre" ("Regrets on My Old Dressing-Gown") establishes a regrettable precedent in arousing public interest in the private lives of celebrities. From the ancient lives of saints, the chronicles of kings recorded by paid historiographers, and the memoirs of aristocrats and adventurers, intimate literature now moves, in the late eighteenth century, toward its modern forms. Rousseau must answer for the plethora of confessions and autobiographical romances, Diderot for the "trips around my room," the "little journeys to the homes of the great"—to use the rubric immortalized by Elbert Hubbard—and, finally, the "releases" of twentieth-century press secretaries and publicity agents.

Gide's public image is presented with less fantasy but with even greater attention to the theatrical art of *préparations*, and with a playwright's view of the impression to be left on the audience when the final curtain comes down. Diderot was often amused by his paradoxical part in life's comedy. Gide was but rarely. Most of the time, he pondered his fate like a latter-day Hamlet, presenting a grim soliloquy on "life, a comedy when it is viewed as a show, a tragedy when it is taken as real." [9] His role as featured player in his own production called less for jests, in his opinion, than for gestures.

What has been taken at times as a tendency to narcissism in Gide—the many allusions to mirrors, images, and reflections in water—is primarily an awareness of himself as a public figure, actual or potential. His *vie grimacière* (public posture) reveals his person and his personality as he wants them presented. The removal of his beard to show his sensitive lower face is as deliberate a gesture as the affecting of a cape and broad-brimmed hat. All add studied touches to his self-disclosure in words. With better press services available than in Diderot's day, plus executive status in the large publishing firm he helped found, and the privileges he earns as contributor to reviews and newspapers, he has a wealth of opportunities for personal publicity and the artistic shaping of a legend. His interviewers and visiting reporters find him charming, hospitable, sometimes profound, and always quick of wit. He is not reluctant to be photographed and he proves to be an excellent subject, whether in thoughtful pose (often at his desk) or relaxing in his garden. Among his favorite photographs are those taken of him as a handsome young intellectual and man of the world, and some later studies showing him in stocking cap and English-style scarf, playing the piano or reading a manuscript. Asserting that he feels still young in his seventies—it will be remembered that he was already old in his thinking at twenty—he confesses that being a septuagenarian seems like a role he is playing. When he is tempted to forget his age, he adds, his infirmities and failings act like a prompter to remind him of his years. "Then, like the good actor I want to be, I slip back into character and pride myself on playing the part well." [10]

In Diderot's first works, the few references to death reflect the tone of English free thought and his own nascent materialism. One of Shaftesbury's observations, for instance, is passed on without elaboration as "The true Martyr awaits death. The man of enthusiasm runs toward it." There is no evidence that the *philosophe* brooded over this thought or felt inclined to end his life in either fashion. The dramatic idea, however, obviously appealed to him. Years after the *Pensées philosophiques,* he gave it a new cast of characters in his own "La Mort" ("Death"), a section of the *Eléments de physiologie:* "The child runs toward it with his eyes closed; the man remains stationary; the old man comes to it facing in the opposite direction." Saunderson's resoluteness on his deathbed, according to the Diderot version in the letter on the blind, was in the best Montaigne tradition of skepticism. From 1749 on, there was to be no defection by Diderot from a realistic attitude and the treatment of dying as a simple physical phenomenon. His short article "Sur la mort" ("On Death") and his endorsement of Seneca's treatise on the brevity of life make it clear that death will have little or no spiritual significance for him when it comes.

During the trying mid-century years, death was no stranger to the Diderot household. His first child, his mother, then two more children died in less than a decade, without his railing against malevolent fate. His sense of loss was strong, but it did not become an obsession. Nor was there inspired in him a reawakening of religious sentiment, even when death came, in 1759, to his father. Deeply grieved by the passing of the worthy and kindly *père de famille,* whose ethical counsel he had welcomed if not followed, Diderot made no concessions of principle. His father stayed in his memory as "a man with excellent judgment, but a pious man." It was difficult to forget his parent's urging him toward holy orders and arranging his enforced stay in a monastery to prevent his marriage to Antoinette, the shirtmaker's daughter. Home for the family funeral in Langres, he was not too overwhelmed by grief to recall an anecdote he found apposite. It concerned the quiet remark of a dying man, whose son was reverently closing the old man's eyes: "Mon fils, dans un instant" ("Not just yet, son").

What did dawn on Diderot at the time of the funeral, twenty-five years before his own death, was that he was no longer a young man himself. Until then, life with its toils and its modest rewards had seemed to stretch endlessly before him. At forty-six, he was "eternal," as he wrote Sophie. He had no idea, of course, that the testing years (as Arthur Wilson so aptly calls them) were over. The darkest moments of the struggle to publish the *Encyclopédie* were past. The Jesuit opposition would soon collapse. In the next few years, the attitudes of the *philosophes* would not only prevail but also have the sanction of those in high places. Too busy to pamper himself, he was forced by his wife, from that time on, to admit to an occasional illness or feeling of fatigue. He did so with little grace, since he considered her a hypochondriac and "the only woman who had never learned how to suffer." He also confessed to being a very difficult patient to tend, in spite of (or perhaps because of) his wide acquaintance with doctors and medicine. In any case, the process of aging ceased to be a vague question for philosophic speculation only; it was now one of the essential elements of physiology, an immanent and material fact.

During the months that follow, living matter, its duration, and its destiny are among the favored topics at d'Holbach's gatherings at Grandval or the Rue Royale "synagogue." The discussions are usually echoed or reported at length in Diderot's letters: the merits of fatalism, the inevitability of life's ending, the futility of man's efforts to change the laws of nature, the shortness of the human span, the insignificance of each separate organism, the questions of gladness and sorrow, the equalizing effect of death, the unrelenting passage of time. But the general gravity of tone, in the letters to Mlle Volland, is alleviated by frivolous tales, playful protestations of "undying" love, and such postscripts as that mentioned earlier: "This sad philosophizing is inspired by an upset stomach." In similar vein, as he meditates on the role of chance, the mysteries of fate, and the possibility of an afterlife, he pauses to welcome the prospect of our rejoining those we love, particularly if the meeting takes place in hell.

The pursuit of personal happiness is the crux of the code Gide formulated for himself in 1893: "May each thing yield all the life possible in it. It is a duty to make oneself happy." What he termed "perfectly natural laws" were to direct him to a pleasing sense of balance, an existence that was "vigorous and fulsome," a superior wisdom, and a total experience unfettered by staid conventions. It was obviously an ambitious program, regardless (as it was) of its social implications. As an antidote to everything that was ordinary and routine, the prescription proved efficacious, when taken in the large, experimental dose recorded in the *Journal* and the *Nourritures terrestres:* "This was the great rest after the long fever; my former anxieties became incomprehensible to me. I was amazed that nature was so beautiful, and I called everything nature." [11] Fifty-eight years later, in his last written note, Gide intimated that he had lost little of his capacity for enjoying the pleasures and beauties of the earth: "My own position in the sky, in relation to the sun, must not make me consider the dawn any less beautiful." [12]

Perhaps the best explanation of the serenity with which he approached "the only experience still before him"—to use Jean Schlumberger's turn of phrase—was that he was determined to die "desperate" but undespairing: "Let me have no other rest but the sleep of death. I am afraid that every desire, every energy I have not satisfied during my life may survive to torment me. I hope that after I have expressed on this earth all that was waiting in me to be expressed—I *hope* that I may die satisfied and utterly *hopeless.*" [13] There is a strange parallel between these thoughts of Gide in his mid-twenties and those of Diderot at twice that age. When his spirits and his energy were at low ebb, he confessed to Sophie that death had become a very pleasant prospect, like a long sleep, with his shroud as a bed and the earth as a pillow. Continuing the theme in another letter, he wrote: "Why is it that the fuller life is, the less a person is attached to it? You detach yourself from it, you get tired of it, your strength lessens, you get weaker, you want life to end—just as, after you have worked hard, you want the day to end."

In rebuttal to Jean Schlumberger's assertion that Gide rarely thought of death before his heart attack (in the late nineteen-forties), Roger Martin du Gard insists that it was a leitmotiv in his thinking and conversation during their many years of friendship. It was present, as a matter of fact, much earlier—twenty-odd years before Gide "discovered" Martin du Gard. Deaths in the Gide family and among his friends made it a reality to him; the reading of such favorites as Montaigne and Goethe made it a subject of serious reflection. When his father died of tuberculosis at forty-eight, André was in his eleventh year. The loss of his mother, when he was in his mid-twenties, was a much greater blow to him. Grandfather Tancrède, with a firmness of will worthy of his namesake, died without allowing a doctor to call. An aunt's funeral in 1890 found young Gide as dry-eyed and observant a mourner as young Meursault (in *L'Etranger*) at the services for his mother: "My mind told me what impressions to have." The copious tears of one relative struck him as unfortunate, the sobbing of a maid heart-rending. His own emotions were interesting, but too distorted by the presence of others, and at the same time too "spontaneous" to lend themselves to verbal analysis.

As he wrote the melancholy chronicle of André Walter, Gide considered the possibility of doing a story on Anna Shackleton, his mother's faithful companion, and calling it *L'Essai de bien mourir* (*Essay on Dying Properly*). Later, he used the tentative title of *Mort de*

Mlle Claire (*Mlle Claire's Death*). In the plot of the *récit*, which evolved into *La Porte étroite* (*Strait is the Gate*), there is a direct transposition of his mother's dying wish that he marry his Norman cousin, Madeleine Rondeaux. When "Em" herself died (after more than forty years of a union he called "the secret drama of my life" and "a comedy of happiness"), he admitted to feelings of grief and loss, unalloyed by guilt or remorse.

If Diderot was a trying patient during his confinements to bed, Gide was a worse one. He was overcome by loneliness and insisted on sympathetic understanding during his several encounters with ill health. Some of these, in all fairness, were serious; incipient tuberculosis, for instance, led to a long convalescence in the mountains, which in turn provided Gide with some material for later stories, renewed his conviction that he must return often to sunny North Africa, and warned him to be solicitous of his health in the future. He was. When not yet fifty years old, he noted: "Not a day passes but what I say to myself: all the same, old man, take care, for tomorrow you might wake up mad, idiotic, or not wake up at all." And two years earlier: "Every time I make a gesture, I calculate: how many times already? I compute: how many times more?" [14] At the prospect of death, he felt the mixed emotions he attributed in his "Considerations" to Theseus, who went to meet his fate "with horror and rapture." Like Orpheus, he could count only on himself: "Whoever starts out toward the unknown must consent to venture alone." Yet he accepted his role without complaint: "The last act of the comedy is no less good because I must play it alone. I must not sidestep it." Shortly before he died, he wrote, as though surprised by his stoicism: "I bury people and things, and myself, with disconcerting ease." [15]

In the *Eloge de Richardson,* published in 1761, Diderot speaks of the English novelist much as he did of Montesquieu, when he attended the funeral of the *président* six years before: "Richardson is no more. What a loss for literature and for humanity!" In his closing words, there is a personal touch: "And I move on toward the date of expiry without attempting anything that may commend *me* to the future." [16]

Gide too writes eulogies, several of them collected as a separate volume (*Eloges,* 1948). Included are Jacques Rivière and Charles-Louis Philippe, who both died of typhoid fever; Verhaeren, whose death (like that of Camus in 1960) was "early, accidental, absurd"; Rimbaud, Conrad, Jammes, Valéry, Ghéon, and Ramuz, among others. Each of them, as he dies, widens and deepens Gide's perspective on death; none of them inspires portentous moralizing in the tradition of Bossuet. The manner of dying, however, provokes considerable thought in personal terms. Gide is impressed by "spiritual" courage, but not by physical heroism, as he avers in the preface to *Vol de nuit* (*Night Flight*); he is intrigued by Montaigne's wish to die on horseback, and he is particularly taken with Goethe's achievement in dying—without grace, without pangs, and "surfeited with everything." In his own life, he views death many times at close range, literally as well as figuratively—as a sufferer from lung trouble, a heart injury, and assorted minor disorders; as a frontline observer in two global wars, in the auxiliary services in the first and as a refugee in the second. Showing noteworthy calm when faced by major threats to life or freedom, he allows himself to be irked only by petty annoyances.

As he approaches and enters his fifties, Diderot realizes that time and energy are not inexhaustible. The thought adds a sense of urgency to his desire to make his greatest possible contribution to letters and to his fellow men. He resolves to be less impulsive and disparate in his undertakings, more indulgent in his dealing with others, holding his temper when confronted by unreasonable attitudes and striving to become used to dealing with stupidity. But the mood of philosophic resignation and of unswerving devotion to intellectual pursuits is shattered by the discovery of LeBreton's treachery in expurgating the *Encyclopédie* without consulting him: "In eight or ten days then, I shall see the end of this undertaking that has kept me busy for twenty years, which has scarcely made me a fortune, which has made me run the risk of leaving my country or losing my liberty, and which has eaten up my life, which I could have made more useful and more famous." [17] With growing vexation, he reviews the wasted years, the spending of his forces, and the pittance he has been given: "Is it not strange that I have worked for thirty years for the *Encyclopédie* publishers, that my life has gone by, that they have two million from it and I haven't a sou? To hear them tell it, I'm very lucky just to have stayed alive." [18]

It was not Gide's publishers but his wife who "betrayed" him. While he was traveling abroad with a young friend, she "mutilated" some of his cherished manuscripts, many of them on matters she felt were too intimate for profane eyes, since her husband had purportedly written them to her as love letters. Gide was inconsolable—he broke down, sobbed and wept for days at the loss of what he called "the best there was in me." He was *in extremis*, "already dead," living a "posthumous life." He did manage to survive the shock, however, and to hold to the tenuous thread of life for another thirty-two years, during which he mourned her perfidy in *Et nunc manet in te . . .* and its accompanying *Journal intime.* Curiously enough, he "dies" again just before he recommences his *Journal* after many blank years. When Mme Gide dies, after long service as his companion, hostess, nurse, and (unheeded) moral counselor, he is overcome by loneliness and lassitude: "I have merely pretended to live, without taking any further interest in anything or in myself, without appetite, without taste, or curiosity, or desire, and in a disenchanted universe; with no further hope than to leave it." [19] The mood lasts several months, inspiring such notations as "I have no longer any great taste for living. I already belong to the past." Some years before, he talked over the detailed arrangements to be made for his funeral, including possible cremation. Then he added, "Not that I want to die, my good friend. . . . But very often I should like to no longer be alive." [20] By the nineteen-forties, having "had his fill" on this earth, he feels he has within him unlimited possibilities of accepting whatever may be his lot: "A certain happy equilibrium is worked out and one reaches the end of the banquet without much wanting it to go on longer. Others are waiting for one's place; it is their turn." And two years later, after his liberation by the Allied troops, "Without being too impolite, I should like to take leave of myself: I have decidedly seen enough of myself. I no longer even know whether or not I should still like to begin my life over again." [21]

Notwithstanding his pathetic tale of decrepitude and penury, Diderot in his fifties is blessed with reasonably good health and relative affluence, assured him since 1765 by Catherine II's largesse. As imperial custodian of his own library, he has leisure to devote to his writing. Manuscripts and drafts long laid aside now receive attention. He writes Sophie often. His chats and conversations with friends are full of spirited observation and advice. His exchange with Falconet is a protracted discussion of the future, with little intimation of defeat by the past. To add to his over-all peace of mind, life at home is all he could hope for—Mme Diderot, no longer querulous, shows constant solicitude for his comfort; little Angélique, now a fine young lady, has her dowry assured. The world seems full of promise to the *philosophe* when, before he reaches his sixtieth year, he sees his daughter become Madame Caroillon de Vandeul.

A few months later, the placid existence is interrupted. Acceding to the insistent invitation of the Empress, more through admiration and gratitude than because of enthusiasm for travel, he sets out for Russia. Haunted by a vague premonition that he will never return to taste the joys of being a grandfather, he packs some manuscripts and boards the coach with a sigh: "But I tell myself that the earth is as light in St. Petersburg as it is in Paris, that the worms there have as good an appetite, and that it doesn't matter much what part of the earth we fatten them in." [22] The fears are real, despite their lighthearted expression. But they prove groundless. After a year abroad that is both interesting and productive, Diderot returns to Paris, somewhat surprised by his own hardiness. His capacity for literary toil seems undiminished; in his bags are several studies and works of fiction, some of them near completion, some merely sketched. He has agreed to direct some elaborate publishing of official documents for the Czarina and to prepare a complete edition of his own works. When a new version of the *Encyclopédie* is projected, with Catherine's sponsorship, he writes: "Let's do the *Encyclopédie* and leave some worthy soul the task of gathering up my rags and tatters after I'm dead."

Gide thoroughly enjoys traveling, both in France and abroad, on foot or by train, boat, or plane. He visits many parts of his country and of North Africa, is fond of England and knows some areas of Russia and the Near East at first hand before he dies. One of his regrets is that he has to refuse an invitation to the United States late in his life. As he meditates on what he would do if he had life to live over, he observes: "Oh, what a good Mentor I should now be for the man I was in my youth! How effectively I should be able to drive myself to extremities! If I had listened to my own advice (I mean: the man I once was, listening to the one I am today), I should have gone around the world four times . . . and I should never have married." [23] If given a second chance, moreover, he would revisit Russia (not the "wild" part, he adds), travel to Tahiti, study Greek, learn to speak English and German fluently and, above all, be more adventurous and less "held down, held in check, held back by the feeling of *duty*." Such musing is as close as the aging Gide comes to a palinode on his experiences or an Orphean "backward look." It is perhaps a projection of his theory, in more material terms, of palingenesis or "re-naissance."

Gide's inclusion of himself among the incongruities of the world comes with old age, as a privilege he grants himself. In his youth and middle years, a studied seriousness of mien and a straight-faced intensity accompany his jokes and witty remarks. As he grows older, he is still "little disposed to laughter," but he reveals to the public a sprightliness and gaiety long veiled from all but his closest friends. He finds the world not only tolerable, but often amusing. Whimsical thoughts come to him, quips and cracks intermingle with his solemn observations, especially when boredom or brooding threatens. One sign of his increasing indulgence with others is his relaxing of self-discipline, which he proposes with "At my age it is permissible to be a little free-and-easy. *Amen.*" He expects no miracles of energy ("I don't really know what keeps me alive except the habit of living") or of juvenile enthusiasm, "The age of eighty is not the time to try leaping forward." [24] In the words he once used in more serious context, he is "a stranger on this earth, playing at the game of life without too much believing in it." [25] The *étranger* note and the gambling metaphor are both, as we have seen, reminiscent of Diderot. The first is struck again in "I am merely occupying the seat of someone who is mistaken for me." The games-of-chance figure of speech is among Gide's favorites. He is, for instance, "at death's door, not so much because my strength is at an end, but because the game is over and

I am already leaving it." And the subtitle of *Ainsi soit-il, les Jeux sont faits,* is an ironic juxtaposition of Biblical and gambling expressions.

It is not lassitude, as he sometimes pretends, but other lively interests that keep Diderot from spending the last decade of his life compiling and editing articles. His preoccupations are morals, esthetics, and progress through education. A comprehensive treatise on Seneca, two new *Salons,* and a detailed curriculum for a Russian state university give ample scope for all three. All explore new ground and look toward the future—the recast *Encyclopédie* and collected edition, had they been done, would have been repetitive and retrospective. The general sobriety of tone that marks these last works is relieved only occasionally by gaiety, as Diderot's humor becomes less exuberant and the years take their inevitable toll. How precarious life is comes home to him: "There is certainly a nice inconsistency in setting a terminal date for oneself and living from one day to the next. The fact is that people don't believe too much in that terminal date," as he confides to Sophie. After his Russian and Dutch sojourns, he writes another friend: "And as far as life is concerned, I tell you I should leave mine as readily as I should pour a glass of champagne, if only to shut up anyone who dared contradict such an assertion. Nevertheless, whether I hasten the *finale* of this clumsy and insipid farce called life, or I patiently slow its ending beyond its time, I remain, madam, your devoted servant." [26] The erstwhile leader in battle seems ready to arrange a truce with time and troubles. He doubts that he still has the strength to defend his own cause, finding it irksome that only the dead are judged equitably by the living. Posterity, however, can be counted on, if contemporary judgments cannot, and its opinion is an afterlife worth working for: "Time is all that is needed for genius and stupidity, vice and virtue to get their just deserts. A worthy man, a clever man can die too soon; as for the imbecile and the evil man, they always die in time." [27] The *philosophe* determines to carry on his work—at a somewhat slackened pace, now that there is less pressure from others—and to make light of infirmities as long as his thinking remains sound. The prospect of senile decay bothers him. He has no desire to have his body outlive his mind—that would be worse than the fate of Marivaux and Crébillon, who outlived their eras and their reputations. As for death itself, it holds no terror for him. He is prepared to set out on the "long journey" whenever the date is set—preferably with his mental baggage intact.

The standard ingredients of the youthful romantic hero, with the exception of religious fervor and morbid introspection, are to be found, combined with the more stable components of his character, in the sexagenarian Diderot. His ill-starred love affairs, talk of suicide, travels to exotic lands, and vague ennui have been mentioned. To them can be added traits he notes in himself, especially his extreme *sensibilité* and a somewhat unexpected sentimental penchant for solitude. In the city, he is happiest when he limits his company to the family and a few intimate friends; at every opportunity, he escapes to the country or the coast. His declaration that only the evil man flees the gregarious life—which wounded Rousseau so deeply—seems to be conveniently forgotten. The year Rousseau and Voltaire die, he takes stock of his own "poor machine"—"I am in quite good health, but beginning to feel I am growing old. All my teeth are getting loose; before long, I shall have to eat gruel as children do. At any moment, I shall no longer be able to talk, which will be a rather considerable advantage for others and a very slight inconvenience to me. In a short time, I shall grow hard of hearing and my sight will grow dim. I shall set out, bag and baggage, for the other world. I can see the preparations for the big trip being made without feeling very much concerned." [28] As it turns out, he waits nearly six years for the protracted journey to start, years filled with affection at home, reading dictated by pleasure and not by deadlines, and short excursions from the capital to the peaceful countryside. News comes to him of the deaths of several acquaintances in quick succession. After Voltaire and Rousseau, among others are Condillac, Turgot, d'Alembert, Mme d'Epinay and his beloved Sophie Volland. His reactions vary from nonchalance in Rousseau's case to poignant regret in Sophie's. Viewing death as a natural phenomenon, which he will soon know himself, he feels neither gratitude nor hostility toward it. As implacable a materialist as ever, he approves of Voltaire's deathbed intransigence, and he resolves to make no concessions to religiosity himself, even for the sake of his family. Fidelity to principle also keeps him from sanctimonious praise, after their deaths, of those he has been unable to respect during their lives. Speaking of Jean-Jacques, for instance, he leaves to future judges the unbiased estimate of his onetime friend, as he leaves to posterity the evaluation of his own worth. All men, knowingly or otherwise, stride toward eternity: "Posterity is for the *philosophe* what the 'other world' is for the religious man. Eternity is the religious man's posterity." Without even waiting until "the pronouncement of the future corrects the idle chatter of the present," humanity can know the special eternity that is to be found in earthly happiness. But "admirable people and men who are great in any respect all look to posterity." Secure in the approval of his own conscience, in the approbation of a few friends and in the belief that intelligence will one day recognize his contribution to mankind, Diderot is not dismayed as he comes close to "the final date when everything fades from sight." Conviction and rhetoric combine in his affirmation that "there is but one virtue, Justice; but one duty, to attain happiness; but one corollary, not to overestimate life and not to fear death." [29]

In the last five years of his life, Gide's suspicion that he is merely marking time (or taking up useful space) combines with a busy schedule of travels and of accepting awards to keep him from any major writing. He does continue his diary "to be systematic," feeling like Baron Münchhausen pulling himself from the swamp by his hair. Time is too short, he tells one correspondent, for him to answer an interesting letter at length. Death is too near to justify his having a chair repaired. His energies no longer respond to his calls on them. Words like "joy" and "fervor" now connote only past experience. Logical and sustained reasoning are more difficult than they were. "My thoughts escape me," he comments, "like spaghetti slipping off both sides of the fork." What he presents is the "outcome" of his thoughts, which he writes down with a nonchalant "Let him understand who can or who will." Even as he concedes that he is "old and already as if obsolete," he marvels at how robust and lighthearted he often feels: "I don't hit it off, I have never been able to hit it off completely with reality. I even believe that at the moment of death I shall say to myself: 'Look! He's dying.' " In spite of the conviction that his life has been well spent, when the time comes to die, he says, he may have to go back to his childhood games (*boquillons*) before deciding that he is ready. And that will be only if his failing memory has reduced his luggage to the minimum kit for a one-way voyage.

In the last pages of the *Journal* and in *Ainsi soit-il*, it becomes obvious that he feels his deliberate detachment from possessions is nearly complete. There is an abundance of reflections on "consenting" to death, accepting it, and leaving everything to "time and gravity." A typical valedictory is, "Death has already slipped in between me and things (people somewhat less) and the union cannot be repaired. I have taken my leave; my leave has been granted; there is no turning back." In the same mood: "I consider it very beautiful at times to see people cling to life and be unwilling to let go . . . ; but not always; not when one has lived; and in certain cases, like mine, it is proper to consent."

Gide's concern with his public image is closely related to his hope of enjoying "smiling" old age and to his wish to die "authentically." After the death of his wife, he declares: "If I cannot succeed in attaining serenity again, my philosophy is bankrupt." The success of his campaign is remarkable, as both his friends and his critics testify. "At a time when the universe appears to be in chaos," says one, "he sinks into serene old age." [30] And the editor of his "complete" works, published in the nineteen-thirties, sees him more than a decade later as "having entered the tonic era, when efficacy prevails over responsibility." [31] In 1947, he explains his situation to a fellow novelist: "I think of death with complete indifference, if that's what is meant by serenity." [32] His close friends are impressed, as Jean Schlumberger points out, by the "serene grandeur" of his long and productive life, which "advanced to meet death, considered it and accepted it." [33] Such equanimity is not accidental. Gide works for it and counts on it as proof of his fidelity to himself and to his career. In 1926, he remarks self-assuredly: "This profound fidelity of heart and mind I believe to be extremely rare. Name me those who, before dying, can see accomplished what they proposed to accomplish, and I take *my* place beside them." [34] It is small wonder that many readers mistook Theseus's farewell message to his city as Gide's literary leave-taking.

In his concern with becoming, through effort and skill, the Gide he wants people to remember, there is a personal illustration of one of his favorite notions—the "becoming" he proposes for man and God.[35] In its broad lines, the concept recalls Diderot's ideas of the great chain of being, of evolution from the nonsentient to the reasoning entity, and of the gaining of a "spiritual" end by material means. Gide speaks of "a propensity, an inclination encouraging the groping, vague, and unconscious progress of matter toward life and consciousness; then, through man, toward God." [36] The ethical implications are clear: "As soon as I realized that God was not yet but was becoming and that his becoming depended on each one of us, a moral sense was restored in me."

Once committed to "obtaining" God, the former critic of "that consuming belief in progress" is convinced that "real old age would be giving up hope of progress." [37]

Gide sees no easy solution of the world's problems. During the First World War, with the Germans at Château-Thierry, he comes close to despair: "All around us I see nothing but disorder, disorganization, negligence, and waste of the most radiant virtues—only falsehood, politics, absurdity." When the Nazis overrun France, he seriously considers collaborating with the new regime. After World War II ends, he claims he needs all his courage to go on living in "this atrocious world." Aware of the incongruity of man's involvement in a universe oblivious to his fate, long before *condition humaine, absurde, angoisse,* and *engagement* become clichés, he refuses to capitulate entirely.

Gide will not, moreover, hold God responsible for problems that result from chance or are of man's own making. Irked at times by injustices and inequities, he is quick to criticize abuses, but slow to indict individuals. Even when he finds it hard to believe he is part of what is taking place in the world, he assumes his share of responsibility, declares himself less than satisfied and refuses to accept as inevitable what is remediable. The remedy, he insists—and repeats when he is awarded the Nobel Prize—will be found by men who scorn facile solutions, by the "unsubmissive" few who are the "salt of the earth." This declaration of the obligation, rather than the rights, of intelligent man is paralleled in the philosophy of revolt expressed by Camus, as it is in Diderot's resistance to bad laws and in Gide's own observation: "Daedalus can no longer make his way out of the labyrinth he himself constructed. No way to get out, excepting upwards." An oblique allusion, years earlier, to the title of some poems by Mauriac is in less lofty words: "If the ship is to be saved, it will not be by clasped hands."

Far from indifferent to the world while he is in it, Gide is hopeful when he thinks of its fate after he leaves it:

> I have often shown myself (or more precisely pretended) to be more optimistic than I was in reality. Some days, if I let myself go, I should scream with despair. But a few glimmers of true virtue, self-sacrifice, nobility, and dignity are enough to obliterate the discouraging accumulation of stupidity, gluttony, and abjection. The sparks of virtue seem to me more dazzling by contrast. And I am willing to admit that, without them, our sorry world would be but an incoherent tissue of absurdities. But there they are, nevertheless, and I intend to count on them.[38]

In nature as in mankind there are promises that lift Gide's heart. When he is among the refugees in North Africa, during the months when all seems lost for the allied cause, a magnificent autumn day reminds him of the delights he has known. He finds the world so full of love and beauty that the very thought of war seems impious. And after he is forced to give up an American trip on his doctor's orders, he tells a friend, "I shall leave this earth with the idea that there are some fine people in the world." [39]

Past eighty, Gide amuses himself by trying "artesian" writing, vowing he will not even reread, much less edit, his notebooks. If there are repetitions and the ramblings of an old man, so much the worse. He begins what will be called *Ainsi soit-il,* determined that everything will "come forth all of a sudden from my heart and mind, without any affectation." Then he finds he is cheating when he crosses out a few words. As keenly interested as ever in verbal effects, he invents *orgueillite* ("priditis") to describe a contemporary writer's malady, speaks of his own "personal radar" and is delighted with "anorexia" as an apt expression for loss of appetite, both physical and intellectual. Considering his own *anorexie,* he admits that he is all too aware of a lessening in his hungers and taste for pleasures, even in the *gourmandises* that supplanted his youthful asceticism. What is more, he smokes too much, his fine singing voice is failing, his heart is weak and he is often short of breath. He recognizes the ravages of time, stops reminding himself of his age, and decides to let infirmities do what they will.

Although he does not feel threatened with becoming an old crybaby, as Diderot said of himself, Gide shudders to think he may become ungracious or disagreeable. He tends, for that reason, to monopolize conversation, then regrets doing so. One result is that he becomes somewhat more withdrawn from society than in previous years. Nostalgic reminiscences of places he has been happy—particularly Normandy and North Africa—are noted in his diary, with lyric outbursts on the weather and on his sadness at seeing summer's end. Poignant memories come to him of the "new harmony" that was almost supernatural or superhuman, which finally blessed the Gide household. His late successes cheer him, too: the critics' ranking of *Les Faux-Monnayeurs* among the twelve best modern novels; the general acclaim accorded the dramatization of *Les Caves;* his winning of the Nobel and Goethe prizes; and the awarding of an honorary doctorate by Oxford University.

But there are times when he sees himself as an unprepossessing old nuisance: "I no longer have any great curiosity as to what life may still bring me. I have said more or less well what I had to say, and fear repeating myself. But idleness is a burden to me. Yet the thing that would keep me from killing myself (although I do not at all consider suicide reprehensible) is that some would try to see in that deed a sort of confession of failure, the obligatory result of my error. Others would assume that I was giving Grace the slip. It would be hard to convince people that, simply, I am surfeited with living and don't know how to use the little time left me. Anorexia. The hideously inexpressive face of Boredom." [40]

There is a pensive postscript: "Oh, how hard it is to age well! You would like to do a favor for others, and you feel yourself becoming a burden." Even the mild diversion of posting his journal is no longer always a pleasure. Since it is getting to be as baleful a habit as smoking, he gives it up—several times—with such "final" entries as "I am giving up keeping this insipid report. I might as well set down the menus of my meals." [41] But, like the artist who claims to have finished a painting, Gide returns now and then to add a figure or a brush stroke to his work.

Disposed though he is to accept the prospect of dying, Gide is revolted by the thought of a funeral, with its family anguish, artificial postures, and ceremonial pomp. Since suicide solves nothing unless the body is lost, he considers cremation, which strikes him as "not unattractive": "I am rather tempted by it, but I confess that I prefer being nibbled by worms and absorbed by the roots of plants and trees to being sniffed haphazardly by a lot of halitosis-ridden *jean-foutre* (what-the-hell-do-I-care's)." [42] But even such macabre speculations are variations on his theme—that the time, place, and manner of his death are of little consequence to him, provided he meets death well. They add a colorful touch, as well, to the self-portrait, giving the lie to Martin du Gard's conviction that it is scarcely fitting to lay out one's own shroud. What really matters to Gide is that his life has been rich in satisfactions: "After all, as for the game I was playing, I have won it. But I have ceased being really interested in it."

Despite the refrain of protestations that "it's been all over for some time," Gide's mind is far from senile, his curiosity is still lively, and he has flashes of energy. Resistance to temptation is another matter, however. It is so far beyond his powers, he confesses, that he rarely attempts it: "If I believed in the devil (I sometimes pretend to believe in him; it's so convenient!), I should say that I came to terms with him at once." The newer poetry may also be beyond him, he reflects, as he looks back at errors (such as underrating the novels of Dorothy Bussy and Proust) in his critical judgment. Perhaps, he rambles on associatively, he has had his fill of poetry, as he has of music and—he is tempted to say—of love. He turns to Virgil, works on a dramatic version of *Les Caves*, and starts a collection of anecdotes, witticisms, and "shaggy dog" stories for a projected *Manual of the Complete Conversationalist.*

One temptation he has little trouble resisting is that of

sectarian religion—he wants none of the "supreme lies" (an improvement on Diderot's "impudent lie"?) sometimes indulged in to bring solace to devout survivors, particularly to those left to mourn unbelievers. It seems pointless to him, as it did to the *philosophe*, to gamble with nonexistent souls as stakes: "We simply admit what we are, without priding ourselves in it, but without grieving about it either." When he attempts the pious gesture of turning back to St. Augustine, he finds it gives him a "mystical nausea." His many Catholic friends, abetted for a time by his wife, strive to save him before it is too late. Grateful but unconvinced, he declines the invitation to "enter into the House," since "too many things must be left in the cloakroom." His position has been on record for some time: "I have lived too long and too intimately . . . in the thought of Christ to agree to call on him today as one rings someone up on the telephone." [43]

For Gide, the "soul" is mortal: "As for the soul, it goes without saying that I believe in it! Why, of course I believe in the soul. I believe in it as in the glow of phosphorus. But I cannot imagine that glow without the phosphorus that produces it." [44] Considering promises of immortality, he suggests that the church has misread the scripture: "The eternal life Christ offers . . . has nothing future about it. It is not beyond death that it awaits us; and indeed, if we do not attain it at once, there is no hope that we may ever achieve it." Later, " '*Verily, verily, I say unto you,*' Christ repeats everywhere, '*He that heareth my word . . . HATH* (not: *will have*, but *already has*) EVERLASTING LIFE.' " [45] Such statements based on conviction do not, of course, endear Gide to Catholic critics. Other jibes are calculated to tease, to bedevil, or even to offend. He says of one anti-Gidean that he "speaks as a Catholic and addresses himself to Catholics; nothing is more likely to distort judgment." He quotes Claudel's alleged remark on the 1947 Nobel jury: "A Protestant clique!"

Regretting that form is as important in religion as in art, he feels little urge to conform: "I should have been quite capable of being 'converted' at the last moment" —but if he had, it would have been to save his wife some anguish. Bypassing the church's kind of redemption, he intends to "detach himself from life, without weakness or bravado, simply and decently." It is on this note, following a long monologue on the only immortality he hopes for (in the hearts and minds of future readers), that the printed entries of the *Journal* end: "Of what concern to me are *revelations?* I want to call on nothing but my reason, which is the same and was the same throughout all time for all men." [46]

What meager information there is on Diderot's last days, leading up to his death in 1784, stems largely from Mme de Vandeul and Grimm. The best known legend is his supposed reply to the priest, who called on him to repudiate his atheism in a little retraction that would have an excellent effect on the public. The gesture, said the *philosophe,* would be "an impudent lie," since he did not believe in "the Father, the Holy Ghost, or anyone in the Family." Another personal glimpse is of his lack of interest in a new bed, delivered the day before his death—he probably would not be using it for long, he told the workmen. According to his daughter, the last words she heard from him were, "The first step toward philosophy is skepticism." Apocryphal (or anachronistic) though they may be, they express the unwavering and serene disbelief with which Diderot approached the end of life. That end came, suddenly and fittingly, as he sat at the family dinner table, reaching for an apricot. An impressive—and expensive—funeral, with burial in the Chapel of the Virgin at Saint-Roch parish church, was provided at the insistence of his son-in-law. It was an almost ludicrous epilogue to Diderot's unregenerate manner of living and dying. By accident or design, his grave did not become a shrine. Its location remains among the unanswered questions Diderot bequeathed to posterity.

Gide's death occurred "as he wished it," to summarize the more favorable reports. One of his intimates, who was close to him for nearly forty years, said, without malice, "Probably no author of 'Confessions' has ever been so astutely sincere in modeling his statue in advance and in setting up its base so solidly." Few public figures, it must be admitted, have had their last hours chronicled in such detail or their supposed last pronouncements debated so extensively. François Mauriac, another longtime friend, mixing eulogy of Gide's art with censure of his conduct, sows the seeds of a pious legend —Gide, at the end, *may* have submitted to God like a humble, repentant child. Mauriac finds the possibility in a remark attributed to Gide in his last lucid moments: "It is always a struggle between what is reasonable and what is not." [47] Martin du Gard hastens to correct what he fears may become a second "Mehr Licht!" by pointing out that the comment was made three days before Gide's death and well before several lucid conversations with others; the one person present, a medical professor, had simply asked the patient whether he was suffering; the conclusion: "There is nothing sibylline about the remark, nor is it laden with any mystical sense." [48] Actually, Gide's last audible words, a few hours before he died, were not exactly oracular. He said "C'est bien. . . . C'est bien . . . ," intimating politely that the conversation had lasted long enough. "And so," as one report expressed it, "with his customary courtesy, he took leave of life." [49] There were ten witnesses: Jean Schlumberger, Roger Martin du Gard, Pierre Herbart, Mme Van Rysselberghe, Catherine (Gide) Lambert and her husband, two medical professors, and two other doctors.

The body was taken to Cuverville for interment. By request, there was neither funeral nor commitment service. The coffin was borne by seven employees of Gide's Norman estate and a personal servant. Throughout the world, people of many lands and creeds paid homage in countless eulogies and tributes. Two were peculiarly appropriate. The first was the pause in memory of the author during the performance of *Les Caves du Vatican* at the Salle Richelieu. The other was the quiet observation by one of Gide's admirers, Albert Camus: "It seems to me that a fitting death redeems a bit of creation. If I were a believer, Gide's death would comfort me." [50]

Influences and Inferences

The author who is fully aware of the influence another has had on his work is even wiser than the child who knows his own father. It is a demonstrable fact that Gide was, *lato sensu,* influenced by Diderot. How well he knew him, how much he admired his works, how often he echoed his sentiments are perhaps questions of major importance to those seeking evidence of imitation or plagiarism. They were academic to Gide. He recognized many uncles but virtually no ancestors—like his unencumbered Lafcadio. Whatever traditions of thought, technique, or morals erudites have chosen to place him in, he always felt that he was unbound or, like the new Prometheus, *mal enchaîné.*

An ideal spiritual affinity is one in which each of the creative artists is blissfully ignorant of the existence and the products of the other. By such a definition, the Diderot-Gide relationship is considerably less than perfect. References to the *philosophe* in Gide's writing, scattered though they are, are frequent enough to show that the two were no strangers. If there was any marked coincidence of ideas and interests, however, Gide seems to have been completely unconscious of it. His allusions, for the most part brief, are to various aspects of Diderot's thought and activity. They range from mild approval to enthusiastic endorsement in one direction, from slight distortion of meaning to complete incomprehension in another. They begin at the turn of the century and end in the late nineteen-forties. The most elaborate (and those that invite most speculation) occur shortly before the appearance of *Les Faux-Monnayeurs*. But at no time, then or later, is there an obvious pattern of formulated critical attitude or an acknowledgment of any conviction of kinship. The reader has a tantalizing impression that Gide might have said much more of his interest in Diderot. That he failed to do so is not the result of a diabolical plan to confound those with what he calls "this modern craze for seeing influence in every resemblance." It was simply because he looked on Diderot as an interesting figure—in a century that he, like Valéry, preferred to any other. The *philosophe* was more than a casual acquaintance, but neither an idol nor an admitted "ancestor."

In 1900, when he delivered his "apologia for all influence" before a Belgian audience, Gide opened his arms and mind to every kind of inspiration.[1] As the author of some ten appreciable (if not uniformly famous) works, he explained that he found each book was an "explanation" of himself. Condemning the timorous who saw influence as a "crime of lèse-personality," he asserted that great minds seek influences with a sort of eagerness. Even the weather could play its part, he added, quoting Diderot: "When the wind is high, I feel madness in my spirit." But the catholic welcoming of influence from all quarters must be done intelligently. If the *disponibilité* is carried too far, the result is mediocrity. Diderot makes the same point in his article on "Distraction": excellent qualities, such as associative thinking, need discipline and direction. "With a little self-control, one can protect oneself against this mental meandering." [2] The lure of the wanton thought (Diderot's *idée-catin*) concerns Gide less, in his lecture, than the danger he dramatizes in *Le Roi Candaule*—that of being too receptive. One way to avoid it is by selection. In the words of André Walter: "Let us choose influences so that everything becomes an education." When the choices have been made, "the true artist will seek the man behind the work and learn from him." Deliberately or by chance, Gide apparently chose to look into (and behind) the works of Diderot.

His broad reading of everything from newspaper fillers to the classics of antiquity left few authors, French or foreign, beyond Gide's ken. His mind was ready to assimilate whatever was useful or unusual, regardless of its source—all contributions were grist to the Gidean mill, provided he did the winnowing personally. Apart from countless allusions and brief evaluations in his journals, in *Eloges* (*Eulogies*) and in *Rencontres* (*Encounters*), Gide did major critical studies of Dostoevsky, Montaigne, and Le Bruyère, shorter studies of many other literary figures; he translated (from English, and sometimes in collaboration) Shakespeare, Blake, Whitman, Conrad, Pushkin, and Tagore. Conversely, he became one of the most widely translated of modern writers. Asked by a prominent periodical to name his favorite ten French novels, he listed works by Stendhal, Laclos, Mme de La Fayette, Furetière, Prévost, Fromentin, Balzac, Flaubert, Zola, and Marivaux—in that order.[3] To find his own most effective expression, he claimed, he needed to be compassed about by a host of sympathetic spirits, past, present, and future: "A body can produce a sound only when it feels around it a possibility of overtones." In musical metaphor again, he welcomed the attitudes of others for their evocative effects: "I am like a well-tuned harp." Such artistic imagery reflects Gide's refinement of response as strikingly as the high winds and weathervane exaggerations convey the idea of Diderot's rugged sensitivity. But Gide is no more a plaything of prevailing winds than the man from Langres. His receptivity implies no surrender of his own personality, no subservience to his unseen guests: "At the most they helped me disentangle my thought. And even then? I took pleasure in hailing those in whom I recognized my thought. But that thought was mine, and it is not to them that I owe it."[4] They are rewarded in hospitality, but may expect little praise. Gide counts on minimum plaudits himself, at least in his own time: "It is not for today that I am writing." There is a certain irony, perhaps, in his wish to "overflow" his epoch, to become one of the most influential authors through the heritage he, like his Theseus, leaves to posterity: "It is not enough to exist, then to have existed. One must bequeath." But he clarifies his intention in the *Journal:* "It is the spirit that is important to hand on, not the 'letter that kills.' "

Diderot fares better than many others (including Voltaire and Rousseau) in Gide's company from the literary past. An assortment of references to him indicates that he was a regular visitor (though sometimes a perplexing or an irritating one) who came early and stayed late. What is perhaps the most revealing comment is in an undated collection of "detached pages," which are omitted from separate editions of the *Journal.* Probably written about 1923 or 1924, this is Gide's most elaborate and sympathetic picture of the *philosophe:* "What a strange man Diderot is! Nothing is more contradictory than his work. He goes from the best to the worst, from the most natural to the stilted, from licentiousness to virtue, from atheism to piety; he welcomes everything, takes on all shapes without becoming distorted and is never more like himself than when he is in those very diverse forms." In several respects, these words might serve as a self-portrait of Gide. The observations continue: "The Germans sometimes claim him, going so far as to see something Germanic in his genius and a corruption of the name Diederich in his name. Sainte-Beuve encourages them: 'The most German of our minds,' he writes (page 375), 'a mind in which there are at once something of Goethe, something of Kant and something of Schiller'—and yet I know few authors who are more French." [5]

In the same pages, Gide recalls Sainte-Beuve's remark that Diderot was the "father and first model" of modern journalists. Mentioning the editor's scornful definition of weekly newspapers in the *Encyclopédie,* he concludes: "You can imagine what he would think of *dailies.*"

In some other detached pages, dated 1911, Gide quotes Diderot's definition of manners as "a general submission and conduct consistent with good or bad laws." The sentence is from the *Supplément au Voyage de Bougainville,* which was written as a dialogue on "the disadvantage of attaching moral ideas to certain physical actions incompatible therewith." Both the subtitle and the argument (that some savages have a better concept of reasonable customs and restraints than the French) must have appealed as much as the definition to the author of such recent problem-tales as *L'Immoraliste, La Porte étroite, Isabelle,* and *Le Retour de l'enfant prodigue.* In 1911, the question of submission is still unanswered for Gide. He has posed it himself in terms of self-centered disregard of convention, incarnate in Michel; of Christian ethics in his own early piety, Alissa's sacrificial gesture, and the exodus of the prodigal's younger brother; of preferring of art and other people to self, from *André Walter* through the *Nourritures;* of tragic family relations in *Le Retour* and *Isabelle.* Such preoccupations with conduct and its implications, private and public, will continue throughout his life.

By 1914 Diderot has taken on such a special personality in Gide's mind that he uses the name metaphorically, as though speaking of a character from ancient history or legend. When he sees his friend Jacques Copeau (with whom he was associated in founding the Théâtre du Vieux-Colombier), he finds him "younger, more Diderot than ever, eagerly embracing every new project." [6] However apt the description is of Copeau, it makes a good sketch of Diderot as Gide then imagines him—lively, experimental, almost gluttonous in his enthusiasms. The conjunction of Copeau's and Diderot's names becomes less mysterious when it is remembered that in 1914, while he is giving the final touches to *Les Caves* and laboring as a volunteer in the new theater project, Gide is also busy reading the authors of the eighteenth century—a task to which he intended committing himself as early as 1891 "to dry up my heart," as he said. At that time he ranked, among the readings he was planning to do, the *Encyclopédie* and Condillac, as well as Swift, Stendhal and such robust writers as Aristophanes, Shakespeare, and Rabelais. More than two decades later, he is evidently carrying out his reading program. Still later, he will examine Grimm's commentary on the writing of Rousseau's first discourse and the question of whether the ideas in it were invented by Rousseau or merely became his with the passage of time. Diderot is not mentioned by name, incidentally, but Gide already has a considerable acquaintance with the Diderot circle. He has read the Centenary Edition of the *Supplément.* He has delved into Mme d'Epinay's memoirs, and compared them with Rousseau's *Confessions.* He has, too, noted Grimm's "charming passages" and gone through Sainte-Beuve's double article on Grimm—without much benefit, he admits, since it is a mediocre piece of work.[7]

It is not until ten years after the remarks on Copeau that Gide next refers to Diderot's work: "I buy in the Carnoules station *Les Bijoux indiscrets* [*The Indiscreet Jewels*], which I am reading with rapture." [8] The approval of these indecent tales confirms the worst suspicions of puritanical critics. It is evident that both authors have lewd tastes in reading as well as writing, since they admit to enjoying Rabelais and his ribald successors. Like Créon in Gide's *Oedipe,* overhearing the libidinous talk of the youngsters, crusaders against prurience may cry, "Two nasty-minded fellows!" And yet, apart from (or in addition to) its Crébillonesque indelicacies, the collection has much to commend it, especially to those who are themselves tellers of tales, students of narrative techniques, and admirers of conceptual wit. Echoing Gide's musing on Diderot's opinion of weekly newspapers, some readers will wonder what Gide would have said of *La Religieuse*, if he had read it. The 1924 entry in the *Journal* continues, "I believe, however, that I prefer *Jacques le fataliste*." Here, too, there is a regrettable lack of elaboration. It is virtually a mystification, since this is the only mention of the Diderot work considered to have most in common with Gide's one novel, published two years later—in themes, techniques, and contrived relationships between author and reader, narrator and narrative.

Some months later, the letters to Falconet are cited as the source of a maxim: "Ofttimes more is owed to an unusual error than to a common truth." [9] The paradox evidently appealed to Gide, who had recently posed one of his own in *Si le grain ne meurt . . .* and was soon to amplify two others in *Numquid et tu? . . .* and *Corydon*. The statement is rich in possible applications to his own life and works, but once again Gide is disappointingly reticent. He refrains from discussing his own inferences and deductions, leaving to the reader whatever extrapolation or exegesis he chooses.

Toward the end of the same year, there is a notation that helps date Gide's most extensive and enthusiastic companionship with Diderot—as his own novel moves closer to publication: "Read . . . much Diderot. When he is good, he is bewitching." [10] The critical terms "bewitching" and "with rapture," by the way, are signs that a book has earned high praise from Gide, since his scale of values is based at least as much on the pleasure actually given the reader as on the intellectual stimulus hoped for by the author. His translation of "Anthony and Cleopatra," some of Sainte-Beuve (read with "unequal rapture"), *Les Goyescas,* Meredith, and Tristan are among the works and artists earning the accolade. Diderot is demoted from the group some four years after his elevation to it, when Gide reproaches him for failure to understand Spinoza, and especially for his treatment of Spinoza's atheism. The entry ends: "It takes a bit of reflection to realize the moralizing position of those great theists of the eighteenth century: Rousseau, Voltaire, Diderot, etc." [11]

The question of true understanding raised here begs another: Did Gide ("an unbeliever but never an ungodly man") ever succeed in understanding Diderot's attitudes as an early deist, later atheist, and constant moralist, if indeed he took the time to consider them? There is little evidence of such comprehension. He shows plainly, during the years of composing his *Oedipe,* that he no more subscribes to the brand of materialism—suggested by Diderot and illustrated by Crudeli in *L'Entretien d'un philosophe avec la Maréchale de * * ** (*Conversation of a Philosopher with Maréchale* X)—than he does to orthodoxy. Yet the human answers Oedipus gives the Sphinx and Teiresias, like Gide's theory of man becoming God, have much in them of Diderot's "moralizing position." The *philosophe* insists, as Gide does, on human attainment without divine guidance or salvation; Crudeli conjectures that God (if there happens to be a God) will welcome an honest atheist to Paradise (if by chance Paradise exists). Is the resolution of Oedipus basically different from the dedication to virtue proposed by Diderot? Is the zeal for bequeathing personified in Theseus anything other than a concern with serving posterity? And are Gide's challenges to divine power more "godly" than Diderot's? In *Numquid et tu?* . . . , he apostrophizes a God presumed to be merciful: "O Lord, if you are to help me, what are you waiting for?" Concerning the proper state of mind for salvation, his tone is flippant, even if his thought is sincere: "I know, moreover, just how that state is achieved; I have the recipe. But on my part there would be, today, a certain element of pretense; I am loath to do it." [12] The wholly human moral stance he advocates, including turns of phrase popular with atheistic gamblers such as Diderot, is summarized in the *Feuillets d'automne*: "To take things as they are. Play with the cards one has. Require one to be what one is." To this he adds a paragraph on the dangers of accepting as inevitable what is modifiable. The comment ends, "For one does not make a better *likeness* of oneself by giving way to the less good." The statement is reminiscent of Diderot's insistence that each man make his own best contribution to human betterment. From *Oedipe,* which had as an early subtitle "The Triumph of Morality," to "Dieu fils de l'homme" ("God the Son of Man"), which he had thought of calling "Dialogue avec Dieu," Gide considers the pursuit of happiness and the question of what he calls the "blooming" of man. His firm refusal to accept the Deity on the church's terms, his confidence in man's moral resources, and his dialectical presentation of argument place him in a moralizing position very much like the one he found so perplexing in eighteenth-century thinkers.

Gide's respect for Diderot is at its lowest point in 1929, when he comments on the opposition to the *Encyclopédie*. While he grants that some caution is to be expected when censorship is severe, he cannot justify

Diderot's handling of his subject in some of the articles. That on Spinoza, for example, is a "monument of misunderstanding and injustice," the one on Christianity an "excellent apology for what I expected to see him attack." [13] His disappointment at Diderot's resorting to indirection when under close surveillance is somewhat naive, since he realizes the technique may have been intended to baffle the opposition. But he finds himself bothered by the tricks of evasion—such devices as cross-references and seemingly unnecessary allusions, interpolated paragraphs, extreme generalizations in the middle of orthodox articles, precise definition by illustration. All of these have troubled readers other than the censor and Gide. He takes Diderot to task for some of the *Pensées philosophiques* (although the ideas are sometimes taken verbatim from Shaftesbury), accusing him of lack of intelligence, even complete stupidity, for pleading his adversaries' cause to reinforce his own argument. Gide's disapproval of Diderot's distortion of Spinoza suggests a failure on his part to appreciate how the *philosophes* adapted formal philosophy to serve their aims. He seems equally blind, incidentally, to his own adoption and adaptation of ideas from Nietzsche.[14] Unless he is being ironic, which is always possible, he is unusually obtuse in presuming that such articles as the one on Christianity were intended to contribute much to the propagation of the faith.[15]

More than two years later, Diderot's name reappears in a strangely cryptic allusion, during a discussion of a Martin du Gard play with a homosexual theme. Some people, Gide avers, are able to remain unmoved by the beauty of the nude youths in the Sistine Chapel and "unable to see anything but aberration in the passage from Diderot's letter that the *N.R.F.* printed last year (quote it)." Gide does not follow his bracketed suggestion, perhaps because the letter actually appeared more than two and a half years earlier. The extract reads:

> But it would indeed take courage to hide nothing. One would perhaps accuse oneself more readily of a scheme to commit a major crime, than of a small and obscure feeling that was vile and base. It would be less painful perhaps to write in one's notebook: *I coveted the throne at the expense of its occupant's life, than to write: one day when I was at the baths with a number of young men, I noticed one who was surprisingly beautiful, and I could not keep myself from approaching him.* This sort of examination would not, what is more, be useless for oneself.[16]

This evidently appeals to Gide as corroborative proof of the existence of much unrecognized homosexuality, and of the validity of his own crusade for public admission that it exists and is natural. He could scarcely infer that Diderot too was an apologist of the practice, if the *philosophe* found even the thought of it a "feeling that was vile and base."

Gide's sympathy with Diderot returns in later comments in the *Journal.* Leafing through the *Oeuvres complètes,* he comes on a quotation from the *Salon de 1767:* "Imagination creates nothing, it *imitates.*" [17] Delighted by his discovery, he feels he now understands Wilde's aphorism (in *Intentions*) on imagination as an imitator and the critical spirit as a creator. When he quotes the dictum later in a magazine article, Gide is annoyed at seeing *imitates* given as *invents,* so that his readers miss his point—and Diderot's *pointe.*

Those who consider Gide to be in the classical tradition will appreciate his enthusiasm for the maxim on imitation. No less than Diderot, he is concerned with the nature of genius and the development of maximum talents, although not so much as the *philosophe* with the fine distinction between *être un génie* (being a genius) and *avoir du génie* (being endowed with genius or having developed talent).[18] Like Diderot's *homme de génie,* Gide's creative artist is distinguished by his ability to absorb and reintegrate available materials, blending them with fresh ideas and techniques to produce his own masterpieces. No writer, painter or sculptor, fortunately, must create his basic working material by sheer invention, notwithstanding Racine's much quoted saying, "Creating anything consists of making something out of nothing." Imagination draws on infinite resources, concepts, and manners of presentation, often unconsciously and frequently at the moment when the artist is being most "original." The genius of Shakespeare is not held less for his having imitated or adapted themes, settings, characters, and plots already known; the painter's creative ability is shown in his choice and use of colors, not in his manufacture of canvas, brush, and paint. If Diderot turns to account whatever seems useful in past and contemporary thought, and Gide, in turn, subscribes to classical "imitation" of the tales of myth and scripture, the cause is not paucity of ideas. Both take full advantage of their remembrance of things encountered, in their own lives or in others' lives, deliberately or casually, and whenever it will serve their artistic or artful purposes. There is a pleasant incongruity, as well as a certain appropriateness, in this meeting (on the classical ground of imitation) of two of the most original and imaginative authors of modern literature.

Diderot is divorced from his usual company when Gide refers to him in his *Interviews imaginaires* (1943): "Catholic writers indict Renan, Diderot, even Montaigne." With men of resolute fibre, independent thinkers in the great tradition, Gide is himself associated by choice and by public profession of his faith in free thought. Few contemporary writers of the first order have waged so sustained a campaign against accepted Roman Catholic doctrine, resisted so organized an effort of well-meaning friends to convert them, or been so completely and unconditionally placed on the index of "damned and forbidden" books.

In the later *Journal*, the *philosophe* is mentioned three times. He is among the writers being "devoured in huge quantities" by the son of Gide's Tunisian host. When the intractable youngster's mind shows signs of improvement ("He is engaged in sorting; he is informing himself"), it is largely because he is reading the good authors of the eighteenth century, according at least to Gide.

A 1944 quotation from the letters to Sophie Volland pertains more to ethics than to intellectual progress: "I am at ease with myself only when I am doing my duty." Gide adds as his comment, "That is very well said; but the trouble is that one doesn't always know what one's duty is." [19] Whether the remark is taken as serious or playful, it restates the problem of choosing that has confronted Gide for over half a century—the privilege and plague of ethical man. During that time, as an individualist and as a humanitarian, he has been keenly interested in "what one's duty is." Much of his strength has been spent in the search for a definition of duty that will guide him to a full "flowering" of his own capabilities. Like Diderot, he thinks of duty not as stultifying restraint but as a positive vitalizing force, a kind of spiritual regimen. Like Diderot, too, he is concerned with duty as something personal and practicable rather than with Duty in the abstract or ideal sense. The inner satisfactions he hopes to earn, like those implicit in Diderot's conception of *bienfaisance,* reward the man who performs worthy actions. Chief among them is a feeling of personal fulfillment, which he equates with true peace of mind, with the serenity that comes to the man who finds a sense of achievement in carrying out self-imposed obligations.

In the three years preceding Gide's death, several collected editions appear, grouping shorter prose pieces such as sketches, portraits, eulogies, reminiscences, and periodical articles. The last to be published covers the period 1930 to 1938. It constitutes (with the reports on Russia and the Journal for those years) a sixteenth volume of the so-called *Oeuvres complètes.* Called *Littérature engagée* (*Literature of Commitment*) by its editor, it makes a "proletarian" author of Diderot—at a time when Gide is still an admirer of the brave new Soviet world of the arts. Two days after his arrival in Moscow in 1936, he says, in a funeral oration on Maxim Gorki: "It could be asserted, no doubt, that intelligence did not necessarily go with wealth: In French literature, a Molière, a Diderot, a Rousseau came from the proletariat. But their readers were still people of the privileged classes." [20]

A year before, in a monarchist newspaper, Gide had made the same point: "What reinvigorates our French literature in the eighteenth century, which really needed reinvigorating, is not Montesquieu, not even Voltaire, in spite of all their genius; no, it is the commonalty, the plebeian. It is Jean-Jacques; it is Diderot." [21] Another "presence" of the *philosophe* is in a typical *cas de conscience* Gide proposes to Soviet children, concerning the shooting of a dog by the man who had saved its life. This is later revealed a matter of *déformation professionnelle,* since the man involved is a breeder of thoroughbred dogs. The question of whether he was right or wrong elicits many replies, published in *International Literature.* In answer to another periodical's question on what he considers to be his public, Gide virtually quotes Diderot's pronouncements on posterity.

Gide's close friend Valéry died shortly after World War II. It was reported that he read Voltaire on his deathbed. Praising him for his brilliant use of intelligence, Gide singles out Valéry's approach to his reader: "Just like the actor whom Diderot praises in his *Paradox on the Actor,* it is not a matter for him of being moved but of moving others." [22]

In *Rencontres,* a miscellany of real and spiritual encounters plus sketches, portraits, essays, and anecdotes, there is a seven-page piece with the punning title of "L'Art bitraire" in which Gide melds devices that are usually associated with Marivaux and Musset with a moral problem presented in the manner of Diderot.[23] More important in the collection—and in any evaluation of influence on Gide—is a eulogy of Goethe, to whom he claims to owe more than to all other writers combined.

He speaks of his discovery of Goethe, "toward whom so many natural affinities inclined me," professes undying gratitude for the reassurance and self-confidence the German genius has brought him: "It is because I recognized myself in him constantly." [24] This is an unconscious tribute to Diderot, since Goethe spoke with equal enthusiasm of the contribution the *philosophe* had made to him, to letters, and to humanity.

Considering the number and length of these references, it would be critical folly to draw sweeping conclusions with regard to Diderot's influence on Gide or Gide's debt to Diderot. What is apparent is that Gide's acquaintance with Diderot the author and Diderot the spirit is more than passing. He does a verbal portrait, relates him to writers he himself admires, mentions his rapports with his associates such as Grimm. He talks of Rousseau, Voltaire, and Mme d'Epinay. He evaluates some articles found in the *Encyclopédie*. He endorses the free thought of the eighteenth century, without accepting it *in toto*. His knowledge of texts is first-hand, often supported by critical reading of commentators such as Sainte-Beuve. He quotes directly from the *Supplément*, the letters to Falconet and Sophie Volland, paraphrases ideas from other works, cites definitions, maxims, and paradoxes. He admits to browsing through the *Oeuvres complètes*, buying the *Bijoux indiscrets*, preferring *Jacques le fataliste*, and reading "much Diderot," some of it "bewitching." Approving of such reading for others, he comes to Diderot's defense against unfavorable criticism on occasion, without being an apologist of all that he represents. In short, the variety of the allusions, the range of their topics, and the coincidence of several of

Diderot's preoccupations with some of his own give the total impression that Gide enjoyed Diderot's spiritual company. But there is no evidence that he felt inordinately indebted to him, as he did to Goethe and at times to Montaigne.

Since the nineteen-twenties, there has been a tendency among critics to link the names and some of the devices of Diderot and Gide. Pierre Hermand entitles one section of his thesis "Diderot immoraliste." Paul Souday likens the reactions of Gertrude, in her idealized love of the pastor before the catastrophic operation which restored her sight, to Diderot's comment on young Mélanie de Sallignac's inability to distinguish between charming youth and wrinkled old age, "one of the advantages, especially for women, of not having one's eyesight." Ramon Fernandez and Denis Saurat see the two as having some literary ancestors in common. Otis Fellows and Norman Torrey suggest "L'Immoraliste" as a subtitle for the *Neveu de Rameau*, which Jean Fabre feels could be called a *sotie* more appropriately than the *Caves du Vatican*. André Billy, Robert Loy, and Pierre Mesnard all apply the term to *Jacques le fataliste*. In the foreword to his edition of *Jacques*, Charly Guyot proposes that Diderot's "deliberate disorder" was in the mind of Gide as he wrote *Les Faux-Monnayeurs*, a thought that is echoed by George Havens. Jean-Paul Sartre, in *La Nausée*, groups Gide, Diderot, Baudelaire with medical treatises as works that are not accessible to schoolboys in the library where his self-educated man studies. Otis Fellows considers Gide's remark about the absence of focus in the *Faux-Monnayeurs* singularly apt for the *Neveu.* Arthur Wilson, discussing Diderot's most published work, the scabrous and lively *Bijoux,* alludes to Gide's having read it "with rapture." Georges May discerns a parallel between Diderot's dismay at having accomplished so little by the time he was in his forties, which spurred him to write the *Neveu,* and Gide's creative anguish at a like age—a state of mind that helped him decide to make *Les Caves* his last ironical work and to correct the public impression he was giving of himself before it became completely unrecognizable. Gide's penchant for *dédoublement* was implicit in Diderot's character. "I am two people, I play two roles," Diderot says in his treatise on drama. In the *Neveu,* similarly, "I am able, too, to become a stranger to myself, a talent without which one can accomplish nothing of value." Roland Mortier uses the Gidean term to describe the essential feature of the *Lettre sur les sourds et les muets.* Robert Loy uses a variation on Gide's variant of a proverb; he characterizes Diderot by saying "The extremes meet in him." And Robert Niklaus's portrayal of Diderot could equally well be that of Gide: "an artist-philosopher who is 'committed' and yet 'uncommitted,' if we may so express it, who studies himself as well as others, who splits himself into two, becomes a stranger to himself, and is creative." [25]

For many years, Diderot's reputation as a militant atheist, encyclopedist, and anachronistically "modern" thinker obscured his claims to fame as an admirer, a critic, and a theorist of the arts—claims that the Germans recognized early.[26] Most appreciations of Gide's writing, inversely, stress his achievements in prose style and artistic effects, passing over his philosophic ideas in virtual silence. One chronic difficulty is that critical evaluations are prone to deal more with the man than with his works—few commentators can dismiss from their minds, as they judge Diderot or Gide, the complex personalities and eccentric public figures they present as they divulge their idiosyncrasies, parade their enthusiasms, and advocate unconventional causes.

The personal philosophies of Diderot and Gide evolve from their surveys and their casting off of dogmatic systems. Their uninhibited inquiry into the nature of things, beings, and the universe exemplifies the spirit of a special breed of thinking man that extends from Leucippus to the experimental naturalists of the present era. Scientists by disposition, they interpret material and perceptible nature without recourse to theology and its metaphysics—their abiding faith is in mortal virtue and in human advancement through human endeavor. Monists by conviction, they labor to earn the approbation of a public "scattered in the future." Relativists by negative reaction to fixed doctrines, and humanists by choice, they have a purview of a vast and changing universe, where physical man is at best a puny creature, but where intellectual man has infinite possibilities, if he mines and spends his resources well.

Diderot welcomed the epithet *le philosophe* (with the definite article that indicates the archetype), conferred on him by his contemporaries. He gave it a dignity not intended by his adversaries, who invented the term "Cacouacs" ("nasty-quacks"?) as the *philosophes* grew in public esteem. Voltaire, whom Diderot addressed as "dear Master," dubbed him "Tonpla," an anagram of Plato. But Diderot is remembered by intellectual historians less for his sobriquets than for his thought-provoking questions, his call for intelligent revaluations, and for the impetus he gave to the thinking of his own and later times.

Gide, in like manner, has a significant place in the thought and a negligible one in the formal philosophy of his day. Particularly during and after World War II, he devoted much of his time to philosophic problems. Basing his meditations on premises that were never clearly defined—suggested by experience and by his own speculation, therefore necessarily contingent—he found rational, emotional, and artistic bearings that were satisfying to him and of possible meaning to potential readers. Like Diderot, he was intrigued by ideas, analogies, and associations but bored by conventional combinations of thoughts. Opposed to bigotry, the accepted divinities, and all tyranny, he believed in deterministic science, individual rights, and man's capabilities. In the encouragement he gave others to scorn mediocrity, to adopt new patterns of thinking and living, to help their fellow men to progress, he combined the traits of the revolutionary, the humanist, and the *philosophe.* Because of these qualities so often ascribed to the men of the "age of enlightenment," he was as much an anachronism as Diderot was.

Both Diderot and Gide took a sociological interest in the institutions, mores, and issues of their times. Neither distinguished himself by inventing a new theory of the origins, history, or total pattern of society, although each surveyed current utopias as an interested spectator, regretting that dreams were so rarely realized. Without professing to be *engagés* (Gide's Russian adventure excepted), they were not at all isolationists—they examined promising concepts and trends, weighed relationships and prospects, considered even the most extravagant panaceas in the hope that they might contain some provisional answers to social man's questions.

As a political philosopher (in the broad sense) and as a social scientist (before the study of human society was called a science), Diderot examined biological man and primitive societies. He contended with Locke that civilization had its beginnings in understanding and not, as Hobbes had asserted, in strife. In agreement with Montesquieu on the social necessity of virtue and on the efficacy of democratic rule in small nations only, he claimed that the ideal state was to be communal, if not communistic. Unfortunately, he admitted, that state must remain an ideal, since in practice it would be an economic impossibility. In spite of an avowed hatred of dictators (from the Greeks to Frederick the Great), he admired the one benevolent despot he knew (Catherine of Russia) and concurred with his French contemporaries, from Montesquieu and Voltaire to Rousseau and Beaumarchais, that France should be a constitutional monarchy.

Diderot wrote no "social contract" as such, unless it is to be found—as René Hubert and Antoine Adam suggest—in the liberal views expressed in Rousseau's article on "Political Economy" and in his own on "Natural Law." His version of the much discussed *volonté générale* (general will), as a case in point, emphasized the reasoned concession to public policy of each individual citizen, not the total social faith of the group. Universal suffrage and the concept that all men are politically equal was as patent an absurdity to him as the contention that all are intellectually equal. Supporting the idea of maximum opportunity for education at all levels of society, he insisted that enlightened leadership and human progress would prevail only if there were an elite, endowed with special privileges because of capacity, accomplishment, and a sense of responsibility for the welfare of others. But it was as a student of human behavior and of public morality that Diderot contributed most to modern social theory. In his inquiries into laws and conventions, their validity and their effects, he moved from Montesquieu's historical relativism and Rousseau's specious utopianism toward principles of legal reform and criminal rehabilitation that are basic in twentieth-century jurisprudence and penology.

Gide's sociological activity, like his political orientation, was an outgrowth of his conviction that the intelligent individual must "manifest," provide an example and help improve humanity's lot. For the opportunities it promised, communism appealed to Gide. He said so, loudly and repeatedly. Invited to Moscow with much fanfare, he was struck more forcibly by the obvious shortcomings of the Russian experiment than by its achievements. On his return to France, he was equally vociferous (and honest) in his public admission of error. That error was, he insisted, in his judgment of the ideology and not of the Russian people, for whom he had a lasting affection. His admiration of German genius, personified in Goethe, of German efficiency, and of the language, were matched by his fondness for some of his German acquaintances. Yet he had an implacable hatred of nazism, after a momentary acceptance of France's collapse, and of all that nazism stood for. He opposed fascism and narrow French nationalism with the same vigor—any abuse of individual rights, legalized or illegal, was taken by him as a personal affront, as well as a crime against humanity.

Since each man, as he often remarked, interested him more than Man, Gide's concepts of society revolved about the individual. For that reason, laws, conventions, and codes must be changed if they restrict any man's freedom to do his best for himself and others. But he concurred with Diderot in the belief that even bad laws were to be respected until the change was effected; otherwise the unintelligent, seeing some laws disregarded, would scorn all laws. Unimpressed by promises of heavenly redress of earthly inequities, Gide devoted himself to the cause of "human and approximate" justice, since Christian charity is so rare a practice among men. His support of Dreyfus, visits to court sessions, investigation of celebrated cases and minor miscarriages of law were typical of his effort to be *ressemblant*—a good likeness of what he felt he should be. The same could be said of his defense of homosexuality, his challenge to the vast colonial exploitation companies, and his acceptance of the mayoralty in his Norman village. But the gestures were not purely selfish or for the sake of the "image" in the public mind—they expressed a social consciousness and conscience that are rarely met to such a degree in men of letters. If Gide was a sociologist and a crusader at the same time, it was largely because of an unusual combination of scientific observation, moral indignation, and sense of duty. In his outspoken resistance to social oppression, his intolerance with those who impose it, and his impatience with those who accept it, he made common cause with such literary humanitarians as Voltaire, Diderot, and Zola, and with such proponents of human dignity as Montaigne, Goethe, and, in our times, Camus.

In the realm of the arts, Diderot and Gide earned places of some prestige: Diderot, for his criticism of the fine arts, for his experiments in prose forms and in drama, as well as for his anticipations of new resources in poetry; Gide, for his innovations in narrative modes and in the theater, his refinements of prose style, and his sponsoring of talent in others. Their own creative art has such a stamp of individuality that their works represent at once many traditions and no specific school or "ism" in the history of literature. A statement by a modern critic concerning Diderot could equally well have been made of Gide: "The impossibility of enlisting his support of a thesis or a system shows him to be one of those indomitable beings who are, by definition, the true writers." [27]

There is, then, ample evidence in the writings of Diderot and Gide that their multilateral minds had many facets in common. Similarities appear in their attitudes, themes, techniques, and goals; there is intellectual incidence in the aggregate, in detail, and in implication; there is a peculiar harmony in their beliefs—and disbeliefs. There remains, among the questions passed on unanswered to their readers, the considerable problem of characterizing their total relationship.

Diderot the "pantophile" had no compunction about accepting contributions to his own thinking. This was the privilege of a man eager to learn, the reward of one seeking wide experience: "We do not know where we got significant and really important parts of our knowledge. It is not from the books printed at Marc-Michel Rey's or somewhere else, it is from the book of the world. We read that book without cease, without plan, without application and without suspecting we are reading it." [28] Gide voiced the thought as, "The only thing that is worth anything in literature is what life teaches us." Other views of Gide on imitation and assimilation were fundamentally the same as Diderot's: "It is not that I hope to be taken as more original than I am; but certain ideas are, as they say, 'in the air,' and one need only raise one's nose to see them. But very few people manage to raise their noses." For, as Gide noted early in his career, "In every relationship lies a possibility of influence." And, within three years of his death, "Great minds have never feared to testify to others' contributions to their work, and with gratitude." [29]

Can anything more than extreme chance have caused the apparent coincidence of thought that seems implicit in the circumstantial evidence we have adduced? Answering one question by posing another (supposedly an American verbal tic), both authors might say: Need there be something more, in a world where everything is fortuitous? And Gide could add: "Influence; people often mistake it, for they judge by external appearance. As soon as they see an analogy, a resemblance, they check the chronology, they conclude that this has influenced that. It's really too simple!" [30] Or he might suggest, as he did on another occasion, when it was alleged that he knew Nietzsche in the eighteen-nineties: "There is intellectual relationship but no descent." [31] How then, without resorting to so threadbare a phrase as "spiritual affinity" or Diderot's "imperceptible links," can the bonds that exist between independent minds be defined? With his customary verbal ingenuity, Gide has spoken of the blending of subconscious imitation and coincidence by like inclination as *influence par ressemblance.*[32] He invents another expression to describe the slow transmission of the creative artist's message to the public and to the later "poet" capable of appreciating it: *communion à retardement.*[33] Few phrases describe the rapports between Diderot and Gide more appropriately than "influence via resemblance" and "eventual recognition of kinship."

Elysian Epilogue

Diderot.—*Ave,* Gide. Welcome to the afterlife. Relax and enjoy yourself, now that Mauriac has your telegram. Do you suppose he passed on your *faire-part* to Claudel? There's no cloakroom here, by the way, so you won't need to check anything. And we don't go in for the courtesy visits required of other immortals-elect. Incidentally, we have been expecting you for some time. Trying to revise the three-score-and-ten rule? You certainly took an unconscionable time in dying. How did you leave Paris?

Gide.—Quietly, without ill feeling (to quote a latter-day Prometheus), and via Cuverville. "Serenely" was the word some of the obituaries used. I left unencumbered by possessions, with all hopes spent, and—if I may say so—pretty much according to plan.

Diderot.—So we hear. And with no last-minute recanting, no services, and no *bossuétades,* to coin a phrase. That was almost wicked of you, but commendably consistent. A nice gesture, too, that of having your old chauffeur and seven tenant farmers as bearers. How Gidean a Parthian shot, dramatizing the *Caves du Vatican,* then your own burial! To paraphrase our old friend Montaigne, a man's way of dying often sums up his thinking. Both of ours, come to think of it, were *dulce et decorum* —you were able to die *dénué, désespéré,* and *authentique* and I, luckily enough, at the dining table, surrounded by my family and my favorite fruits. Just desserts, as it were.

GIDE.—The pun is atrocious, Diderot, and the zeugma only passable. But the *pointe* is well made. You know, *philosophe*, I find you good company, both in what you have to say and in the way you say it. In the next few eons, we must get together often. We have enough in common and enough differences of opinion for many a chat. Do you realize that in a sentence or two, you mentioned several subjects I should like to discuss with you at length, from gestures and Montaigne to families and fruits of the earth? They rank among what you would call my true sentiments—concerns that I have turned from frequently but come back to constantly. As you know, I am not unacquainted with your works. I have sometimes thought how much I should like to talk over with you some of the questions we both asked and for which we found so few answers.

DIDEROT.—An excellent idea! We certainly have the time, as well as the topics. And I must say some of us from the old d'Holbach crowd like the shape of your mind, Gide, as much as your skill with words. I have been thinking of proposing you for honorary membership in the *philosophe* society, posthumous division. You seem to have broken your vow to shun all honors by accepting that Nobel award and the Oxford doctorate. What do you say? You will enjoy Galiani, I'm sure, and Father Hoop, not to mention our lusty Baron d'Holbach, God's personal enemy and our sometime genial host at Grandval and the "synagogue" in Rue Royale. They are all quite mad, as you know.

GIDE.—I feel honored, whether I should or not. But I look forward particularly to our own conversations. Is

Fontenelle life secretary here, too? *Perpétuel,* I mean. He could be our amanuensis and add a volume to his dialogues. Too bad I did not bring a tape recorder, but I always travel light. Still, we can manage. You are not writing Sophie, I presume—she must be here. And I have finally and irrevocably given up my diary.

DIDEROT.—A sort of do-it-yourself *Interviews imaginaires?* Why not? We can use your title again, if you like —you own the rights to it—and perhaps my epigraph *Piscis hic non est omnium* . . . What a literary event this will be! A post-posthumous publication!

GIDE.—Something new, at any rate, for both of us. We can't complain, though. We had our share of slow-fuse works and delays in reaching our public, didn't we?

DIDEROT.—Not always by our own choice, either. But that's another story. Let's turn to publics and posterity. This record of our talks could run to several volumes, given the incidences, as you would say, or the *correspondances* (fine word, that!) of our meandering minds. As far as publishing is concerned, you might act for the *Nouvelle Revue Française*—or rather *faire agir* the N.R.F. Publishers of the kind *I* dealt with are rare birds in Elysium, thank heaven!

GIDE.—Watch those clichés, Diderot! Did you mean "Thank goodness," or "Thank virtue," or some such phrase? Linguistic habits are hard to break, but I expected better of you, one of the first experts on what is now known as communication theory.

DIDEROT.—You really are unregenerate, Gide, as they said when you died. For a man with your Biblical background, you seem to take a fiendish delight in misinterpreting things and terms held sacred by us true believers.

GIDE.—Drop the "us" and I'll agree. The *mésentente cordiale* has been commented on, by friends and others. But we can dispense with the sanctimonious pose here. You are scarcely a candidate for canonization yourself, in spite of your teen-aged tonsuring and family connections. I wonder how we fared at the recent ecumenical congress, you and I. Rumor has it that the Index was to be revised. Unpredictable things . . .

DIDEROT.—. . . are all written on the Great Scroll up yonder, as Jacques used to tell himself. If the council gave its blessing to the writers of *Les Caves du Vatican* and *La Religieuse*, the act would be gratuitous, disarming, and highly Christian all at once! But there I go at my *marivaudage* again. My guess is that we can count on few readers and fewer votes of confidence from the holy, Roman, and apostolic church. If they looked at our essays in and on religion at all, it was probably risking only one jaundiced eye.

GIDE.—Or by divination, without removing the blindfold. There are none so blind as those who, having eyes . . .

DIDEROT.—Gently does it, Gide. That smacks of plagiarism, if there is such a thing. I had staked out a pioneer's claim, I thought, on that blindfold and blindness area, though I must say you mined it pretty well, from your *André Walter* days to *Ainsi soit-il*. Which reminds me —I'd like to hear more some time of young Mouton and of your near-blind music teacher, M. Dorval. Was that honestly his name? You should write *Dorval et Moi II* when you get time. I'd appreciate one of those sly dedications of yours, if you do. What a shame, while we're on the subject, that you changed your *récit* title from

L'Aveugle to *La Symphonie pastorale!* It would have driven translators out of their minds, except for the English. They could have kept the ambiguity with *The Blind One*. But the other poor devils—translation is no picnic, as you are well aware—might have been a bit embarrassed.

GIDE.—You know how much I like to *gêner*, in all senses of the word. So it was not to save trouble, or *fil à retordre*, for later translators. The new title strikes me, to tell the truth, as singularly apposite.

DIDEROT.—It is. It's clever without being *précieux*, which is unusual these days. Especially in our country, where an ill-chosen word or two can ruin a good writer's reputation.

GIDE.—And where *La Chanson de Roland* is considered a masterpiece and Victor Hugo (if I may be allowed to repeat myself) the greatest of poets, alas! But titles do fascinate me, as do names of characters, even if the choice of an apt one—like all choices—often entails the rejection of what might have been better.

DIDEROT.—It was simpler to name a work in classical times, when the protagonist's name or title, or a nicely generalized epithet, would do. Even in what we fondly called the "Age of Enlightenment" the system prevailed, though the characters changed from ancient to modern names. Marianne had quite a run, but Sophie won the popularity contest, which seems reasonable to me. I'd like to know where you dredged up some of those names of yours, Gide, particularly the wild ones in *Les Caves* and *Les Faux-Monnayeurs*. You reached far out for some of them, and in all directions. Did you ever notice how harsh you twentieth-century fellows are with the Huberts and Roberts? They have a worse time of it than C in arithmetic problems—the inept and nameless third-person fellow who is always weaker, slower, and much more stupid than A and B.

GIDE.—Nothing personal, unless it's subconscious with me. Robert's a Gide family name, as a matter of fact. But they really are clods, now that you mention it. No punning associations, please, with your Claudius. . . . When you were speaking of titles, the thought of subtitles came to me. In your day, you used them to compensate for any dullness of titles or characters' names, didn't you? With luck and ingenuity you could hit on one that filled so much of the title page that you had to move the epigraph off. Perhaps they will come back into vogue, but not by the yard. Did you happen to see the one given in *Ainsi soit-il?* Sartre may have been annoyed, but "Les Jeux sont faits" was not exactly original when he used it. In any case, legal or otherwise, I left it to the publishers.

DIDEROT.—Don't let me get started again on *libraires*, the scoundrels!

GIDE.—I know the cross you had to bear, and what a Judas that LeBreton was, if I may misplace an epithet or two. Would that all publishers were blessed with unadulterated good sense—and editors as well as *éditeurs*. I'm still a bit touchy myself when I think of having rejected that Proust manuscript. And there was one proofreader I could have strangled for his tampering.

DIDEROT.—At least the author has *some* protection now. And there are copyright laws in most countries.

GIDE.—Try collecting Russian royalties some time! They must be hoping to recoup that largesse showered on you by your friend Catherine the Great. Things have changed considerably in the years between our visits to

Russia, but tyranny is still the fashion there. If they had not produced Dostoevsky, I'd find it hard to justify the existence of the Russians. No doubt you have seen a pirated edition of my *Retour de l'URSS*. But where were we when I got off on that tangent?

DIDEROT.—On authors and copyright. I was thinking, as you spoke, of the unauthorized cut-rate editions now pouring out of Hong Kong. It reminds me of the book business in my time and that sharp operator, Panckoucke, who battened on the toil of others.

GIDE.—In case you are being very subtle, Diderot, and alluding again to my plagiarism, let me go on record as saying that I have taken from nobody and from everyone. I borrow without incurring debt, as all of us artists do. Was it Molière who said, "I take my material wherever I find it"? The only true indebtedness we have is to the work we undertake; if we do it well, the account is paid. I readily admit, for example, prospecting in the blindness area. But there is no such thing as an exclusive claim to what is in the public domain. In his *Oedipus*, Sophocles was a pioneer, to use your term. And in the beginning was the scriptural word—or rather phrase—you worked in so neatly with the title of the *Lettre sur les aveugles*. You would be the first to agree that there are certain ideas floating about at any given time, inviting inquiry. Even the books we have read and forgotten stay with us. Each person we meet reveals us to ourselves one way or another. You once said something like that, I believe, of such eccentrics as young Rameau. So please don't imply, my good Diderot, that any author is influenced, unless you mean the gratuitous, uncompromising sort of influence that acts *par ressemblance*.

DIDEROT.—You're hypersensitive, Gide. That well-tuned harp you compare yourself to is sometimes an octave or so high, twanging like an overtaut longbow. Always on the defensive—or counteroffensive—at the wrong time! You are what we used to call *sensible* and Nietzsche later dubbed "human, all too human." You should have lived in the eighteenth century. I happen to agree entirely with your theory of influence. You should know that I'm an old "public-domain" man myself, by necessity *and* choice.

GIDE.—Please accept my apologies, if they seem called for. At times I interpret general questions in personal terms. In spite of the resolutions I make to think and act sensibly, I'm like Voltaire's Memnon, who planned a full day of perfect *sagesse,* then spent it in *sottises.*

DIDEROT.—Don't we all, most days? That is one of the qualifications for admittance to Elysium. But, speaking again of subconscious borrowing—"involuntary recall" always sounds pretentious to me—I'll wager you were not even thinking of La Bruyère when you said, "Tout est à recommencer" and "Toutes choses sont dites déjà." He worded it, as you recall, "Tout est dit, et l'on vient trop tard depuis plus de sept mille ans qu'il y a des hommes, et qui pensent." All of us "poets" subscribe to Solomon's *Nil nove sub sole,* and most of us to the Biblical "Judge not . . ." you are so fond of. What is important is that we say what needs to be said—or resaid—and that we say it honestly and well.

GIDE.—You put it succinctly in "L'imagination ne crée rien—elle imite." I had thought that was Wilde's until I reread my Diderot.

DIDEROT.—A Wilde idea, but far from an original one,

with him or me. It is best stated, in my opinion, in the couplet, "True fancy is to advantage dressed/ What oft was thought but ne'er so well expressed." My quotation may not be exact, but my endorsement is complete.

GIDE.—We do have to put our talents to good use, sow seeds in fertile ground, and, in less parabolic phraseology, play with the cards we are dealt.

DIDEROT.—Were you warning *me* against clichés, Gide? You missed that other favorite of yours, "To thine own self be true. . . ." In all seriousness, though, we are in full agreement; without advocating the idea that the creative artist has a messianic role, we believe in the existence of an intellectual élite. Those who have much talent—or even some genius, which represents a still greater step—are morally obligated to interpret the nature of things to their fellow men, to improve the famous *condition humaine* in a world man did not fashion and cannot fully control.

GIDE.—Spoken like a *philosophe*, old boy—and many another humanist from Montaigne to Malraux and Camus. Was it Montaigne who coined the expression, *condition humaine?* He used it, in any case. When I was in my twenties, I read a lot of the things you Encyclopedists wrote, plus most of Stendhal, to stiffen my intellectual fibres. It certainly was not for what is called the "good of my soul." And I have the impression you were inclined to overdo the faith you had in reasoning power, not to mention your consuming belief in progress and human betterment. Am I right?

DIDEROT.—Perhaps, but even unattainable ideals can have practical results, if they avoid becoming dogmatic and ending up as cults. All accomplishment, particularly in the arts, involves a touch of exaggeration. Would you prefer stagnation, mediocrity and eternal ignorance? Are you disowning *Paludes?*

GIDE.—Far from it, as I am sure you realize. But if man's lot is ever improved, it will be by individual men, by the "moi" we so often decry and Pascal detests—not by the formless, faceless third person the grammars speak of, or "of which the grammars speak," if you prefer. That English structure always strikes me as being as artificial as some of our French "rules" for the subjunctive. But I digress, which is not unusual. Were we on banality? Goethe, your devoted admirer and translator, is still one of my idols, but his theory of banality bothers me as much as the inordinate importance given his casual remark about "Mehr Licht."

DIDEROT.—Legends help the image, you know. Sometimes we all do a little posturing, once we have become public figures. Your own cryptic comment, in somewhat similar circumstances, has stirred up some brisk controversy. How did it go? "Always the struggle to decide what is reasonable and what is not," or words to that effect.

GIDE.—*Touché.* Perhaps I should leave well enough alone and join Goethe as an accidental oracle, just to add to the confusion. It was Goethe himself who said that what marks the perfect work of art is the artist's ability to have more seen in it than he intended or even suspected.

DIDEROT.—Your own definitions are, I must say, becoming proverbial: "la collaboration du lecteur" is good and "la part de Dieu" is masterly. They rank with Montaigne's "suffisant lecteur" and the classic "substantifique moelle."

GIDE.—Ah, Montaigne! Let's compare notes on him

some time soon, Diderot. On the whole question, for that matter, of how writing is written, to use Gertrude Stein's revolting title. We have both given some thought to the creative process and its problems. While I was doing my *Faux-Monnayeurs* (which someone called "le roman du roman," and someone else "le roman du romancier"), I was particularly interested in techniques of composition. Among the novels I read, by sheer chance and by choice, was *Jacques le fataliste.* And I enjoyed the *Bijoux indiscrets* I picked up one day while waiting for a train. It seems to me you went in for the experimental novel some time before it was the vogue. But then, everything an artist does should be experimental, I feel, or mental rigor mortis will set in. We both have had our *expériences* in prose forms, dabbled in verse, and convinced ourselves that we missed our true vocations as dramatists. How about a colloquy on the art of composing?

DIDEROT.—Nothing would suit me better. It can be as revealing as an autopsy—and I always enjoyed them. We may establish a new trend in amateur post-mortems. And if we interrupt ourselves or each other to digress, who cares? A bit of the unexpected always adds zest. And chains of thought with a few missing links are the most interesting. I don't think we are in great danger of being too systematic. Systems, like time and prescience, are among the taboos here. *Disponibilité* is the nearest thing we have to a law in Elysium. Epicureanism is, as you have probably guessed, the popular philosophy.

GIDE.—You've done it again, Diderot—started my thoughts in several directions at once: the *imprévu, chaînes, systèmes,* and *disponibilité* all in the same breath! We may be talking forever, if we are to cover all the promising topics that come up.

DIDEROT.—So much the worse—or better. When everything has been said, we can start again, to paraphrase an expression I've seen somewhere. Incidentally, if you are reporting our conversations, my good friend, you had better resurrect *divers* as a rubric for this one. What started as a *rencontre* became a *voyage* and now threatens to qualify as a *sotie*.

GIDE.—It certainly is not a *conte*, as someone once said. Nor a *récit*, by my definition. Let's consider it a *préface* to later *entretiens*.

DIDEROT.—Agreed. We certainly ran that list of categories into the ground, didn't we? It's fortunate you are as prone as I to be carried away by verbal associations. Some sensitive souls abhor them.

GIDE.—That's their privilege as well as their loss. Labels themselves are not worth much as indications of contents—I gave them up long ago, after years of indulgence. It was easier than giving up some other habits, such as smoking.

DIDEROT.—I'm glad you said "smoking." My own vice was coffee. Labels, indulgence, and habits—more items for our infinite agenda! We may very well out-memoir poor old Chateaubriand, ensconced as we are here in the *outre-tombe*. This eternity, I confess, has much to commend it. I like its reassuring *durée*, the feeling that time is working for instead of against us. What was that definition of *durée* you used? Something about "works the changing times cannot affect." It could define "classic," too.

GIDE.—Not so fast, Diderot. Eternity admittedly suits

us fine now. But a belief in it on earth is such an invitation to inertia, to accepting the status quo, that it makes any real progress impossible, even by revolution. When I said that in the thirties, you may remember, the communists cheered. You're quite a fellow-traveler yourself, I hear. Are they doing an edition of your works in Russia, or just reinventing your *Encyclopédie?* It is reported that you rank as a good pre-Marx-and-Engels "dialectical materialist"—or did a while ago. Hoist on your own petard of skill in dialectic and atheistic materialism!

DIDEROT.—I'm afraid that's all over for both of us, Gide. They know me better now. In some mysterious way, when it comes to the Russians, I never seem to improve on acquaintance. As for eternity, the only time I felt "eternal" before I arrived here was when I was in exuberantly good health. It was a matter of animal spirits, not faith or philosophy. In the material sense, however, all things are eternal. Life comes from death as well as to it. I'm an earth-and-worm man, myself, though metempsychosis is a tempting thought. Dead molecules nourish live molecules, as we used to say; there is a bit of rearrangement and there you are—or there your palingenesis is. It was "spontaneous generation" in my day. The inanimate and the animate are both matter, and one becomes the other if the circumstances are favorable. I used to tell Sophie that with any luck our dissolved particles would eventually get together. It was a dream I cherished, just as great men do the dream of immortality. Immortality is not an academic question—it can be attained by those who strive for it, I feel convinced.

GIDE.—In the memories of men, yes. Provided memory is not a tombstone, but a living heritage of thought. Like Theseus, we all want to bequeath, hoping that our heirs will be grateful. But the immortality reasonable men aspire to is not the one my good wife "Em" believed in. Her kind of afterlife was beyond me, although she prayed that I might share it. Obliging though I am, the detachment within my powers does not include that of the soul from the body. The idea of the soul outliving the flesh seems to me inadmissible, unthinkable, quite unacceptable. After death, there is probably nothing—and no one is there to see that there is nothing, or to find that natural. Yet it would be strange if there were, whatever it might be! Just think: something instead of nothingness! Reminds me somewhat of your fable of the young Mexican who drifts to the uncharted island and meets the Old Man.

DIDEROT.—Lower-case for those last two words, please. Remember, it's an apologue. You sounded perilously close to conversion in that last outburst, Gide.

GIDE.—To tell the truth, there have been times when, if I'd let myself go, I should have rolled right under the communion table.

DIDEROT.—Fortunately Claudel is not with us. Didn't he make it clear that your refusal of Christianity meant opting for the *néant?*

GIDE.—A worthy fellow, Claudel. Bad case of proselytis, but otherwise sound. Mauriac is a fine type, too, speaking of devout souls.

DIDEROT.—I wish I could say the same of my very Christian brother. But let's get back to our *moutons* and leave the *agneaux* to their own green pastures. Where were we? On immortality?

GIDE.—We had gone from there to the Christian paradise, I believe. What did you mean when you called paradise an abstraction? That it is merely a term for something that does not exist?

DIDEROT.—Abstractions, like ideals, exist—in the sense that they are vague concepts, ideas with no real sense in them. They are the counterfeit money metaphysicians use in their black-market dealings. Artists attempt to realize abstractions by attributing sense to them—usually nonsense, or hyphenated non-sense, unfortunately.

GIDE.—Counterfeit coin and nonsense are now as equitably distributed as Descartes says common sense was in his day. But you are behind the times in your art criticism, Diderot. A few of the recent abstractionists may surprise you by outlasting your eighteenth-century masters.

DIDEROT.—Possibly. If they hope to, they cannot afford either to scorn the future or to count on it too naively. Its portrait should be constantly before their eyes—glued to their noses, in fact—unless they are geniuses, speaking directly to posterity. Or seers, like our friend Teiresias, whose eyes were sealed to his own times but open to the future. Artistic immortality, posterity, and the urge to deserve emulation are inseparably bound—unlike your Prometheus, his rock, and his eagle. The *philosophe* has the same regard for his beneficiaries-to-be as the religious man has for his "other world." Posterity is, in a word, the echo of the present, corrected by experience, always just, ever ready to reward those who have respected it. . . .

GIDE.—In several words! You need not be carried away by your own rhetoric, Diderot. I was convinced even before I read your letters to Falconet, with their "thirty-five final reasons." You cover the *gens de bien* quite nicely, too, in the piece on posterity. But you are really at your most eloquent and eurythmic in the article on "Encyclopédie," where you speak of "hommes qui viendront après nous," "siècles qui succéderont" and "nos neveux . . . plus instruits . . . plus vertueux et plus heureux." You would have done better than I in politics. I presume the "neveux" were not intended to include Rameau?

DIDEROT.—Do I sense a baleful English influence in your penchant for puns? It's definitely un-French of you. Some of them are not bad, but frankly I prefer to hear you pontificating on posterity, as I have been. Would you vouchsafe a few Gidean intimations of immortality?

GIDE.—An infinite number, if you like. For many a year it has been among my favorite subjects. As a premise, then, my theory of eternity; *secundo*, immortality; *tertio*, posterity. "Eternal life" has never meant "future life" to me. It is present, immediate, in us and with us, rather than something after death. The man who loves his life must lose it, figuratively speaking, to find himself and realize his possibilities. Dostoevsky and the parable of the seed both illustrate the point. Whoever loses his "life" for the betterment of mankind will be born again. As Daedalus tells Theseus, he will be "inépuisablement recréé par la reconnaissance des hommes." That's a Grail worth Galahading for (*La Table Ronde* please quote). And a man—or a god—must *manifester* if he is to *devenir*. The best type of commitment I know is not even to the next generation, but to the one after that. Your genius may have such an aim unconsciously; the talented man—"celui qui a du génie," to use your distinction—must adjust his sights himself, or at least estimate his range. The unknown artist may well have a receptive public scattered somewhere in the future. Think of Stendhal and his confidence in the "happy few." Or Baudelaire and Rimbaud. And what of Lautréamont, that "maître des écluses pour la littérature de demain"?

DIDEROT.—How about Gide and his "flying fish," present and future? Du Bos claims that you confuse *temps* and *intemporel*, which may be a good idea at that. Laurent says you confuse posterity with malicious intent. He turns a nice phrase sometimes. In my opinion, his "engagé solitaire" tops Mauriac's "virtuose du tirage limité" and Maulnier's "grand veilleur attentif et ironique." You must have overliberated Laurent. He not only threw away your book, as prescribed, but he picked it up again and tried to bludgeon you with it. He was quite snide in that jibe about "writing of people's slightest faults for their children's maximum delight." Not that he was entirely wrong. . . .

GIDE.—Some of us have a magnetic attraction for epithets and capsule criticisms, especially from onetime friends and holier-than-thou critics. You were not immune yourself. Palissot was cruel, but occasionally witty, in his caricature of you. Rousseau was malevolent, the Jesuits vindictive. La Harpe and his ilk were simply obtuse.

DIDEROT.—Popularity can be the kiss of death, approval by the majority a poor substitute for achievement, unless you are writing for the newspapers. Did you know Rousseau and I came close to starting a literary journal?

GIDE.—I liked the name: *Le Persifleur*, but Rousseau's

sample copy was less than brilliant and his ideas on editorial policy were absurd. You were wise to drop it. Sainte-Beuve might not have called you "our first journalist." I am an old *Figaro* hand myself—a professional *journaliste,* if I may risk the word—and I still read the papers avidly. Especially the *faits-divers,* which are full of gems. But I define as journalism anything that will be less interesting tomorrow than it is today. *Le Temps* est mort! Vive l'intemporel!

DIDEROT.—That has the odor of the Academy's "A l'immortalité." Considering the views we share on lasting forever, perhaps we should have tried for one of the forty seats, instead of the forty-first. Beards are optional, you know.

GIDE.—You've heard of my aversion to them, I see. Actually, those courtesy calls were too much for me to stomach. And laurels have a bitter taste, at best.

DIDEROT.—D'Alembert joined enough learned societies for all of our crowd. The "Société de gens de lettres" was enough for me. Membership in academies can become a devil and possess you.

GIDE.—Makes me think of Radiguet and Dostoevsky, both of whom I consider personal discoveries. Had we got to my *secundo* or *tertio?*

DIDEROT.—To both, since they interrelate. We were on immediate popularity, if my memory is correct. A propos of that, you managed to win a solid reputation in your own time.

GIDE.—Time to come may revise it drastically, as it has changed yours. Being in fashion is not to be despised, but the later the fashion the better. The artist who has the most influence fifty years after his death has the best chance of lasting. It is, after all, the work that survives and deserves to survive, if the creator has preferred it to himself. What really assures perenniality is the ability of the artist—your "poet" again—to transmute himself, or parts of himself, into his creatures. If he does so with style and taste, he is present and eternal in an unobtrusive way. There is something pathetic about Chateaubriand and Rousseau, whose lives are more interesting than their works. At one time, when my wife burned my letters to her, I thought the one part of me that deserved to survive had been destroyed. I wept for three days, beyond all consoling. The letters were good, undoubtedly, but now I feel she may have done me an unintended service.

DIDEROT.—We all have strength enough to be critics of others, as well as to bear troubles that are not our own. The philosophic "Know thyself" and "Physician, heal thyself" are both antidotes to overconfidence. Perhaps what makes life bearable is the understanding of a few perceptive contemporaries and an innocent confidence in the intelligence (and taste) of later generations. We have to ask ourselves why, how well, and for whom we toil.

GIDE.—Too bad you missed Louis Aragon's poll. He merely asked, "Pour qui écrivez-vous?" I used both your phrase, "ceux qui viendront," and a paraphrase, "Ceux à qui mes livres s'adressent ne sont pas encore nés." That may be why my *Nourritures terrestres* sold only five hundred copies in twenty years. Fortunately, I am patient.

DIDEROT.—I am not, by nature, though I have some self-discipline. My works, with the exception of the *En-*

cyclopédie, never rated what you call the best-seller lists. Of course, the book business has changed since I knew it. But I should have risked becoming a posthumous author sooner than I did, if some of my manuscripts had appeared when they were first written. What is more, the scandal might have hurt some good people. You have to think of others, as you and Casanova have so aptly remarked, as well as of art and catharsis.

GIDE.—There are those who feel that much of my work should not have appeared before my death *or* after it. I don't agree. Some things must be said by those capable of saying them. *Corydon,* for instance, is my most important work. Apart from that, I leave judgments and inferences to those who like to reach conclusions. I let my books choose their readers patiently.

DIDEROT.—That's a system that has merit and virtue—if you care for systems, that is. And virtue is another topic. Were you ever nominated for the "Prix de vertu"? I like to consider myself its godfather, since I suggested it.

GIDE.—Do you ever miss a word, Diderot, or an *idée-catin?* Sometimes I fear you are beyond redemption.

DIDEROT.—*Num quid et tu?* May the misfortune of being *irrécupérable* continue for both of us, *immoraliste*—*ad infinitum. Vale.*

GIDE.—Classically said, except for the Sartrian allusion: *Et nunc manet in te,* to recoin a phrase, and *ne quid nimis, philosophe.* May we enjoy the delights of Elysium as we both did the fruits of the earth. And may chance soon bring us together again, among the dead and the quick. *Vale.*

Bibliographical Notes

Works of Diderot, unless otherwise indicated, are referred to here by title, volume number, and page in the Garnier edition, edited by J. Assézat and M. Tourneux. Where the French source alone is given, the translation is my own. *LSV* in these notes refers to Diderot's *Lettres à Sophie Volland,* Babelon edition (N.R.F., 1938, 2 vols.).

References in these notes to those of Gide's works found in the Gallimard-N.R.F. collection, edited by Louis Martin-Chauffier, will be by title, volume number, and page, followed by a bracketed allusion to the author and page of the English translation. References to the French *Journal* are shown by date only, followed by the volume and page in the Justin O'Brien translation, *The Journals of André Gide* (Knopf, 1947–51, 4 vols.).

Open Minds and Open Questions

1. Such terms are frequent in the letters to Mlle Volland: "a fairly faithful history of my life" (14 July 1762), "the continuation of my journal" (6 September 1762), "my journal interrupted once more" (9 September 1762), "writing my journal again" (23 September 1762), "whether I can go on with my journal" (10 September 1767).

George Roth's voluminous edition of Diderot's correspondence (Editions de Minuit, 1955– –) is a milestone in progress toward total publication of the letters. It amends and expands earlier collections, notably those of Babelon (1931), Assézat and Tourneux (1875–79), Paulin (1830), Brière (1821–23), Belin (1818), and Naigeon (1798).

2. Gide's correspondence, scattered through his published works and in various private collections, periodicals, and appendixes to studies, completes his self-portrait. His exchanges of

letters with famous contemporaries—among them Paul Valéry, Francis Jammes, Paul Claudel, and Charles Du Bos—have appeared at length.

3. Mme de Vandeul's memoirs, in the Assézat-Tourneux edition of Diderot, I, xxv-lxviii; André Billy, *Vie de Diderot* (Flammarion, 1932); Franco Venturi, *La Jeunesse de Diderot* (Skira, 1939); Jean Pommier, *Diderot avant Vincennes* (Boivin, 1939); Lester G. Crocker, *The Embattled Philosopher* (Michigan State, 1954); Arthur M. Wilson, *Diderot: The Testing Years, 1713–1759* (Oxford, 1957). Useful biographical detail is also to be found in early studies by Joseph Reinach, Daniel Mornet, and Hubert Gillot, as well as in recent ones by Herbert Dieckmann, Charly Guyot, Jean Fabre, Georges May, Roland Mortier, and Jean Mayer.

4. Ramon Fernandez, *André Gide* (Corrêa, 1931); Léon Pierre-Quint, *André Gide, sa vie, son oeuvre* (Stock, 1932); Paul Archambault, *Humanité d'André Gide* (Bloud et Gay, 1946); Justin O'Brien, *Portrait of André Gide* (Knopf, 1953); Germaine Brée, *André Gide l'insaisissable Protée* (Les Belles Lettres, 1953).

5. Detached pages (*feuillets*) preceding 1924–25 journal entries in *Oeuvres complètes*, XIII, 440. Cf. Diderot's comment on the need of rereading his d'Alembert series, in *Oeuvres complètes*, IX, 252.

6. *Journal*, 26 October 1924 (O'B II, 356).

7. *De l'interprétation de la nature*, II, 7; *Les Nourritures terrestres*, II, 223. Cf. Diderot's advice on throwing his work in the fire. *Essai sur les règnes de Claude et Néron*, III, 373.

8. *Journal*, 3 June 1924 (O'B II, 350).

9. See I. K. Luppol, *Diderot, ses idées philosophiques* (Editions Sociales Internationales, 1936), Jean Luc, *Diderot* (Editions Sociales Internationales, 1938), Jean Stewart and Jonathan Kemp, *Diderot Interpreter of Nature* (International Publishers, 1943) for Diderot as an ancestor of Marx and Engels. For Gide's Russian adventure, see Richard Crossman, *The God That Failed* (Harper, 1950).

Gide is given a special, if less reprehensible, interpretation in most studies. Charles Du Bos, in *Le Dialogue avec André Gide* (Au Sans Pareil, 1929), speaks as a close and concerned friend; Paul Archambault strives to demonstrate "la sinueuse unité de ses démarches" (*Humanité d'André Gide*, p. 11) by applying "psychological" techniques of criticism; Jean Hytier, in his *André Gide* (Charlot, 1938– – English translation by Richard Howard, Doubleday-Anchor, 1962), deals primarily with the esthetic point of view.

10. Cf. Jean Mayer, *Diderot homme de science* (Rennes, Imprimerie Bretonne, 1959), which supersedes such earlier studies as those of Mme Doublet (1934), Tribouillet (1921), Paître (1904), and Caro (1880).

11. Of the several theses done for medical degrees, the best is that of Mme S.-M. Doublet, *La Médecine dans les oeuvres de Diderot* (Bordeaux, 1934). Her opinions are shared by the profession. Cf. Dr. Cabanès, "Diderot et les Sciences médicales," in *Médecins amateurs* (Albin Michel, 1932).

12. See my article, "Diderot's Teratology" in *Diderot Studies IV* (Droz, 1963).

13. *LSV*, 28 July 1762.

14. *Journal*, 25 May 1931 (O'B III, 162); *Journal* 3 May 1916 (O'B II, 142); *Interviews imaginaires* (Schiffrin, 1943), p. 96 (English translation by Malcolm Cowley, *Imaginary Interviews*, Knopf, 1944, p. 59); *Interviews imaginaires*, p. 142 (Cowley, p. 89).

15. *Corydon*, IX, 236.

16. *Journal*, 8 June 1942 (O'B IV, 114).

17. "Feuillets d'automne" and *Journal*, November 1947 (O'B IV, 276). Cf. Diderot's discussion of the *comment* and the *pourquoi* in *De l'interprétation de la nature*, II, 54.

18. *LSV*, 21 September 1768.

19. *Journal*, following August 1893 entry (O'B I, 29–30).

20. *Journal*, 12 May 1892 (O'B I, 21); *Journal*, June 1927 (O'B II, 404).

21. *LSV*, undated fragment in Babelon edition, II, 265.

22. *Journal*, 15 May 1892 (O'B I, 21).

23. Herbert Dieckmann, review of Eric M. Steel, *Diderot's Imagery* in *Romanic Review* XXXV (1944), 347.

24. See Eric M. Steel, *Diderot's Imagery* (Corporate Press, 1941); Margaret Gilman, *Baudelaire the Critic* (Columbia, 1943); Gita May, *Diderot et Baudelaire* (Droz, 1957); Anne de Commaille, "Diderot et le Symbole littéraire," in *Diderot Studies I* (Syracuse, 1949); Eleanor M. Walker, "Towards an Understanding of Diderot's Esthetic Theory," in *Romanic Review* XXXV (1944).

25. Antoine Adam, in "Rousseau et Diderot," *Revue des Sciences Humaines* (1949), lists several examples of Diderot's obtaining effects usually associated with Jean-Jacques, often better than Rousseau himself. Jean Pommier illustrates Diderot's borrowing Rousseau's heart to write "Délicieux" as though he were doing the *Rêveries*. *Revue d'histoire de la philosophie* (1942). See also Jean Fabre, "Deux frères ennemis: Diderot et Jean-Jacques," in *Diderot Studies III* (Droz, 1961).

26. *Salon de 1767*, XI, 267; "Extraits d'un ouvrage anglais sur la peinture," XIII, 36.

27. Leo Spitzer, "The Style of Diderot," in *Linguistics and Literary History* (Princeton, 1948), p. 139.

28. Daniel Mornet, *Cours de lettres, 1947–1948* (Paris, 1948), p. 214.

29. See O'Brien III, 445–50, for a listing of Gide's "poetry" under the heading used by him and his publishers until 1935. Compare Diderot's identification of the poet with the creative artist, as interpreted by Margaret Gilman, "The Poet According to Diderot," *Romanic Review* XXXVII (1946), 37n.

30. "Feuillets d'automne" in *Journal*, November 1947 (O'B IV, 276–77).

31. *Journal*, 4 May 1893 (O'B I, 25), 10 June 1891 (O'B I, 9), following 9 May 1893 (O'B I, 25), 22 July 1891 (O'B I, 12), 10 October 1893 (O'B I, 33).

32. *Journal*, August 1893 (O'B I, 27).

33. Letter to Grimm, 27 November 1776; *LSV*, undated fragment, Babelon II, 280.

34. *Poétique* (Neuchâtel, Ides et Calendes, 1948), p. 11.

35. *Paradoxe sur le comédien*, VIII, 367; *Poétique*, p. 12.

36. *LSV*, 6 November 1760; *Le Neveu de Rameau* V, 387; *LSV*, 10 November 1760; *LSV*, 20 September 1765.

37. Maurice Tourneux, *Diderot et Catherine II* (Calmann Lévy, 1899), p. 452. This section, "Sur ma manière de travailler" (pp. 448–52), helped destroy the legend that Diderot wrote "au courant de la plume."

38. *Journal*, November 1890 (O'B I, 8); undated pages following 1893 entries (O'B I, 36); 18 March 1890 (O'B I, 6). For an elaboration of Gide's *manière de travailler* that is strangely consonant with Diderot's, see the Justin O'Brien translation in *Pretexts* (Meridian-Greenwich, 1959), pp. 306–07.

Extremes and Emphases

1. André Cresson, in his *Diderot, sa vie, son oeuvre, sa philosophie* (Presses Universitaires, 1949), speaks of Diderot as an "esprit universel et bouillonnant"; Rousseau called him "cette tête universelle"; Alice Scheyer entitled her thesis *Diderot als universaler Denker* (Berlin, Ebering, 1932). The Faustian theme of "possession" is recurrent with Gide, from Prometheus bedeviled by his *conscience* to Dostoevsky and James Hogg, the "justified sinner" whose confessions fascinated Gide.
2. "Réflexions sur Térence," V. 234.
3. *Ibid.*, p. 237.
4. *Lettre sur les aveugles,* I, 301.
5. *LSV*, 2 September 1769.
6. This notion seems to be taken at face value by Gide, who quotes Grimm's letter in the *Journal,* 29 September 1921 (O'B II, 271). Among modern critics, few are convinced of inordinate debt on Rousseau's part. This question, and others of influence, have been debated continually since G. Gran's 1911 article—by F. Vézinet (1924), L. G. Krakeur (1937), G. Havens (1939, 1942, 1961), H. Guillemin (1942, 1943), J. Guéhenno (1948), A. Adam (1949), J. Pommier (1952), J. Fabre (1961). The names of Diderot and Rousseau are again coupled in an article by Robert Niklaus, *Diderot Studies IV* (1963).
7. *LSV*, 30 October 1759.
8. See Carl Becker, "The Dilemma of Diderot," *Philosophical Review* XXIV (1915), 54–71, as a case in point. Gide's bemused reaction to Diderot's technique is discussed in his *Journal,* 1 April 1929 (O'B III, 46).
9. Cf. Joseph E. Barker, *Diderot's Treatment of the Christian Religion in the "Encyclopédie"* (King's Crown, 1941).
10. O'Brien I, xiv.
11. IV, 199–218 (translated by Angelo P. Bertocci in *Pretexts,* pp. 59–73).
12. X, 461–62.
13. *LSV*, 20 October 1760. Diderot's only major use of the term *inconséquence* in its usual sense is in the title of the story of Mme de la Carlière: *Sur l'inconséquence du jugement public de nos actions particulières.* In a lecture on the importance

of the public (translated by Angelo P. Bertocci in *Pretexts*, pp. 48–59), Gide deals primarily with the artist's task.

14. Cf. the first-person-pronoun outlook in the *Nouvelles Nourritures:* "Yes, I do feel, throughout my diversity, a constancy; I feel that what is diverse in me is still *myself*. But for the very reason that I know and feel the existence of this constancy, why should I strive to obtain it?" *The Fruits of the Earth,* trans. D. Bussy (Knopf, 1949), p. 259.

15. *Le Neveu de Rameau,* V, 487–88 (Stewart and Kemp, *Diderot Interpreter of Nature,* p. 328).

16. Jean Hytier, *André Gide,* Chapter VII.

17. *Ibid.,* pp. 232, 234 (English translation by Richard Howard, pp. 205, 207).

18. *De l'interprétation de la nature,* II, 7.

19. *Ceci n'est pas un conte,* V, 311; *Jacques le fataliste,* VI, 15, 285.

20. *Paludes,* I, 369.

21. *Journal,* 23 June 1930 (O'B III, 113), 2 January 1931 (O'B III, 137), 22 August 1926 (O'B II, 386).

22. *Satire* I has the subtitle, "Sur les caractères et les mots de caractère, de profession, etc."

23. *Journal,* 16 November 1917 (O'B II, 217); *Interviews imaginaires,* p. 189 (Cowley, p. 123); *Journal,* 14 July 1940 (O'B IV, 32); *Interviews imaginaires,* p. 119 (Cowley, p. 75, translates *geste* as "deed"), p. 114 (Cowley, p. 71, uses "occupational disease"); *Journal,* 30 October 1931 (O'B III, 198–99).

Fools and Their Play

1. *LSV,* 10 May 1759, 30 October 1759, 20 October 1760, 28 September 1767.

2. *Ibid.,* 20 October 1760.

3. *Ibid.,* 30 September 1760.

4. *Ibid.,* 30 October 1759, 20 October 1760, 24 September 1767, 30 October 1759, 28 October 1760, 30 October 1759, 28 September 1767, 10 May 1759, 8 October 1760, 2 October 1761.

5. *Journal,* undated entry preceding 2 May 1923 (O'B II, 324). In the foreword to the 1926 edition of *Num quid et tu?* . . . (O.B II, 187), Gide is "grateful" to M. Massis, who has been waging religious war on him since 1914. The allusion to

the distortion in *Verve* is in the *Journal,* 15 December 1937 (O'B III, 365).

6. *LSV*, 30 September 1760.

7. *Ibid.*, 19 October 1761, 26 September 1762.

8. *Ibid.*, undated fragment, Babelon II, 266, 7 October 1760, 20 October 1760, 25 July 1762.

9. *Les Caves du Vatican*, VII, 408. Parts of the letter and unused preface are entered in the *Journal,* 12 July 1914 (O'B II, 39).

10. Retold myths, parables, and Biblical tales abound in Gide: *Narcisse, Ajax, Proserpine, Philoctète, Oedipe, Thésée; Le Retour de l'enfant prodigue, Saül, Bethsabé.*

11. Eugénie Droz, *Le Recueil Trepperel* (Droz, 1935), p. lxvii. See also L. Petit de Julleville, *Répertoire analytique du théâtre comique en France au moyen âge* (Cerf, 1886); E. Picot, *Recueil général des sotties* (Didot, 1902–12, 3 vols.); E. Viollet le Duc, ed., *Ancien Théâtre français* (1854).

12. Gringoire's title was actually *mère-sotte.* L. Petit de Julleville, *Les Comédiens au moyen âge* (Cerf, 1886). A list of religious comedies is given in C. Hastings, *The Theatre* (transl. London, Duckworth, 1902), pp. 168–69.

13. Paul Thiry, *Le Théâtre français au moyen âge* (Brussels, Lebègue, 1944), pp. 69–70.

14. *Le Prométhée mal enchaîné,* III, 134.

15. Diderot, like Gide, ranks the ability to move others to action above purely personal effort: "l'être rare par excellence, c'est celui qui réunit la force qui fait agir et le génie qui fait dire grandement." "Fragment inédit," III, 539.

16. *LSV*, 11 September 1769.

17. *Ibid.*, 7 October 1762. J. Robert Loy, in *Diderot's Determined Fatalist* (New York, King's Crown, 1950), suggests that Sterne knew and used *Jacques,* despite the latter's claim to "plagiarism."

18. *LSV*, 30 September 1760, 15 October 1760, 25 November 1760, 12 November 1765.

19. *LSV*, 2 September 1769, 5 September 1762, 30 September 1768.

Blindness and Blindfolds

1. Extract given in IV, 108.
2. *Lettre sur les sourds et muets,* I, 357.
3. *Ibid.,* I, 290–92; *Les Bijoux indiscrets,* IV, 244–49.
4. *Lettre sur les aveugles,* I, 289, 310, 307.
5. *LSV,* 30 October 1759, 15 November 1768, 12 August 1762, 30 September 1760.
6. Passage reputedly written by Diderot and inserted in Pézay's *Eloge de Fénelon,* given in IV, 106.
7. *Poésies,* IX, 16.
8. *LSV,* 30 September 1760.
9. *Ibid.,* 22 September 1761.
10. *La Symphonie pastorale,* IX, 19–20.
11. *Ibid.,* p. 85. Gertrude's quotation of Romans VII:9 occurs again in *Num quid et tu . . . ?,* VIII, 314 (O'B II, 170).
12. *Ibid.,* pp. 67, 13, 10, 54, 64.
13. J. T. Sheppard, *The Oedipus Tyrannus of Sophocles* (Cambridge, 1920), p. lx.
14. *Journal,* 22 January 1932 (O'B III, 215–16).
15. *Cahiers d'André Walter,* I, 119.
16. *Thésée,* pp. 117–18.
17. *Journal,* 13 January 1929 (O'B III, 36); *Interviews imaginaires,* p. 56 (Cowley, p. 31); *Attendu que . . . ,* p. 18; *Journal,* 24 June 1940 (O'B IV, 24) and *Interviews imaginaires,* p. 162 (Cowley, pp. 101–02).
18. *Journal,* 14 June 1926 (O'B II, 380).
19. "Extrait," IV, 108.
20. *Journal,* 7 May 1927 (O'B II, 400).
21. *Thésée,* pp. 117, 122.
22. "Dieu, fils de l'homme," in *Pages de Journal,* p. 158.

Dilemmas and Directions

1. Carl Becker, "The Dilemma of Diderot," *Philosophical Review* XXIV (1915), 54–71; *Journal,* 11 January 1892 (O'B I, 19).
2. Letter to Father V. Poucel, 27 November 1927, given in XIV, 407.

3. Joseph Barker says of Diderot's attitude: "Religion in general and by inference the Christian religion, is shown to be not only unnecessary to insure the moral life, but as actually harmful to the only morality that is natural and universal." *Diderot's Treatment of the Christian Religion*, p. 128. See also Aram Vartanian, "From Deist to Atheist," in *Diderot Studies I*, 46–63.

4. Gide's "Dieu, fils de l'homme" in *Pages de Journal*, pp. 149–70. Compare Diderot's "Dieu et l'homme," IV, 93.

5. *Encyclopédie* article "Passions," given in VI, 220.

6. *Journal*, 4 October 1931 (O'B III, 194).

7. *LSV*, 7 November 1762, 31 July 1762.

8. *La Religieuse*, V, 88.

9. *Ibid.*, p. 119.

10. *Corydon*, IX, 179 note. See also "Feuillets inédits," IX, 359.

11. *Ibid.*, preface to 1924 edition, reprinted in IX, 178.

12. *Ibid.*, preface to the second edition (1920), given in IX, 182.

13. *Ibid.*, p. 200.

14. "Feuillets," (1911), VI, 365.

15. *Journal*, 19 January 1937; *Si le grain ne meurt . . .* , X, 32, 376.

16. *Eloge de Richardson*, V, 214; Letter to the Princess of Nassau-Saarbruck in *Le Père de famille*, VII, 184; *De la poésie dramatique*, VII, 312.

17. *De la poésie dramatique*, VII, 313; *Sur l'inconséquence . . .* , V, 342.

18. *Le Neveu de Rameau*, V, 442, 422, 423 (Stewart and Kemp, 284, 266, 267).

19. "Pages inédites," XI, 30.

20. *Journal*, 6 October 1916 (O'B II, 153).

21. "Feuillets d'automne," in *La Table Ronde* VI (1948), 917–28. Both quotations are on p. 919 (O'B IV, 277).

22. *Ibid.*, p. 925, 919–20, 919 (O'B IV, 281, 277, 278).

23. *Le Neveu de Rameau*, V, 413–14 (Stewart and Kemp, 286).

24. Letter to Landois (1756), XIX, 436. Addressed to Naigeon in Babelon I, 311.

25. *LSV*, 31 July 1762.

26. Letter to Montgomery Belgion, 22 November 1929, in the

N.R.F. XXXIV (1930), 196, included in different form in *Journal,* 4 November 1929 (O'B III, 78).

27. *Journal,* undated pages, 1925, XIII, 432 (O'B II, 377).
28. *Entretien d'un père avec ses enfants,* V, 307–08.
29. *LSV,* 15 October 1760.
30. *Sur l'inconséquence . . . ,* V, 357.
31. *Réflexions sur quelques points . . .* (1897), II, 423; *Le Prométhée mal enchaîné,* III, 130 and *Journal,* 12 January 1941 (O'B IV, 57); *Journal,* 16 January 1941 (O'B IV, 59).
32. *Réflexions sur quelques points . . . ,* II, 420; *Journal,* "feuillets" following 1937 entries (O'B III, 370).
33. *Journal,* 27 September 1940 (O'B IV, 48).
34. Jean Thomas, *L'Humanisme de Diderot* (Les Belles Lettres, 1932), p. 160. Compare R. Mauzi, *L'Idée du bonheur au XVIIIe siècle* (Colin, 1959) and "Diderot et le Bonheur," *Diderot Studies III,* pp. 263–84.
35. Letter to Falconet, 6 September 1768.

Mortality and Eternity

1. Dr. Henry Ronot, "La Maladie et la Mort de Diderot," in *Cahiers Haut-Marnais,* 1951, no. 24.
2. *Le Figaro Littéraire,* 5 January 1952.
3. *Journal,* 3 January 1892 (O'B I, 18).
4. François Mauriac, "La Victoire de Spartacus," *La Table Ronde* XL (1951), 13.
5. *LSV,* undated fragment, Babelon II, 274.
6. *Eléments de physiologie,* IX, 428.
7. *LSV,* undated fragment, Babelon II, 265.
8. *Ibid.,* undated fragment, p. 280.
9. Quoted by Louis Guilloux, "D'un voyage à l'U.R.S.S.," *N.R.F.: Hommage à André Gide,* p. 245.
10. *Journal,* 6 March 1941 (O'B IV, 62).
11. *Ibid.,* 10 October 1893 (O'B I, 33).
12. 13 February 1951. *Ainsi soit-il, ou Les Jeux sont faits,* pp. 197–98 (translated by Justin O'Brien, *So Be It or The Chips Are Down,* Knopf, 1959, p. 166).
13. *Les Nourritures terrestres,* II, 229 (Bussy, p. 14).
14. *Journal,* 26 July 1919, 16 November 1917 (O'B II, 254, 217).
15. "Considérations," IX, 153; *Journal,* 12 May 1927 (O'B

II, 403), 26 August 1938 (O'B III, 399); *Ainsi soit-il,* p. 159 (*So Be It,* p. 134).

16. *Eloge de Richardson,* V, 222, 227.

17. *LSV,* 25 July 1765.

18. Letter to Sartine, 13 October 1769.

19. *Journal,* 21 August 1938 (O'B III, 394).

20. Notation in *Et nunc manet in te,* dated 8 February 1939; remark quoted by Roger Martin du Gard, dated July 1932.

21. *Journal,* 5 May 1942, 12 June 1944 (O'B IV, 107, 243).

22. Letter to Falconet, 20 May 1773.

23. *Journal,* 9 September 1940 (O'B IV, 45).

24. *Ainsi soit-il,* pp. 4, 6, 7 (*So Be It,* pp. 12, 14, 16).

25. *Et nunc manet in te,* p. 70.

26. *LSV,* undated fragment, Babelon II, 270; letter to Princess Dashkoff, 25 January 1774.

27. *Réfutation de . . . l'Homme,* II, 292.

28. Letter to his sister, 29 November 1778.

29. *Eléments de physiologie,* IX, 429. Cf. Chanoine Marcel, "La Mort de Diderot, d'après des documents inédits," *Revue de l'histoire de l'église en France,* 1925, pp. 25–52, 202–26.

30. *Journal,* 26 August 1938 (O'B III, 398–99); R.-M. Albérès, *L'Odyssée d'André Gide* (La Nouvelle Edition, 1951), p. 263.

31. L. Martin-Chauffier, in *Mercure de France,* April 1948.

32. To Julien Green. *Entretiens,* p. 39.

33. *Le Figaro Littéraire,* 24 February 1951.

34. Preface (1926) to *Les Nourritures terrestres,* II, 229 (Bussy, pp. 4–5).

35. "Dieu, fils de l'homme," in *Pages de Journal* 1939–42, pp. 149–70.

36. *Journal,* 8 June 1942 (O'B III, 114).

37. *Ibid.,* 2 June 1942, 13 October 1942 (O'B IV, 113, 127).

38. *Ainsi soit-il,* pp. 55–56 (*So Be It,* p. 44).

39. Julien Green, "Entretiens avec André Gide," *La Table Ronde,* XL (1951), 42.

40. *Ainsi soit-il,* p. 45 (*So Be It,* p. 35).

41. *Journal,* 8 May 1942 (O'B IV, 111). Compare 21 August 1938, 12 June 1949, 25 January 1950 (O'B III, 393; IV, 306; IV, 306).

42. *Ainsi soit-il,* p. 87 (*So Be It,* p. 72).

43. Conversation with Jacques Maritain, *Journal,* 21 December 1923 (O'B II, 340).

44. *Journal*, 15 May 1949 (O'B IV, 300).

45. *Num quid et tu . . . ?*, following 15 June 1919 (O'B II, 186).

46. *Journal*, 12 June 1949 (Omitted from O'Brien translation, though autograph entry that follows is given).

47. *Le Figaro*, 27 November 1951.

48. "Sur la mort d'André Gide," *Le Figaro Littéraire*, 5 January 1952.

49. Robert Mallet, *Le Figaro Littéraire*, 24 February 1951.

50. "Recontres avec André Gide," *N.R.F.*: *Hommage à André Gide*, p. 227.

Influences and Inferences

1. "De l'influence en littérature," III, 249–73 (translated by Blanche A. Price in *Pretexts*, pp. 22–39).

2. XIV, 287. Cf. Herbert Dieckmann, "La Pensée et ses Modes d'expression," in *Cinq leçons sur Diderot* (Droz-Minard, 1959), pp. 69–94.

3. "Les Dix Romans français que . . . ," VII, 447–58 (translated by Blanche A. Price in *Pretexts*, pp. 243–50).

4. *Journal*, November 1892, 12 May 1892, 4 November 1927 (O'B I, 22; I, 20; II, 420).

5. "Feuillets," XIII, 416.

6. *Journal*, 8 August 1914 (O'B II, 69).

7. *Ibid.*, 10 June 1891, 29 September 1921, 2 December 1905, 10 January 1906, 7 and 8 April 1906 (O'B I, 11; II, 271; I, 161; I, 168; I, 178).

8. *Ibid.*, 28 March 1924 (O'B II, 349).

9. *Ibid.*, 8 December 1924 (O'B II, 362).

10. *Ibid.*, 13 December 1924 (O'B II, 363).

11. *Ibid.*, 13 January 1929 (O'B III, 36–37).

12. *Numquid et tu?* . . . , VIII, 329 (O'B II, 180); *Journal*, 21 December 1923 (O'B II, 340).

13. *Journal*, 1 April 1929 (O'B III, 46).

14. The Gide-Nietzsche rapports are touched on by Elsie Pell, in her *André Gide*, p. 10. They are investigated at length by Renée B. Lang, "André Gide et Nietzsche," *Romanic Review* XXXIV (1943), 139–49, and in her *André Gide et la Pensée allemande* (Libr. Univ. de France, 1949).

15. Cf. Barker, *Diderot's Treatment of the Christian Religion . . . , passim.*

16. *Journal,* 4 October 1931 (O'B III, 194). The allusion is to *LSV* 14 July 1762; the source is *N.R.F.* XXXII (1929), 355.

17. *Ibid.,* 15 December 1937 (O'B III, 365), quoted from the *Salon de 1767,* II, 131.

18. Cf. Herbert Dieckmann, "Diderot's Conception of Genius," Journal of the History of Ideas, II (1941), 151–82.

19. *Journal,* 25 June 1944 (O'B IV, 243), quoted from *LSV,* 8 October 1760.

20. *Littérature engagée,* ed. Yvonne Davet (Gallimard, 1950), p. 132.

21. "Défense de la culture," *Action Française,* 13 June 1935. Reprinted in *Littérature engagée,* p. 88.

22. "Paul Valéry," in *Eloges* (Ides et Calendes, 1948), p. 104 (Pell, p. 97). First printed in *Arche,* October 1945 (translated by Elsie Pell in *Autumn Leaves,* Philosophical Library, 1950, pp. 95–115).

23. *Rencontres* (Ides et Calendes, 1948), pp. 137–44.

24. *Ibid.,* p. 87.

25. Pierre Hermand, *Les Idées morales de Diderot* (Presses Universitaires, 1923), pp. 88–119; Paul Souday, *André Gide* (Kra, 1927), p. 54; Otis Fellows and Norman Torrey, *The Age of Enlightenment* (Crofts, 1942), p. 210; Jean Fabre, *Le Neveu de Rameau* (Droz, 1950), p. xcv; Otis Fellows, "The Theme of Genius in Diderot's *Neveu de Rameau,*" *Diderot Studies II* (Syracuse, 1952), p. 174; Arthur Wilson, *Diderot: The Testing Years, 1713–1759* (Oxford, 1957), p. 86; Georges May, "L'Angoisse de l'échec et la Genèse du *Neveu de Rameau,*" *Diderot Studies III* (Droz, 1961), p. 307; Herbert Dieckmann, *Cinq leçons sur Diderot* (Droz-Minard, 1959), pp. 80–81; Roland Mortier, "Diderot et le Problème de l'expressivité," *Cahiers de l'Association Internationale des Etudes Françaises,* XIII (1961), 291; Robert Loy, "L'Essai sur les règnes de Claude et Néron," *Cahiers de l'AIEF,* XIII, 242; Robert Niklaus, "Diderot et le Conte philosophique," *Cahiers de l'AIEF,* XIII, 314.

26. Schiller, Goethe, and Lessing among the first, as noted by Sainte-Beuve. See also Roland Mortier, *Diderot en Allemagne 1750–1850* (Presses Universitaires, 1954).

27. Jean Fabre, *Le Neveu de Rameau,* p. lxxxvii.

28. Review of *Principes philosophiques,* IV, 99.

29. "Feuillets," XIII, 441–42; *Journal,* following 13 October 1894 (O'B I, 42), 25 January 1948 (O'B IV, 289).

30. "Feuillets," XIII, 441.

31. *N.R.F.* XXXIV (1930), 322.

32. "De l'influence en littérature," III, 256–57 (Price translation, *Pretexts,* pp. 26–27).

33. "Dans l'oeuvre de chacun de ceux-ci respire une force de communion puissante—mais de communion à retardement." *Littérature engagée,* p. 92.

Selected Studies in English

John Viscount Morley, *Diderot and the Encyclopædists,* rev. ed. London: Macmillan, 1923 (1878). 2 vols.

Lester G. Crocker, *The Embattled Philosopher: A Life of Denis Diderot.* East Lansing: Michigan State College Press, 1954

Arthur M. Wilson, *Diderot: The Testing Years, 1713–1759.* New York: Oxford University Press, 1957

Justin O'Brien, *Portrait of André Gide.* New York: Alfred A. Knopf, 1953

Jean Hytier, *André Gide,* trans. Richard Howard. Garden City: Doubleday-Anchor, 1962

Germaine Brée, *André Gide.* New Brunswick: Rutgers University Press, 1962

Selected English Translations

WORKS OF DIDEROT

Diderot, Interpreter of Nature, trans. Jean Stewart and Jonathan Kemp. New York: International Publishers, 1938. Contains extracts, abridgments, and the following complete works: *Conversation between D'Alembert and Diderot, D'Alembert's Dream, Conclusion of the Conversation, Philosophic Principles on Matter and Motion, Supplement to Bougainville's Voyage, Conversation between the Abbé Barthélemy and Diderot, Discourse of a Philosopher to a King, Conversation of a Philosopher with the Maréchale X, Rameau's Nephew.*

A *Diderot Pictorial Encyclopedia of Trades and Industry,* ed. C. C. Gillespie. New York: Dover Publications, 1959

Jacques the Fatalist and His Master (*Jacques le fataliste*) trans. J. Robert Loy. New York: New York University Press, 1959; rev. trans. New York: Collier, 1962

Memoirs of a Nun (*La Religieuse*), trans. Francis Birrell. New York: Elek-Masterpieces of World Literature, 1959

The Paradox of Acting (*Paradoxe sur le comédien*), trans. Walter H. Pollock, intr. Lee Strasberg. New York: Hill and Wang, 1957; New York: Calder, Dramabook, 1958

Rameau's Nephew (*Le Neveu de Rameau*), trans. Sylvia M. Hill. London, 1897; in *Diderot, Interpreter of Nature* (above)

Rameau's Nephew and Other Works in New Translations, trans. Jacques Barzun and Ralph H. Bowen. Garden City: Doubleday-Anchor, 1956

WORKS OF GIDE

Afterthoughts: A Sequel to "Back from the U.S.S.R." (*Retouches à mon Retour de l'URSS*), trans. Dorothy Bussy. London: Secker and Warburg, 1937. Republished with title *After-*

thoughts on the U.S.S.R. New York: Dial Press, 1938; London: Secker and Warburg, 1938

Amyntas (*Amyntas*), trans. Villiers David. London: Bodley Head, 1958, Dufour, 1961

Autumn Leaves (*Feuillets d'automne*), trans. Elsie Pell, with thirty-one other articles, among them "Youth," "Acquasanta," "Goethe," "The Teaching of Poussin." New York: Philosophical Library, 1950; trans. Justin O'Brien in *The Journals of André Gide, 1889–1949*, IV, 275–81.

Bathsheba (*Bethsabé*), in *My Theater*

The Coiners (*Les Faux-Monnayeurs*), trans. D. Bussy. London: Cassell, 1927, Cassell, Secker and Warburg, 1950

"Concerning Influence in Literature" ("De l'influence en littérature"), trans. Blanche A. Price in *Pretexts*

Corydon (*Corydon*), trans. Hugh Gibb. New York: Farrar Straus, 1950; trans. Frank Beach. New York: Noonday Press, 1961

Corydon: Four Socratic Dialogues, trans. P. B. (sic). London: Secker and Warburg, 1952

The Counterfeiters (*Les Faux-Monnayeurs*), trans. D. Bussy. New York: Knopf, 1927, 1947. Republished with *Journal of "The Counterfeiters,"* trans. J. O'Brien. New York: Knopf, 1951

Dostoevsky (*Dostoïevsky*), trans. anon., intr. Arnold Bennett. London: J. M. Dent, 1925; New York: Knopf, 1926; London: Secker and Warburg, 1949; New York: New Directions, 1949. Reprinted with Bennett introduction and new introduction by Albert J. Guérard. New York: New Directions, 1961

Et nunc manet in te, trans. J. O'Brien, with *Intimate Journal.* London: Secker and Warburg, 1952

"The Evolution of the Theater" ("L'Evolution du théâtre"), in *My Theater*

Extracts from the Journals, 1939–1942 (*Pages de Journal, 1939–1942*), trans. J. O'Brien in *The Journals of André Gide, 1889–1949*

Fruits of the Earth (*Les Nourritures terrestres*), trans. D. Bussy.

New York: Knopf, 1949; London: Secker and Warburg, 1949

Genevieve (*Geneviève*), in *The School for Wives*

If It Die . . . (*Si le grain ne meurt . . .*), trans. D. Bussy, limited ed. New York: Random House, 1935; London: Secker and Warburg, 1950; New York: Random House Modern Library, 1957; New York: Vintage Books, 1961

Imaginary Interviews (*Interviews imaginaires*), trans. Malcolm Cowley. New York: Knopf, 1944

The Immoralist (*L'Immoraliste*), trans. D. Bussy. New York: Knopf, 1930, 1948; London: Cassell, 1930, 1953; New York: Vintage, 1954

Isabelle (*Isabelle*), trans. D. Bussy in *Two Symphonies*

The Journals of André Gide, 1889–1949 (*Journal, 1889–1939; Pages de Journal, 1939–1942; Journal, 1942–1949*), trans. J. O'Brien. New York: Knopf, 1947–1951; London: Secker and Warburg, 1947–1949, 4 vols.; with title *Gide Journals.* New York: Vintage, 1956, 2 vols.

Journal of "The Counterfeiters" (*Journal des Faux-Monnayeurs*), trans. J. O'Brien, in *The Counterfeiters and Journal of "The Counterfeiters."* New York: Knopf, 1951

King Candaules (*Le Roi Candaule*), in *My Theater*

Lafcadio's Adventures (*Les Caves du Vatican*), trans. D. Bussy. New York: Knopf, 1927, 1943; London: Cassell, 1927; New York: Vintage, 1960

The Living Thoughts of Montaigne (*Essai sur Montaigne*), trans. D. Bussy. Toronto: Longmans Green, 1939; London: Cassell, 1939

Logbook of "The Coiners" (*Journal des Faux-Monnayeurs*), trans. J. O'Brien, limited ed. London: Cassell, 1952

Madeleine (*Et nunc manet in te*), trans. J. O'Brien. New York: Knopf, 1952

Marshlands (*Paludes*), trans. George D. Painter, in *Marshlands and Prometheus Misbound.* New York: New Directions, 1953

Montaigne (*Essai sur Montaigne*), trans. S. H. Guest and T. E. Blewitt. New York: Horace Liveright, 1929; London: Blackmore, 1929

My Theater (*Théâtre, Théâtre complet*), trans. Jackson Matthews. New York: Knopf, 1952. Contains five plays (*Saul, Bathsheba, Philoctetes, King Candaules, Persephone*), and an essay ("The Evolution of the Theater").

New Fruits of the Earth (*Les Nouvelles Nourritures*), trans. D. Bussy, in *Fruits of the Earth*, pp. 181–293

Notes on Chopin (*Notes sur Chopin*), trans. Bernard Frechtman. New York: Philosophical Library, 1949

Numquid et tu? . . ., trans. J. O'Brien in *The Journals of André Gide*, 1889–1949, II, 169–87

Oedipus (*Oedipe*), trans. John Russell in *Two Legends: Theseus and Oedipus*. New York: Knopf, 1950; London: Secker and Warburg, 1950; New York: Vintage, 1958

The Pastoral Symphony (*La Symphonie pastorale*), trans. D. Bussy in *Two Symphonies*

Persephone (*Perséphone*), trans. Samuel Putnam, limited ed. New York: Gotham Book Mart, 1949; in *My Theater*

Philoctetes (*Philoctète*), in *My Theater*

Pretexts (*Prétextes, Nouveaux Prétextes*), trans. Angelo P. Bertocci, Jeffrey J. Carre, J. O'Brien, Blanche A. Price. New York: Meridian Books, 1959

Prometheus Ill-Bound (*Le Prométhée mal enchaîné*), trans. Lilian Rothermere. London: Chatto and Windus, 1919

Prometheus Misbound (*Le Prométhée mal enchaîné*), in *Marshlands and Prometheus Misbound*

Recollections of the Assize Court (*Souvenirs de la Cour d'Assises*), trans. Philip A. Wilkins. London: Hutchinson, 1941

Return from the U.S.S.R. (*Retour de l'URSS*), trans. D. Bussy. New York: Knopf, 1937; London: Secker and Warburg, 1937

Return of the Prodigal (*Le Retour de l'enfant prodigue*), trans. D. Bussy. London: Secker and Warburg, 1953. Preceded by five other treatises and a play (*Saul*).

The Return of the Prodigal Son (*Le Retour de l'enfant prodigue*), trans. D. Bussy. New York: Bantam Books, 1960

Robert (*Robert*), in *The School for Wives*

Saul (*Saül*), in *My Theater*; in *Return of the Prodigal*

The School for Wives (*L'Ecole des femmes*), trans. D. Bussy, with *Robert, Genevieve*. New York: Knopf, 1929, 1950; London: Cassell, 1929, 1953

So Be It or *The Chips are Down* (*Ainsi soit-il* ou *Les Jeux sont faits*), trans. J. O'Brien. New York: Knopf, 1959; London: Chatto, 1959

Strait Is the Gate (*La Porte étroite*), trans. D. Bussy. New York: Knopf, 1924, 1943; London: Secker and Warburg, 1924, 1943; New York: Vintage, 1956

"The Teaching of Poussin" ("L'Enseignement de Poussin"), trans. Elsie Pell in *Autumn Leaves*

Theseus (*Thésée*), trans. John Russell, in *Horizon*, 1948; in *Two Legends: Theseus and Oedipus*

The Thirteenth Tree (*Le Treizième Arbre*), trans. Robert Gottlieb in *Columbia Review* XXX (1951), 56–74

Travels in the Congo (*Voyage au Congo*), trans. D. Bussy. New York: Knopf, 1929; London, 1930; New York: Modern Age, 1937; Berkeley: University of California Press (2nd ed.), 1962

Two Legends: Theseus and Oedipus, trans. John Russell. New York: Knopf, 1950; London: Secker and Warburg, 1950; New York: Vintage, 1958

Two Symphonies (*Isabelle, La Symphonie pastorale*), trans. D. Bussy. New York: Knopf, 1931, 1949; London: Cassell, 1931, 1949

"An Unprejudiced Mind" ("Un Esprit non prévenu"), trans. J. O'Brien in *Pretexts*

Urien's Travels (*Le Voyage d'Urien*), trans. anon. New York: New Directions, 1952

Vatican Cellars (*Les Caves du Vatican*), trans. D. Bussy. London: Cassell, 1953

The Vatican Swindle (*Les Caves du Vatican*), trans. D. Bussy. New York: Knopf, 1925.